1983

God and the good

GOD AND THE GOOD

Essays in honor of
Henry Stob

EDITED BY CLIFTON ORLEBEKE AND LEWIS SMEDES

WILLIAM B. EERDMANS PUBLISHING COMPANY
Grand Rapids, Michigan

Copyright © 1975 by Wm. B. Eerdmans Publishing Company
All rights reserved
Printed in the United States of America

Library of Congress Cataloging in Publication Data

Main entry under title:
God and the good.

  "Bibliography of Henry Stob compiled by Peter
DeKlerk": p. 221.
  CONTENTS: Smedes, L. Henry Stob.—Essays in
Christian ethics: Berkouwer, G. C. Orthodoxy and
orthopraxis. Bruce, F. F. The grace of God and the
law of Christ, a study in Pauline ethics. Hageman, H.
The law in the liturgy. Smedes, L. Theology and the
playful life. Holmes, A. Human variables and natural
law. Verhey, A. Natural law in Aquinas and Calvin.
Henry, C. Christian perspective on private property.
(etc.)

  1. Theology—Addresses, essays, lectures. 2. Stob,
Henry, 1908-   —Bibliography. I. Stob, Henry,
1908-   II. Orlebeke, Clifton J., ed. III. Smedes,
Lewis B., ed.
BR50.G538   230   74-31479
ISBN 0-8028-3454-X

Contents

5

HENRY STOB

These essays are published to honor Henry Stob. The occasion is his retirement from the chair of philosophical and moral theology at Calvin Theological Seminary. The motivation is gratitude for the spiritual and intellectual enrichment that he has brought into the lives of the writers.

Henry Stob was born in Chicago on June 24, 1908. He was reared in a devout Calvinistic family and educated from the beginning in the Christian day schools that are interwoven into the total religious perspective of his church and community. He graduated from Calvin College in 1932 and from Calvin Theological Seminary in 1935. He took a Master's degree from Hartford Theological Seminary in 1936, and then he went to Europe to study philosophy at the University of Göttingen, in Germany, taking his Ph.D. in 1938. His dissertation, written in German, was an analysis of Max Weber's sociology of religion. Stob stayed in Europe for a year of post-doctoral study to investigate the efforts then being made by Herman Dooyeweerd and D. H. Th. Vollenhoven to construct a Christian philosophical system. He returned to the United States in 1939 as the war closed in on Europe.

Henry Stob began his academic career as a professor of philosophy at his alma mater the year he returned. In 1943 he entered the U. S. Navy and served as a Lieutenant in the Pacific war zone until shortly after the war ended; he was a member of General MacArthur's occupation staff in Japan until the spring of 1946. Resuming his teaching at Calvin College on his release from the Navy, Stob remained there until 1952, when he was appointed by the Synod of the Christian Reformed Church to teach philosophical and moral theology at Calvin Seminary and ordained a minister in the Christian Reformed Church. There he taught, with a year's interruption as a visiting professor of ethics in the Kobe Reformed Seminary in Japan and the Hapdong Seminary in Seoul, Korea, until his retirement.

Stob is married to the former Hilda De Graff, and they have two children, Ellen and Richard.

These are the data that provide the barest schedule of Henry Stob's career. I am torn between stopping here, having said much too little, and going on to speak of him as a person and teacher, knowing that to say

6

much more—even if said in all honesty—will cause him genuine embarrassment. One characteristic of his style has always been a reluctance to talk about himself. His conversation has been with the world of ideas, of events, of problems outside of himself. The depths of his personal life have, for the most part, been exposed only to his Lord. Yet I know that his large circle of friends and colleagues would feel that something very vital is missing from a volume in tribute to Henry Stob if it recorded only the outline of his career. Let me try to offer a few observations that may at least give some clues to the man himself.

Teaching is Henry Stob's life, and he has been a master of his profession. Every class was, for him, a significant event, every lecture a finely finished piece. The classroom was a holy place; it was here that his gifts and energies were poured out as a kind of oblation. His forte was analysis. He believed, with St. Thomas, that the secret of education was the ability to make proper distinctions—to clarify, to distinguish, to peel away the incidentals until the concept was laid bare, clean and single and transparent. I have never heard his equal anywhere in the art of piercing to the core of complex problems. It was not his style to shock students with novelties. Resort to theatrics was totally foreign to him. He was not given to throwing out radical, untested notions as pedagogical gimmicks; he took the world of theological and philosophical thought too seriously for pedagogical game-playing. And he respected his students too deeply to do other than invite, sometimes prod, them to join him in his own struggle for wisdom.

One facet that both amazes and burdens me, on reflection, is that, while he was painstakingly devoted to the well-crafted lecture, he was available to his students—and even to those who were not his students—at all hours. Students took his time, but he gave it freely, often until the early hours of the morning. Whether it was academic, spiritual, or personal, the student's problem became his problem. And yet, the polished lecture was ready for the following morning. As a colleague of Henry Stob, I can recall engaging him, along with other friends, in hard discussions until the late hours, with Stob stubbornly probing and defining the problem with élan and clarity while the rest of us, younger than he, had long since lapsed into drowsy fuzziness. God gave this man an extra ingredient of sheer physical stamina along with his considerable intelligence.

I do not think he ever considered himself a disciple of any modern thinker. It has always seemed to me that in basic religious perspective he is most like Augustine, in intellectual style most like Thomas Aquinas, in theological commitment most like John Calvin. All of his thinking is rooted in Christian faith; out of that faith he has sought understanding.

But he has not despised, in any radical Protestant negativism, the wisdom of natural man. His whole theological program has been dominated not by the dialectic of sin and grace alone, nor of nature and grace alone, but of nature-sin-grace, with solid respect for the reality of all three. He would, perhaps, prefer to speak of creation-sin-grace as the triad of realities which Christian theological thought must always reflect.

He is not a system-builder, nor an epigone of system-builders. For instance, while he has always expressed gratitude for the creative insights of the Calvinistic system-building of Herman Dooyeweerd, he has at the same time been a vigorous critic of that system, especially of some of its practical implications. On the other hand, he has not been anything like a faddish eclectic; yet, when he comes to grips with the thought of even the most radical critic of the Christian faith, he strives to get inside, as it were, of the critic's mind, to understand the deepest motives of his thought, and vicariously to enter into it—and only then to criticize it. He has been satisfied to let the Light "that enlightens every man that comes into the world" play on all thought, philosophical and ethical, and lead him, not to finality, but at least to a maturity of wisdom in Christ.

Stob is a churchman. He has spent his academic life as a servant of what many would call a minor Protestant denomination. But he has had a catholic grasp of both the church and the world. He saw his own communion only in the context of the whole church of Christ. And when he committed himself to his denomination, he did it in commitment to the catholic church. One cannot help wondering how much the labor that he dedicated through the years to theological controversies within his church drained away resources that might, had he been a more aloof academician, have been published and gone further abroad to affect a larger circle. But he could not have done it differently; God set him where he was, and there he served with both dedication and effectiveness.

Perhaps the accomplishment closest to his heart was his founding, along with four colleagues, Harry Boer, George Stob, James Daane, and the late Henry Zylstra, of the *Reformed Journal*. His editorial mind reflected his attitude toward his own and the catholic church. He wanted the *Journal* to address issues that confronted his own denomination, thereby to serve it most directly. This was not parochialism, for he was sure that the challenges of this church were basically catholic; and he was equally certain they could be addressed journalistically in a way that would demonstrate the catholicity of the *Journal*'s mind. The extent to which the *Reformed Journal* has conveyed a catholic spirit is, in large measure, because from the beginning it conveyed the spirit of Henry Stob. A few days before he died, Calvin Bulthuis—then editor-in-chief of the *Journal*—urged the preparation of this volume on its editors; that he did this was typical of Cal Bulthuis and a reflection of his esteem for Henry Stob. I am sure that Dr. Stob would wish Cal to think of this volume as indirectly dedicated to him.

In the winter of 1974, Stob gave three lectures on the subject of love and justice at Fuller Theological Seminary. These lectures were, true to type, compact, complex, demanding; they led the audience through a labyrinth of ideas until the heart of the matter was reached. At the close of the final lecture, the unusually large audience took to their feet to give him a long, and, in academic halls, exceptional ovation. We trust that he will receive the presentation of these essays as a quieter, but no less vigorous ovation, not for a lecture, but for a life.

LEWIS B. SMEDES

PART I

Essays in Christian Ethics

Orthodoxy and Orthopraxis

G. C. BERKOUWER*

The term 'orthodoxy' has played an important role in the history of the church and her theology, particularly in polemical situations. To be orthodox is to be concerned about the true biblical, evangelical teaching. Champions of orthodoxy have always meant to lead the church through the rough seas of what the New Testament characterizes as departure from "sound doctrine" (I Tim. 1:10; II Tim. 4:3; Titus 2:1) or from the "doctrine of God" (Titus 2:10). The true teaching is opposed to the other spirit, the other gospel, and the other Jesus (II Cor. 11:4). The other gospel, which is not a gospel, evokes Paul's vigorous protest (cf. the *anathema* of Gal. 1:9) because everything stands or falls with one's decision in respect to it.

In theology, orthodoxy is a protest from the heart of the New Testament against any teaching that threatens the real gospel. The word 'orthodoxy' by itself has no concrete content and provides no specific understanding of its significance until we know *what* teaching is involved, what doctrine is in contest. Roman and Greek Catholics have used the word, as have Protestants, which means that orthodoxy itself needs to be tested. The intent of orthodoxy within church history is not always self-evident, and it always evokes profound questions.

Moreover, one must be aware of certain dangers in orthodoxy. We have constantly been warned against dead orthodoxy. Dead orthodoxy suggests an intellectualistic shrinkage of the gospel into thought and words isolated

---

*Translated by Lewis Smedes.

G.C. Berkouwer is Professor Emeritus of Dogmatics at the Free University of Amsterdam, and the author of numerous theological studies, including an 18-volume Studies in Dogmatics. *In addition Berkouwer has written important studies of the theology of Karl Barth and of the Roman Catholic Church. In his essay Berkouwer affirms the biblical marriage between correct doctrine and creative morality. He argues that the Bible forbids any hiatus between the two, and that any theology and any church must, if it makes a claim to biblical thought and practice, honor them as organically united. The vertical relationship of grace entails the horizontal demands of love and justice; doctrine and ethics are born of the same womb.*

13

from the heart, from faith and trust, even though the orthodox formulas are in tune with biblical teaching. Concrete problems with orthodoxy arise whenever we face the other term in our title, 'orthopraxis.'

'Orthopraxis' has never been as common a term in the church as 'orthodoxy.' Its meaning is clear enough: *right action*, that is, concrete deeds of Christian faith within everyday life. The relationship between orthodoxy and orthopraxis—between doctrine and life—has often been discussed, but there is good reason for looking closely at it once again. Here the special significance of sanctification comes within our horizon.

It should not surprise us that a revived consideration is being given today to orthopraxis. For we see around us a profound distrust of words for their own sake, words with no power, words like the summer clouds that bring no needed rain. Moreover, the earnest summons to credibility, to actions along with words, is no mere fad: the New Testament itself is sharply critical of words with no corresponding action. Believers are constantly called to be *doers* of the word and not only *hearers* (James 1:22,23). Merely *saying* "Lord, Lord" does not qualify anyone as a disciple of the Lord; discipleship entails *doing* the will of the Father (Matt. 7:21). There must be no minimizing of the large importance that the gospel gives to action.

The New Testament vigorously seeks to separate the hearers from the doers, the sayers from the actors. It protests against words that are not incarnate in deeds. He who says that he abides in God must see to it that he walks as Christ walked (I John 2:6). To make a verbal claim of loving God while one hates his brother is to label the verbal claim as a lie (I John 4:20). The children of God are revealed in their actions of righteousness (I John 3:10). Right believing and right doing are so closely connected in John's thought that any divorce between them poses this radical and incriminating question: "But if any one has the world's goods and sees his brother in need, yet closes his heart against him, how does God's love abide in him?" (I John 3:17).

The gospel is so clear on this point that no church teacher—other than the extreme antinomians—has ever overtly isolated orthodoxy from orthopraxis. The words of a Reformed catechism—"It is impossible for those grafted into Christ by true faith not to produce fruits of gratitude" (Heidelberg Catechism, Lord's Day 24)—express a recognized ecumenical insight that has always summoned the universal church to guard against any faith *vs.* life dualism. The dangers of a dead and therefore actionless orthodoxy were signaled for all time by James in his words about a faith that remains hidden, especially in respect to one's relation to others (James 2:14). No one has ever warned more sharply against a worthless faith that has no works to show for it (James 2:19,20). Luther may have been goaded into saying some deprecating things about James due to the extreme situation in which his Roman Catholic opponents placed him by using James against the reality of *sola fide*. Prior to these polemics, however, he had seen no tension between Paul and James, as is evident in his 1515 *Commentary on Romans*. None of us can escape the earnestness of James' urgent warnings. To ignore him or water down what he says would be a flight from the depths of *sola fide*, a flight from a faith which, while it rules out works as a means of merit, cannot remain fruitless and workless.

We must expand on what we have just said about the biblical self-evidence of the importance of action. It seems to me that, in spite of the clarity with which the Bible unites faith and works, the importance and depth of their unity is frequently underestimated and minimized. This can happen even where the bond between doctrine and life is honored theoretically, where it is indeed an element within orthodoxy itself (as in the doctrines of justification and sanctification), but is nonetheless minimized by making orthodoxy more important than orthopraxis. Correct teaching can be accorded such importance and attention, especially in reaction to false doctrines, that orthopraxis becomes a secondary matter, theoretically as well as practically. The New Testament, however, simply does not allow for one of the elements to be given a stronger accent than the other.

Those who make practice secondary frequently do so in consideration of the fact that sin remains even in the believer. They point out that "only a small beginning" of obedience is found even in "the holiest" (Lord's Day 44, Heidelberg Catechism). Our own life experience can lead us, then, to suppose that our faith ultimately revolves only around the *sola fide* and not around our works of sanctification. After all, is this not the comfort of the gospel, that in spite of much that is lacking in our sanctification, the eye of faith is fixed on a righteousness that comes to us from Christ, from outside of ourselves, in his radical and forgiving grace? Is this not the humble mood in which one comes to the sacrament of communion, the mood of "in spite of everything," of "our sins notwithstanding"? Can we, in view of the humility that the gospel calls for, still insist on the union of orthodoxy and orthopraxis? Is this unbreakable bond not in conflict with the existential reality of the *simul iustus et peccator* that has always played such a large role in Reformed as well as in Lutheran teaching? Are we not, then, compelled by our own life's experience to make faith primary and works secondary?

Contemporary theology has caused concern lest we shrink the horizon of revelation by way of existential categories of one sort or another. The same concern urges us to consider whether, in the sorts of questions just raised, we are in danger of thinking and teaching from the perspective of our Christian life-experience (the experience of the *"simul"*) rather than subjecting ourselves to the clear demands of a gospel that calls us to a faith that lives and reveals its life by actions which can be seen by others, leading them to glorify God (Matt. 5:16). The Bible nowhere minimizes the importance of words, of teaching, of upholding orthodox doctrine; but neither does it isolate right teaching from action or honor orthodoxy for its own sake. In complex situations where believers are closely associated with unbelievers, the latter may be won over by the conduct of the believers without a word intervening (I Pet. 3:1). The New Testament opposition to words without deeds is fierce. The separation of good words from good practices is characterized as a deceptive tearing apart of the unity of life from within.

It is possible for a person theoretically to recognize the law as the incarnation of knowledge and truth, and to see himself as its orthodox teacher (the *didaskalos* of Rom. 2:20), and yet not do the works of the law. A person can preach the commandments and yet steal or commit adultery or rob the temple (Rom. 2:21,22). By such inconsistencies, says Paul, the name of God is blasphemed. Here, one cannot talk about a primary or secondary accent, but only of a deep unity of faith and works.

To respect this union is not to reduce the Christian life to moralism. It does, however, remind us that love for God as the first commandment is not real unless obedience to the second commandment goes hand in hand with it. The second commandment is, after all, like the first. That the unity of orthodoxy and orthopraxis clearly belongs to the true doctrine is not a discovery of the New Testament. The entire life of Israel in the Old Testament was set within the covenant, which contained the unity of life. Whenever Israel defended its religiosity by an appeal to tradition, the prophets stormed against their breaking of the unity of covenant life. The prophets came in the midst of festivals and sacrifices to proclaim divine resistance to a religiosity of custom without redeeming actions: "Let justice flow down like waters, and righteousness like a mighty stream" (Amos 5:24). It was not the religious services of Israel which were disqualified; it was the isolation of religion from works. For lack of justice perverts the festivals and the sacrifices. Isaiah's protest against Israel's fasting is as forceful as Amos' against her sacrifices:

Is such the fast that I choose,
a day for a man to humble himself?

Is it to bow down his head like a rush,
and to spread sackcloth and ashes under him?
Will you call this a fast,
and a day acceptable to the Lord?

Isaiah is indicting Israel for taking flight in all sorts of religious forms. But the right way, the only way of fasting before the eyes of Yahweh, is also made clear:

Is not this the fast that I choose:
to loose the bonds of wickedness,
to undo the thongs of the yoke,
to let the oppressed go free,
and to break every yoke?
Is it not to share your bread with the hungry,
and bring the homeless poor into your house;
when you see the naked, to cover him;
and not to hide yourself from your own flesh?
(Isa. 58:5-7).

The decisive meaning of this divine warning appears when Isaiah says that *only* in this way will light come to Israel itself.

Then shall your light break forth like the dawn,
and your healing shall spring up speedily;
your righteousness shall go before you,
the glory of the Lord shall be your rear guard.
Then you shall call, and the Lord will answer;
you shall cry, and he will say, Here I am
(Isa. 58:8,9).

The prophet's message bears a conditional character:

If you take away from the midst of you the yoke,
the pointing of the finger, and speaking wickedness,
if you pour yourself out for the hungry
and satisfy the desire of the afflicted,
then shall your light rise in the darkness
and your gloom be as the noonday
(58:9,10).

Surely there is no "secondary" accent on action here. It is a summons that cannot be artificially attached to the faith; it is enclosed within faith. Faith is not an abstraction, but something lived. Who could miss the deep harmony between the Old and New Testament evident here? Isaiah's appeal is to live in this world with love for the enemy, with compassion for the oppressed and the poor, an appeal that comes to its clearest expression in the New Testament basis for righteousness: "even as your Father is merciful" (Luke 6:36). It is a summons to put on compassion (Col. 3:12), not as a legalistic appendage to grace, but as the reality of grace itself. Essentially, the two are together so clearly that anyone who fails to forgive another cannot expect to be forgiven (Matt. 18:23-35). The summons is to a perfection like that of the Father, who lets his sun shine over the evil and the good alike (Matt. 5:45), to a love that will eternally be the supreme virtue and on whose practice everything else depends (I Cor. 13:1-3). There is no talk of a moralistic winning of points with God, no place for legalistic boasting, but only of a humble discipleship of Jesus Christ. Following this way, the church can be of service in the struggle against the already disarmed principalities and powers (Col. 2:15). The night is almost past, and the day is coming (Rom. 13:12). What sense, then, can be made of a split between doctrine and life, between orthodoxy and orthopraxis?

The cleavage between right believing and creative doing has sometimes been connected with a fear of moralism, of seeking merit in good works, and of threatening the doctrine of *sola fide*. Orthodoxy is sometimes stressed out of a fear of a horizontalist view of the Christian life which mistakenly believes that we can save and renew the world by our works. But the fear of horizontalism can easily trigger an unfortunate reaction which miscalculates the prophetic witness to how radically new the messianic kingdom is. The life of the earth is open before the power of the coming age (Heb. 6:5), a power that can be experienced even now. The obligation the gospel lays on us can be misunderstood and distorted into a prideful self-consciousness. But it cannot be too strongly stressed. To interpret concern for real people in their real needs and oppression as a form of secularization or a movement away from God's service to the service of men is deeply to misapprehend the implications of discipleship of Jesus Christ (cf. Eph. 5:1). To close up one's heart to another's need (I John 3:17) darkens the biblical perspective on the inner life of God, his inward compassion (Luke 1:78; Mark 6:34). The church is called to offer not a limited concern for the world and the human community, but a total concern on the basis of the divine concern. The believer's concern for the world flows out of God's concern as from a deep wellspring of love. Such was the fantastic perspective that Isaiah had. Isaiah's vision was of the removal of all offenses and the lifting of wrath and corruption from the mountain of God's holiness *because* the earth was full of the knowledge of the Lord as the waters covered the sea (Isa. 11:9). In the environment of this Lord, evil must vanish and distortions must die. This is why the church of Christ, in her concrete acts, goes out to all that threatens, oppresses, and discriminates against the poor. She may not let herself be isolated by a faith that feels at home only in the liturgy; she may not turn away from the world as though the world were abandoned by God to the powers of darkness. Rather, concern for the world and its people is a revelation of the presence of Christ (Matt. 25). He who feeds the hungry, visits the imprisoned, gives the thirsty a drink is ushered to the right hand of God, whither he goes without boasting in his works. Precisely in faith (*sola fide,* at that) human hearts open to the profoundest source of compassion, the divine *philanthropia* (Titus 3:4).

Estrangement from divine compassion causes people to forget that the world's salvation cannot depend on human compassion. But David, it will be recalled, preferred to fall into the hands of God to falling into men's hands (II Sam. 24:14); and Jonah was willing to leave Nineveh to its ruin while God himself could not abandon it (Jonah 4). Estrangement from divine compassion makes us forget the Pharisees, who were capable of casually pronouncing curses on the "crowds who knew not the law." Estrangement from divine compassion erases the memory of human hardness toward the wandering Jewish people, a forgetfulness that led to the worst of human crimes. To forget these things is to make oneself hostage to all sorts of illusions. But if we are aware of this demonic trend within history, we will understand God's calling us to deeds, deeds in which the *divine* compassion is mirrored to the world through a life not only of belief but a life that reveals the inner drive of faith as a light to the world and the salt of the earth (Matt. 5:13f.).

The bond between true doctrine and right action belongs to the most profound aspects of the gospel; but there is more, for the unbreakableness of this bond is underscored in all the warnings that go out to the church. Whenever a break appears in the life of the church between faith and life, the calling comes back again. "Do you not know?" In I Corinthians 6 alone there is a threefold repetition (vv. 15, 16, 19) that points to the glorification of God in the flesh, in the middle of earthly existence. The unity of orthodoxy and orthopraxis is so clear throughout the entire gospel that it cannot help reappearing in the intuition of the church, sometimes redefined within her understanding, not as a self-evident slogan about our human existence, but in fear and trembling, in confession of guilt and deep humility. In that way the church understands that she cannot speak guiltlessly about the sins that remain within us, for those sins are a dark riddle.

The confession of the church reveals numerous tokens of her consciousness of how radical is the passage from death to life (I John 3:14).

In the early church, for instance, Hebrews 6:4 played a problematic role in regard to the need for a second repentance. The believers at that time took seriously the possibility of a return to the old life after once having been enlightened with the heavenly gift. Later, men grew less worried about such a return into sin and apostasy. Often sin was incorporated into the Christian life (by way of self-evident imperfection) and not experienced as a *corpus alienum,* a foreign body. This betrayed a loss of orientation around the gospel, in which keeping the commandments of Christ was seen as a sign of abiding in him and he in us (I John 3:24). John's statement, then, is an alarming note for those who escape into self-excuse: "Beloved, if our hearts do not condemn us, we have confidence before God; and we receive from him whatever we ask, because we *keep his commandments* and do what pleases him" (I John 3:21,22).

The legitimate Reformation struggle against the "meritoriousness" of our works loses all power whenever it casts shadows over the necessary practice of the Christian life within the world. The gospel knows no polarity between grace and work; it knows only the freedom in which faith is practiced as a living faith. Thus Paul can urge his readers on to the riches of good works, forgiveness, and participation, and to all these add (without fear of being misunderstood) that in this way they are "laying up for themselves a good foundation for the future, so that they may take hold of the life which is life indeed" (I Tim. 6:19).

The bond between orthodoxy and orthopraxis, between faith and life, receives a special place in the eschatological promise. This is why there is no need in the Christian life for a defense of the truth for its own sake, but only for a love for the truth that leads to *following the truth,* a characteristic expression of John (III John 3,4).

Finally, we should take note of an aspect of the bond between orthodoxy and orthopraxis which reveals its full seriousness. We have in mind what the Reformation churches call the practical syllogism. It is phrased in the Heidelberg Catechism in this way: "We do good so that we may be assured of our faith by its fruits" (Lord's Day 32). The term 'practical syllogism' is unfortunate, because it seems to imply that the insight here is cast in the form of ordinary logic and to suggest that assurance might come through reasoning from one thing to another outside of faith. But the intent of this "syllogism" is to sustain the close connection between the fruits of faith (good works) and the assurance of faith. The recognition of this bond contains a danger that we let our assurance rest on our own sanctification, and thus to woo us away from constant focus on Jesus Christ towards a concern with our own condition. In view of this real danger, Reformed theology has sometimes been critical of the "syllogism" (in spite of its appearance in the confession and its support by Calvin, who also stressed the relationship between the fruits and certainty of faith). There is actually no talk of a weakening of the *sola fide* in this relationship, nor is there a shred of moralistic self-consciousness. Rather, the authors of the Catechism were under the impression of that profound connection which John saw between action and certainty of the radical passage from death to life: "We know that we have passed out of death into life, because we love the brethren" (I John 3:14).

This passage had an enormous impact on Calvin, and it cannot be minimized by the Reformers' struggle against the meritoriousness of good works. Similarly, Karl Barth accepted the intention of the practical syllogism, not as a new sort of Christian humanism, but as a signal that the light seen by faith is the light of a new life that possesses the believer and cannot remain hidden, and for this reason plays a role in the certainty of his faith. In this it becomes clear that faith cannot be characterized as a rational affirmation of a given number of truths—a distorted idea of faith against which Herman Bavinck warned so frequently. It becomes clear that faith is a lived faith, lived within the uncertainties of concrete existence, and leads to liberty.

In the history of the church the "practical syllogism" is usually related to the individual believer. But there is also ground for noting its bearing on the life of the church as a whole. The church's certainty loses its power whenever she fails to walk in the total truth of active discipleship. Only as she holds doctrine and life together will she be a place of refuge in the wilderness of this world, a house of deep peace. The call to credibility, which has sailed like a comet through the ecclesiastical skies these recent years, is legitimate and meaningful. It rises from the insight that the divorce of orthodoxy from orthopraxis leads to falsehood, to scandal in the world, to great harm for church and world alike.

To stress the bond between true doctrine and true practice is in no way a threat to the comfort of grace, but is indeed a warning against taking comfort in cheap grace. It is an appeal to walk in "fear and trembling," to action within the truth, to obedience to the truth. Only in this way can the church keep clear what is the real scandal in the world, the real scandal of the gospel of grace. She can keep clear the difference between the real scandal and all the other scandals that we create by our disobedience, our powerlessness, our lovelessness, and our darkness. In the scandals that we create lie the real threats to the church's own faith, her certainty, and her *orthodoxy*.

The Grace of God and the Law of Christ: A Study in Pauline Ethics

F. F. BRUCE

If someone currently immersed in Pauline studies is asked to write for a festschrift to be presented to a professor of ethics, it is not difficult to find an area of common interest. Such an area is Paul's ethical teaching—an area which presents real problems, but which repays careful scrutiny because Paul's ethical teaching is no subsidiary concern for him but part and parcel of his Christology. For him the Christian way of life is, in Henry Scougal's words, "the life of God in the soul of man."[1]

I

By birth and upbringing Paul was, in his own words, "a Hebrew born of Hebrews" and a zealot for his ancestral traditions (Phil. 3:5; Gal. 1:14). Like the Jew whom he apostrophizes in Romans 2:20, he had "in the law the embodiment of knowledge and truth." The law was his way of life and the way to life; it comprised the divine ordinances "by doing which a man shall live" (Lev. 18:5). To a pious Jew the law was life itself: Paul might well have said in his earlier days, "For me to live is Torah." To the *ḥasid* who composed Psalm 119 the study of the law brought unending delight, and his sentiments have been echoed throughout succeeding generations by many other godly men. In that entire Psalm there is no hint of the law's association with sin and death, of which Paul became acutely aware.

It is difficult for many students of first-century Judaism to believe that Paul could have been brought up in mainstream orthodoxy, educated at the feet of Gamaliel, as we are told in Acts 22:3. The attitude to the law

---

1. H. Scougal, *The Life of God in the Soul of Man* (1677; reprinted London, 1961).

F.F. Bruce is Professor of New Testament at Manchester University, and the distinguished author of numerous scholarly works in the area of New Testament studies. In his essay, Bruce examines afresh the roles of grace and law in St. Paul's ethics, tracing Paul's development of man's liberation from external codes into the freedom of service to a personal Lord. Bruce concludes that grace is "the Spirit of God in action toward man," freeing him from an ethic that is rule-centered for an ethic that is person-centered.

22

expressed in his capital letters is so utterly unlike that with which we are familiar in the sayings of the great rabbis of Israel that it has seemed more probable that Paul (despite his own statements) derived his ideas from some deviationist group of Hellenistic Jews.

The problem is real, but the solution is ready to hand. Paul had been a devotee of the law, and kept it with such scrupulous care that in respect of the righteousness which it prescribed he was "blameless" (Phil. 3:6). The high-water mark of that righteousness was reached when, in his zeal for the law, he "persecuted the church of God violently and tried to destroy it" (Gal. 1:13; cf. Phil. 3:6). This was the path of duty to which the law pointed him plainly. The idea that he had any misgivings about the rightness of this course of action while he was engaged in it has no basis in the New Testament; it is the result of ascribing to Paul "the introspective conscience of the west,"[2] coupled with a misinterpretation of the 'goads' against which the heavenly voice on the Damascus road warned him not to kick (Acts 26:14). It was at that moment that the goads began to be applied, driving him in the opposite direction to that which he had been pursuing.

But from that same moment, when Jesus the crucified one was revealed to him as the risen and exalted Lord, it became plain to Paul that his persecuting activity had been the sin of sins. He who had set himself so scrupulously to keep all the law's requirements, who had like the Psalmist laid it up in his heart that he might not sin against God, was convicted of a deadlier sin than all those which he had successfully kept at bay. How could this have happened? It was his zeal for the law that had led him to persecute not only the church of God but the Son of God in the person of his people. He had relied on the law to lead him in the way of righteousness, and the law had let him down; it had led him into sin. But how could that be? The law was God's law; there was nothing unrighteous about it. Yet with him it had failed to achieve its purpose: instead of being the way to life it became for him the way of death.

If the fault did not lie in God's law, which was "holy and just and good" (Rom. 7:12), it must lie in the defective human material on which it had to operate. But wherever the fault lay, the law, or at least his devotion to the law, had led him into sin. This discovery must have been a traumatic experience for him, and goes far to explain Paul's continuing ambivalence towards the law. "I delight in the law of God, in my inmost self," he says (Rom. 7:22); at the same time he recognizes that that very

---

2. Cf. K. Stendahl, "The Apostle Paul and the Introspective Conscience of the West," *Harvard Theological Review*, 56 (1963), 199ff.

law provided sin with a vantage point from which to invade and dominate his life (Rom. 7:11). If this attitude is peculiarly Paul's, not to be paralleled in the other sages of Israel, that is because it springs from an experience which was peculiarly his. The leaders of the Jerusalem church knew nothing of such an experience; hence, it was difficult for them to sympathize with the view of the law which sprang from it. Where Paul was compelled to set up a sharp antithesis between the law and Christ, they saw no such antithesis and were willing to attempt a compromise between the two or a higher unity in which the two might be merged.

If until his experience on the Damascus road the law had been Paul's life, thenceforth, as he put it, "to me to live is Christ" (Phil. 1:21). Whereas the law had hitherto been the center of his living and thinking, that center had now been displaced by a new one. As when a magnet is removed from the center of a collection of iron filings that have formed a pattern around it, so the removal of the law from the central place in Paul's life and thought would have resulted in chaos, had the law not been replaced immediately by Christ as the new center, around which the same component elements of his existence formed a new pattern, the pattern of "a man in Christ." His whole perspective was transformed: now he realized that his previous perspective on persons and things, including his perspective on Christ and the law, had been a perspective "after the flesh"—an unregenerate perspective (II Cor. 5:16). For Paul the transition from the era of the flesh to that of the Spirit, from the age of law to the age of grace, took place on the Damascus road; but this was the reproduction in his personal life of a transition which had taken place in the divinely ordered history of salvation with the death and exaltation of Christ.

"Sin," as he wrote to the Romans, "will have no dominion over you, since you are not under law but under grace" (Rom. 6:14). This implies that to be "under law" is to be *ipso facto* under the dominion of sin. This was not inevitably or invariably so: Christ was "born under the law" (Gal. 4:4), yet he was not under the dominion of sin. But for others to be "under law" is to be exposed to the inroads of sin. Paul is not simply referring to the tendency of law to stimulate the very thing it forbids, although he takes this into consideration in his comments on the effect of the commandment "Thou shalt not covet" in Romans 7:7f. He is referring to something more dismaying: in his own experience it was his zeal to obey the law, not his instinctive rebellion against it, that led him into the sin of persecuting the church.

When Paul speaks of law, he thinks mainly of the Mosaic law. So much is this true that he can envisage the period between Adam and

Moses as a period when law was absent: "sin indeed was in the world before the law was given"—and death accordingly followed—"but sin is not counted where there is no law" (Rom. 5:13). Even so, the experience of being "under the law" is not confined to those who consciously live under the law of Moses: "when Gentiles who have not law do by nature what the law [of Moses] requires, they are a law to themselves, even though they do not have the law" (Rom. 2:14). It is pointless to ask if Paul would have modified his language if he had known (say) of the Code of Hammurabi, half a millennium earlier than Moses. He did not know of Hammurabi's law code, but as a Roman citizen he certainly knew of Roman law (of which, indeed, he availed himself when occasion required). Roman law, or at least its administration, was divinely ordained (Rom. 13:1-7), but Roman law was not the law of God in the sense in which Moses' law could be so described, and did not play the part in the history of salvation that Moses' law played.

II

When Paul insists that grace is a surer safeguard against the inroads of sin than law could ever be, he voices an insight that was not peculiar to himself—not even in Israel. Among the seven categories of Pharisee enumerated in the tractate *Berakot* (Palestinian Talmud) there is one described as the "tell-me-my-duty-and-I-will-do-it" Pharisee. His conduct is regulated by the application of an external standard, and he is not regarded as a commendable type. The one category which receives unqualified commendation is the Pharisee who is such "from love of God"; his outward piety springs from an inward motive.[3] This is not far from Paul's statement that "he is not a real Jew who is one outwardly,... he is a Jew who is one inwardly" (Rom. 2:28f.).

But for Paul "grace" is inseparably associated with Christ. That men are freely justified by God's grace, "through the redemption which is in Christ Jesus" (Rom. 3:24), is the central affirmation of Pauline soteriology, but divine grace is equally central to Pauline ethics. The summary of Paul's teaching in Titus 2:11-14 emphasizes this role of grace:

> For the grace of God has appeared for the salvation of all men, training us to renounce irreligion and worldly passions, and to live sober, upright, and godly lives in this world, awaiting our blessed hope, the appearing of the glory of our great God and Savior Jesus Christ, who gave himself for us to redeem us from all iniquity and to purify for himself a people of his own who are zealous for good deeds.

---

3. Palestinian Talmud, *Berakot* 9:7.

Only, in the major Pauline letters grace does not only train the people of God to lead good lives; it supplies the motive power within to enable them to do so. It was God's grace that proved sufficient to empower Paul himself to endure, and even rejoice in, afflictions and to accomplish his apostolic ministry (II Cor. 12:9f.); it was the same grace that moved the churches of Macedonia to give liberally to the Jerusalem relief fund— not only "according to their means" but "beyond their means, of their own free will" (II Cor. 8:1-5). This was their response to "the grace of our Lord Jesus Christ," who became poor himself that his people might be enriched through his poverty (II Cor. 8:9). And when we recall that in Greek one and the same word, *charis,* does duty for both 'grace' and 'gratitude,' we can the better appreciate Thomas Erskine's aphorism: "in the New Testament, religion is grace, and ethics is gratitude."[4]

In 1930 a little book appeared, which excited some interest at the time but to which less attention seems to have been paid in more recent years: *The Grace of God,* by N. P. Williams. Professor Williams' inquiry into the nature of divine grace led him to the conclusion that it could be adequately understood only in personal terms—that it should be equated frankly with the person of the Holy Spirit. In contradiction of Cardinal Newman's well-known lines, he affirmed that "there *is* no 'higher gift than grace'; grace *is* 'God's presence and his very Self, and Essence all-divine'" (p. 110). Certainly this question removes a number of difficulties in our attempts to grasp what grace is: divine grace, we may say, is the Spirit of God in action towards man or in man.

However this may be, there is a close parallel in Paul between the antithesis law/grace and the antithesis letter/Spirit. They are, in fact, one antithesis, not two. "The letter kills," said Paul, "but the Spirit gives life" (II Cor. 3:6), meaning that the law pronounces a sentence of death on the lawbreaker, whereas the Spirit conveys the promise and the reality of life. The "letter" or written code formed the basis of the old covenant; the dispensation of the Spirit is the dispensation of the new covenant. Paul's contrast between the "tablets of stone" and the "tablets of human hearts" (II Cor. 3:3) echoes not only Jeremiah's oracle of the new covenant, in which God undertook to write his law on his people's hearts (Jer. 31:33), but also Ezekiel's prophecy of the day when God would put a new spirit within them: "I will take the stony heart out of their flesh," he promised, "and give them a heart of flesh" (Ezek. 11:19; cf. 36:26). Not by external conformity to a written code, but by the impulsion of an inward power, God's people would do his will from the heart. The old

---

4. T. Erskine, *Letters* (Edinburgh, 1877), p. 16.

covenant declared the will of God without imparting the power—or even the desire—to do it. The new covenant was secured by the indwelling Spirit of God, not only enlightening his people with the knowledge of his will, but supplying the desire and the power to do it. This ministry of the Spirit is expressed by Paul in still more personal terms: it involves the increasing transformation of the people of God into the likeness of Christ here and now, "from one degree of glory to another" (II Cor. 3:18), in preparation for the day of their perfect revelation as "the sons of God" (Rom. 8:19). This increasing Christlikeness, wrought in them by the Spirit, is elsewhere described as "the new man, who is being renewed in knowledge after his Creator's image" (Col. 3:10). Its consummation is that divine glory in hope of which they rejoice at present (Rom. 5:2); "when Christ our life is manifested, then you also will be manifested with him in glory" (Col. 3:4).

The Spirit's law of life in Christ Jesus, then, liberates believers from "the law of sin and death"—the law which stimulates sin and therefore leads to death. "For," Paul goes on, "God has done what the law, weakened by the flesh, could not do: sending his own Son in the likeness of sinful flesh and as a sin-offering, he condemned sin in the flesh, in order that the just requirement of the law might be fulfilled in us, who walk not according to the flesh but according to the Spirit" (Rom. 8:3-4). The Son of God, as we have seen, was "born under law" but was not liable to the death-sentence which the law prescribes because he did the will of God from the heart. His incarnation was a real one; yet in that human flesh which in everyone else proved to be "sinful flesh," in that sphere where sin established its dominion over all others, he remained sinless. More than that, he voluntarily presented his sinless life to God as a sin-offering for sinful men, and thus for himself and for all those united to him by faith he absorbed, exhausted, and overcame the hostile power of sin. "The death he died he died to sin, once for all," and now, since he has been raised from the dead, "the life he lives he lives to God" (Rom. 6:10). In the power of his risen life his people share. Not only has his death as a sin-offering procured them justification before God; it secures them the possibility of living for God, because "the Spirit of him who raised Jesus from the dead dwells" in them (Rom. 8:11). Hence the law's requirements, which by their own strength they were unable to meet, are fulfilled in them as they rely not on their own strength but on the power of the Spirit who now resides within them.

To run and work the law commands,
Yet gives me neither feet nor hands;

But better news the gospel brings:
It bids me fly, and gives me wings.[5]

III

Put this way, it sounds so easy. Paul himself knew that it was not. He is too prone to describe the Christian life in strenuous terms—a race to be run, a battle to be fought—for us to imagine that spiritual victory came to him "sudden, in a minute." The zeal which had driven him to persecute the church was now diverted into other channels, but we can well understand how a man of his qualities found it no simple matter to "crucify the flesh," to bring into subjection the hasty tongue, the premature judgment, the feelings of resentment when others encroached on his sphere of apostolic service. The "meekness and gentleness of Christ" by which he entreated his friends (II Cor. 10:1) were not qualities which came to Paul naturally. The man who pressed forward to the goal of God's upward calling in Christ Jesus (Phil. 3:14) knew that the immortal garland he sought was to be run for "not without dust and heat." There is little of a passive quietism in Paul's understanding of the way of holiness: he knew, as it has been put in more recent times, that it is "all of God in the way of grace, and all of man in the way of obedience."

Paul was no longer "under law" as he had been before his conversion, but obedience to Christ (II Cor. 10:5) was now as central to his moral life as obedience to the law had formerly been: so much so that he can speak of himself as "under the law of Christ" or, more literally, "in-lawed to Christ" (I Cor. 9:21). This "law of Christ" includes the specific rulings of Christ Paul had received from those who were in Christ before him, which he quotes as binding from time to time in writing to his converts. But it includes more: he who is "under the law of Christ" knows it his duty to follow the example Christ set his followers. Thus Paul can say to the Corinthians, "Be imitators of me, as I am of Christ" (I Cor. 11:1); the *imitatio Christi* is involved in being under the law of Christ. Again, when Paul says to the Galatians, "Bear one another's burdens, and so fulfil the law of Christ" (Gal. 6:2), it is plain from the context that to "fulfil the law of Christ" is in practice the same thing as to "walk by the Spirit" (Gal. 5:25). The law of Christ is the law of love: "he who loves his neighbor has fulfilled the law" (Rom. 13:8-10; cf. Gal. 5:14). It is by the Spirit that this law is fulfilled: the love it enjoins is the reflection of God's love, which "has been poured into our hearts through the Holy Spirit who has been given to us" (Rom. 5:5).

---

5. Ralph Erskine, *Gospel Sonnets* (Edinburgh, 1803).

Here we recognize an echo of the teaching of Jesus, who affirmed that the law and the prophets depend on the twofold law of love to God and love to one's neighbor. But when we speak of the law of love, we are no longer speaking of law in the ordinary sense as something which can be enforced by external sanctions. Just as an apple tree produces apples not by legal enactment but because it is its nature so to do, the man in Christ lives a life of love not by outward dictation but because love is the spontaneous expression of the Christ-nature produced within him by the Spirit. This was the principle of Christian ethics Paul laid down for his converts.

It is not surprising that many of Paul's Christian friends, not to speak of his opponents, felt that in this he was impractically idealistic and starry-eyed. It was one thing for Paul himself, or for other converts to Christianity from Judaism, to find this principle sufficient, for they had been brought up under the law of Moses, where the distinction between right and wrong was clearly set forth. But many of Paul's Gentile converts were drawn from a pagan environment: some of them, in his own words, had been "fornicators, idolaters, adulterers, homosexuals, thieves, greedy, drunkards, revilers, robbers" (I Cor. 6:10). How could such people be taught the elements of sound morality? Many Jewish Christians thought that this could be done only by bringing them under "the yoke of the commandments," as Gentile proselytes to Judaism were required to learn and keep the Jewish law. Early in the Gentile mission, according to Luke, some men went down from Judea to Antioch and insisted that Gentile Christians must be circumcised and charged to keep the law of Moses (Acts 15:1-5).

For Paul, this was an impossible course. He knew more about law-keeping than most people did, and had proved its inadequacy. Converts from paganism, like converts from Judaism, had received the indwelling Spirit, with his power to transform their lives into the likeness of Christ. So Paul taught, but would this teaching work? It must have been all too easy for his critics to point to the deplorable moral lapses in a church like that of Corinth and to argue that nothing else could be expected so long as Paul refused to impose the Mosaic law on his converts.

Paul's way was not to impose the Mosaic law on them, but to emphasize the law of Christ—to insist that the gospel which had brought them salvation had ethical implications, and to spell out in detail what those implications were. In some of his letters a transition from his theological teaching to its ethical corollaries is marked by the adverb 'therefore.' "I appeal to you *therefore*, brethren," he says in Romans 12:1, "by the mercies of God, to present your bodies as a living sacrifice, holy and acceptable to God, which is your spiritual worship." "I *therefore,* a prisoner for the Lord," he says in Ephesians 4:1, "beg you to lead a life worthy of the calling to which you have been called." "Put to death *therefore* what is earthly in you," he writes in Colossians 3:5: "immorality, impurity, passion, evil desire, and covetousness, which is idolatry."

In Ephesians and Colossians, too, Paul's ethical admonitions tend to be grouped under easily memorized captions, such as 'put off' (cf. Col. 3:5-11); 'put on' (cf. Col. 3:12-17); 'be subject' (cf. Col. 3:18—4:1); 'watch and pray' (cf. Col. 4:2-6). The old character, with its vices, must be put off; the new character, with its virtues, must be put on. Christians must cultivate mutual deference; their attitude in a hostile world must be one of vigilance and prayer. When the Christian way of life was taught to converts from paganism it was probably easier, for catechetical purposes, to arrange the teaching in this way; and indeed the same general pattern has been traced in non-Pauline writings of the New Testament.

But when Paul uses it, we find an interesting alternation between the indicative and the imperative: "you have put off the old man with his practices," he says to the Colossians (3:9), "put him off," he says to the Ephesians (4:22); "you have put on the new man," he says to the Colossians (3:10), "put him on," he tells the Ephesians (4:24). The "old man" is the unregenerate self, "the man we once were," as it is rendered by the New English Bible in Romans 6:6; the "new man," as we have seen already, is the Christlikeness reproduced in the believer by the Holy Spirit. The indicative statements imply that the old man was exchanged for the new man at conversion, as the death-and-resurrection symbolism of baptism declares. What took place once for all there and then must be worked out in practice. "Be what you are" is the command of Christian ethics: be in active obedience what you are by divine grace.

If we ask, then, how the precepts of the new life differ from those of the old covenant, Paul's answer is plain. The precepts of the new life are not imposed by an external code; they are the outworking of what is already implanted within. The graces which these precepts inculcate are those which make up the "fruit of the Spirit" (Gal. 5:22f.). Those in whose lives such fruit is seen show thereby that they have received the Spirit; those whose lives are characterized rather by the "works of the flesh" show thereby that they have not the Spirit—and "any one who does not have the Spirit of Christ does not belong to him" (Rom. 8:9), whatever his profession may be. "The Spirit of Christ" is personal, but the expression includes the sense of the spirit or mind that characterized Christ: where that spirit or mind is not apparent, the claim to be a Christian lacks conviction.

IV

"Walk by the Spirit," says Paul to his converts (Gal. 5:16); only thus can they avoid gratifying the desires of the flesh and the promptings of the unregenerate ego. To gratify the desires of the flesh may seem at first to be the way of liberty; it turns out before long to be the way of bondage. To try to keep the desires of the flesh in check by submitting to a strict discipline of rules and regulations is only an alternative way of bondage. To walk by the Spirit is the way of release from bondage of either kind: "where the Spirit of the Lord is, there is freedom" (II Cor. 3:17).

We cannot forget Paul's words about the necessity of keeping the body under control (I Cor. 9:27); yet it is plain that he enjoyed his Christian freedom to the full and was the most emancipated of men. None was more free than he from irrational taboos. The perfect liberty he experienced as the bondslave of the crucified and exalted Christ could not tolerate limitations imposed by others, whether on himself or on his converts. But that liberty will readily follow the example of Christ, who "did not please himself" (Rom. 15:3) but lived for others. The "law of Christ," we have seen, is fulfilled when his people "bear one another's burdens" (Gal. 6:2), especially when they "bear with the failings of the weak" (Rom. 15:1).

If the divine law is summed up in love to one's neighbor, then it is our neighbor, the other person, who is important. People matter more than things; people matter more than principles. Things are ethically indifferent. "I know and am persuaded in the Lord Jesus," said Paul, "that no *thing* is unclean in itself; but it is unclean for any one who thinks it unclean" (Rom. 14:14). Morally speaking, food is neither here nor there. Gluttony and drunkenness are works of the flesh, but the fault lies not in the food which is misused but in the people who misuse it. The law in which Paul had been brought up had its food regulations, which he no doubt had observed strictly; but he had now learned a new way from him who in a brief pronouncement "declared all foods clean" (Mark 7:19). The Council of Jerusalem included food restrictions in its recommendations (Acts 15:29); insofar as Paul went along with these he did so because they were calculated to facilitate social fellowship between Jewish and Gentile believers. But if any attempt was made to enforce these restrictions in their own right, Paul could not allow it. What about the flesh of animals that had been offered in sacrifice to pagan deities? The Jerusalem decree enjoined abstention from it; but when the question is submitted to him, Paul sees no obstacle to eating it if the eater takes it with a good conscience and thanks God for it. But if the example of a mature Christian's eating such meat has a harmful effect on an immature Christian, one with a weak and unemancipated conscience—then, says Paul, I for one would abstain from eating it, as I would abstain from doing anything else that had the same effect. It is not that there is any harm in the meat, or in any other *thing,* but there is great harm in injuring my brother's weak conscience. If *things* are morally neutral, people are not; people matter, and matter enormously.

The one limit which Christian liberty can tolerate, then, is the limit imposed by Christian charity. Luther caught the spirit of Paul's argument excellently in his introductory sentences to *The Liberty of a Christian Man:* "A Christian man is a most free lord of all, subject to none. A Christian man is a most dutiful servant of all, subject to all." "Subject to none" in respect of his liberty; "subject to all" in respect of his charity. And this is true of a Christian man because it was primarily true of Christ.

Some of Paul's Gentile converts heartily agreed with his insistence on Christian liberty, but thought that even he was insufficiently emancipated; that he was still enmeshed in old-fashioned Jewish taboos. Of course, said they, food is morally neutral; it is relevant only to this mortal body. But, they went on, the same is true of sex: why should Paul, who was so enlightened with regard to food, be so uncompromising with regard to something so casual as occasional intercourse with a harlot? "Sex for the body and the body for sex"—was that not a corollary of Paul's position on food? No, said Paul: "the body is not meant for fornication, but for the Lord" (I Cor. 6:13). Nothing that involved personal relations, especially at the deep level of sexual intercourse, could be called "casual"; and indeed Paul's language here "displays a psychological insight into human sexuality which is altogether exceptional by first-century standards" when he insists that such intercourse, "by reason of its very nature, engages and expresses the whole personality in such a way as to constitute an unique mode of self-disclosure and self-commitment."[6]

In laying down ethical guidelines for his converts Paul was well aware that, at the opposite extreme from those who wanted to be as permissive in sex as in food, there were others who thought that the interests of the gospel called for the imposition of an unrealistic asceticism on their fellow-Christians. When some of these adopted the slogan "It is well for a man not to touch a woman" (I Cor. 7:1), Paul assured them that he could not agree more, so far as his personal preference was concerned; but he reminded them that the majority of men and women were not

---

6. D. S. Bailey, *Sexual Relation in Christian Thought* (New York, 1959), p. 10.

constituted for such mutual abstention, and that any attempt to impose celibacy would thus lead to far worse evils than the imagined ones it was designed to prevent. Far better, things being as they were, that "each man should have his own wife and each woman her own husband" (I Cor. 7:2)—and so, just when they thought they had Paul on their side, the ascetics found him advocating the very course they had hoped he would discourage.

It is especially interesting to see how Paul appeals to the ruling of Christ when he deals in I Corinthians 7 with marriage problems within the church fellowship. When he can quote no dominical ruling, he gives his own advice. He thinks his friends will be wise if they follow it, but he cannot compel them to do so. But where he can quote such a ruling, there is an end of all controversy: "To the married I give charge, not I but the Lord, that the wife should not separate from her husband . . . and that the husband should not divorce his wife" (vv. 10f.). This is a reference to the ruling we know from Mark 10:2-11. Even so, Paul has to apply the principle of this ruling to a situation not envisaged in its original Palestinian setting but not uncommon in the experience of his Gentile missionary activity—the case of a convert to Christianity whose wife or husband refused thereafter to continue the marriage relationship. In this situation he applies the principle not legalistically but reasonably and humanely, with an eye to the well-being of the persons concerned, as one who recognized that the marriage law, like the sabbath law, was ordained for human beings, and not *vice versa*. Conformity to the likeness of Christ involves obedience to the commands of Christ, but in changing situations it is the spirit of these commands that is of chief importance.

V

Paul is conscious of no discontinuity between the historical Jesus and the exalted Lord. The example and precepts of the historical Jesus remain the rule of life for his people now that he occupies the place of universal supremacy and dwells within them by his Spirit. If Paul's ethical teaching attains its highest expression in his exhortation to love in I Corinthians 13, it does so in a passage where it has been a commonplace of expositors to find the character of Christ portrayed. But it is the character of the *earthly* Christ that is recognized here; if the heavenly Christ is marked by love of this quality, that is because the heavenly Christ is one and the same person as the earthly Christ. The love which was so evident in his life on earth, as he displayed the nature of God among men, remains unchanged now that he is highly exalted; and it is this divine love that he imparts to his people through the Spirit, so that the nature of God may be displayed among men in their lives as it was in his. Thus simultaneously the grace of God is manifested and the law of Christ fulfilled. This is the basis of Pauline ethics.

The Law in the Liturgy

HOWARD HAGEMAN

It is obvious to anyone inspecting even cursorily the liturgies of both Western and Eastern Christendom that one of the peculiarities of the liturgies of Reformed churches is the inclusion of the law as part of the liturgy. To the best of my knowledge, no other liturgical tradition makes this use of the law. The sole exception to that statement is the Order for Holy Communion in the churches of the Anglican communion, in which the reading of the Ten Commandments occurs almost at the beginning of the service. It is universally agreed, however, that this usage, which began in the so-called Second Prayer Book of Edward VI (1552), was the result of pressures from that section of the Church of England which had large sympathies with the Calvinistic patterns in Geneva.

There is an interesting confirmation of this origin in the rubric which accompanies the reading of the Ten Commandments in the Book of Common Prayer. In the Strasbourg version of Calvin's *Forme des Prières,* the singing of the Decalogue was interrupted after the fourth commandment by a short collect, after the reading of which the remaining six commandments were sung. This interruption, which probably had practical as well as theoretical reasons for its origin, was based on the tradition that the two stone tablets mentioned in Exodus contained four commandments on one and six on the other, dividing our duties to God from our duties to our neighbors.

In view of this separation in Calvin's liturgy, it is interesting to read the following rubric in the Book of Common Prayer:

> The responses by the people as hereinafter set forth after each of the Commandments other than the fourth and the tenth may be omitted, in which case the response after the fourth Commandment

Howard Hageman is the President of New Brunswick Theological Seminary, and was for many years the pastor of The North Church in Newark, New Jersey. He has authored distinguished works on theology and liturgy. Hageman here writes about the theological rationale for the use of the law in Calvinist liturgies. He demonstrates that Calvin's liturgical views were rooted in a solid ethical foundation—the conviction that praise of God is inseparable from moral response and moral response to God is fulfilled service to the people of God.

35

shall be *Lord, have mercy upon us, and incline our hearts to keep these laws.*[1]

In other words, the Calvinist origin of the use of the Decalogue in the Book of Common Prayer would seem to be indicated not just by tradition but even by an attempt to reproduce Calvin's liturgical use of the Ten Commandments in two parts, at least as an option, for Anglican worship.

With this single exception, however, the use of the law in the liturgy is a Reformed peculiarity. It would seem to be in order, therefore, to inquire briefly as to its history and significance in this liturgical tradition.

In the thinking of Western Christendom in the Middle Ages the idea arose that every Christian needed to know three things: the Apostles' Creed as the summary of Christian belief, the Lord's Prayer as the model for Christian prayer, and the Ten Commandments as the guide for Christian behavior. These three items became the staple for Christian education during the period, and most of the catechetical material of the time used them as its basis.

In its catechetical practice the Reformation took this medieval inheritance seriously. Almost all of the catechisms from the time of the Reformation use the Creed, the Commandments and the Our Father as the basis for their discussion of the meaning of Christianity. Though they differ in emphasis and understanding, Luther's Shorter Catechism, the Catechism of the Book of Common Prayer, and the Heidelberg Catechism are all alike in using these three items as the basis for much, if not most, of their discussion.

When in the late Middle Ages pressures began to develop for the use of the vernacular in the celebration of Christian worship, especially in German-speaking countries, it is not surprising to find that in the development of the Prone (as the vernacular service came to be called) these three traditional elements came to play an important role. Apparently the Prone had no set form, but varied from one diocese to another. Suggestions as to the content were made by practical theology departments in much the same way as they would be today.

One such suggestion was contained in Surgant's *Manuale Curatorum*, published in Basle in 1506. Surgant had taught practical theology in Basle, and his publication was a kind of priests' handbook, including suggestions for the conduct of the Prone in those places where it was

---

1. *The Book of Common Prayer of the Church of Ireland* (Dublin, 1966), p. 138.

used.[2] Surgant's *Manuale*, in its outline of the Prone, contained the Creed, the Commandments, and the Our Father.

From our point of view the more important point is that the same three items appear in Zwingli's Sunday service, which in the revision made by Farel was the liturgy Calvin found in use when he came to Geneva in 1536. Like Surgant, Zwingli seemed to have no particular rationale for the order in which the three items occurred. Since their usage had been traditionally conceived in a catechetical rather than a liturgical way so that the Prone was actually a kind of catechetical service or *leerdienst,* the inclusion of the three items rather than the order in which they came was the important question. Surgant's *Manuale* and the services of the reformers Leo Jude and Zwingli all have slightly varying places for the three items, but they all include all three.

A striking piece of evidence for the catechetical origin of this Reformed liturgical specialty is found in the work of Martin Bucer, the reformer of Strasbourg with whom Calvin came later to be closely associated. Bucer's immediate liturgical inheritance in Strasbourg was a rather creative translation of the Latin Mass made in German in 1524 by one of the cathedral clergy, Diebold Schwarz. Though recent Reformed liturgical scholarship has hailed the significance of this in the history of Calvin's liturgical development,[3] Bucer himself was obviously not overmuch impressed by it. In the same year he began altering it, obviously to respond to some of the objections he felt were already being raised by the Swiss reformers led by Zwingli.

Since the structure Bucer inherited was that of the mass, there was already a place for the Creed and the Our Father, both of which occur in the text of the Latin rite. But since he was eager also to meet the requirements of the Swiss, what was he to do with the Decalogue, which was part of their service? In his first edition of 1524, he actually inserted it between the reading of the Epistle and the Gospel as a response to be sung by the congregation![4] When in later editions, as a result of his substitution of a single *lectio continua* for the traditional pericopes, that position became impossible, the Strasbourg Reformer, still feeling the necessity of including the law in his liturgy, used it as a kind of call to confession. Such was the usage of the law, certainly a good Lutheran one,

---

2. Surgant's was not the only such manual in existence, but it has come into recent notice because of Schmidt-Clausing's demonstration of the connection between Surgant's Prone and Zwingli's Service of the Word. Cf. Fr. Schmidt-Clausing, *Zwingli als Liturgiker* (Göttingen, 1952).

3. Cf. W. D. Maxwell, *John Knox's Genevan Service Book* (Edinburgh, 1936).

4. A. F. N. Lekkerkerker, *Kanttekeningen bij het Hervormde Dienstboek,* III (The Hague, 1956), 186.

which Calvin found when he came as an exile to Strasbourg in 1538.

Since we are now at the point at which the use of the law in the liturgy is about to receive its peculiarly Calvinist touch, we may summarize the situation as Calvin found it. Following the lead of the Middle Ages, all the Reformation leaders of the Reformed persuasion kept the law in their orders of service, not so much for liturgical as catechetical reasons. As one of three essentials for Christian knowledge it certainly belonged there, and we cannot underestimate the Reformers' understanding of the catechetical possibilities in the liturgy. The exact place at which it came in the liturgy was to them a matter of indifference. It might and did come at the beginning, middle, or end of the service. It might come as a response between the lessons or as a call and stimulation to the confession of sin. The important point was that it be part of the act of worship.

*   *   *

With this point of view Calvin would have been perfectly familiar during his first stay in Geneva (1536-1538). As has been pointed out, the liturgy used there was Farel's French adaptation of Zwingli's service, a service derived directly from the Prone. There is no evidence that Calvin objected to it in any way, though before he left he had raised some broader liturgical questions about the absence of music and the infrequency of the celebrations of the eucharist.

In Strasbourg, however, the situation was different. There, as minister of the congregation of French refugees, Calvin for the first time had to address himself directly to the liturgical question. The town fathers had to know and approve the form of worship to be used in his little parish. Calvin's response was his *Forme des Prières*. Though the earliest printed edition which survives is that of 1542, that edition almost certainly represents accurately the liturgy Calvin prepared in 1539.

There seems to be general agreement that Calvin's *Forme des Prières* was heavily influenced by the German liturgy Bucer was then using, *Von des Herren Nachtmal oder Messe, und die Predigen.* In fact, so acute a critic as Lekkerkerker makes the following comparison: "The Strasbourg order [Calvin's] is practically a translation of Bucer's."[5] Generally speaking, that is doubtless true; but at the point of the use of the law a significant difference appears.

---

5. *Ibid.*

Consider the order of the opening of the two services:

BUCER	CALVIN
Votum	Votum
Reading of the Law	Confession of Sin
Confession of Sin	Words of Absolution
Words of Absolution	Singing of the Law (1st 4)
	Collect
	Singing of the Law (2nd 6)

What has happened is clear. In his adaptation and translation of this part of Bucer's service Calvin has made two changes in his use of the law. First, instead of being read by the minister as in Bucer's service (to be fair, this use of the law occurs only in the third form of that liturgy), the law in Calvin's service is sung in metrical form by the congregation. Secondly, in Calvin's service the position of the law has been changed. Bucer used it in the Lutheran way as a call and a stimulation to the confession of sin, which follows it directly. This use of the law is also that of the third question of the Heidelberg Catechism. Calvin transposed it to follow the confession of sin and the words of absolution.

Let us look first at the change from the reading of the law by the minister to the singing of the law by the whole congregation. This metrical version of the law with accompanying music appeared in the Strasbourg Psalter of 1539, a slight volume of a few metrical Psalms and other liturgical pieces Calvin put together soon after his arrival in Strasbourg from Geneva. Because it contained far less than its great Genevan successor, this earliest Reformed songbook has suffered from long neglect.[6]

Unfortunately for our purposes, Calvin's Strasbourg Psalter gives no indication of the authorship of either the texts or the music. So far as the latter is concerned, we can surmise that the rather sprightly tune given for the law (the corresponding tune in the Genevan Psalter is much more solemn) had its origin either in folk music or in Strasbourg usage.[7] It was only in Geneva that great composers like Goudimel or LeJeune were brought into service.

The authorship of the text is an equal mystery. Somewhere in commenting on the words of the Strasbourg Psalter Calvin says that he was in such a hurry to get the book in use that he provided some of the texts himself, texts which were not part of the Genevan Psalter because he had

---

6. The only English edition of it was published in this century by a Roman Catholic musicologist; R. R. Terry, *Calvin's First Psalter* (London, 1932).
7. There was already a sung version in use in Strasbourg.

subsequently found better poetry. Since this Strasbourg version of the law was one of the texts which was removed in the later Genevan edition, the question can be raised whether the Strasbourg version may indeed be the work of Calvin himself.

That hunch receives further confirmation from a curious characteristic of the Strasbourg version: that each stanza ends with the Greek refrain "Kyrie Eleis." That strange refrain in the original language could, of course, argue that this is indeed a folk usage, since macaronics of this kind were popular at the time. But it could also be interpreted as a strong indication that Calvin himself was indeed the author of the text.

In the Bucer original, which it is agreed Calvin was using as a model, the Words of Absolution are followed by the congregational singing of the Kyrie and the Gloria in Excelsis. To be sure, this was indicated as an option, but it was obviously an indication of Bucer's desire to retain what he could from the traditional Latin mass, especially since the Strasbourg tradition of vernacular worship had begun in 1524 as a fairly close translation of the Latin rite.

There can be no question, therefore, that Calvin saw in the singing of the law a substitute for the singing of the Kyrie and Gloria. We shall shortly be examining some of the theological implications of this substitution. But the use of the law as a substitute for two items, the Kyrie and the Gloria, and the appearance of the Kyrie in the Strasbourg Psalter version of the law, are strong indications that the substitute was created with a very clear understanding of the liturgical position it was to fill. If that does not demonstrate the authorship of Calvin himself, it certainly points to someone who was working closely under his direction.

In speculating about the origin of the Strasbourg Psalter version of the law we have already touched on the reason for the change from the minister's reading it to the whole congregation's singing it. It is clear that Bucer was adapting the use of the Kyrie and Gloria in the Latin rite to make them an act of thanksgiving following the Confession of Sin and the Declaration of Pardon. To this proclamation of forgiveness the congregation made its response by singing its praise. It is equally obvious that this movement in the liturgy, from confession to pardon to praise, appealed to Calvin also.

Calvin's difficulty was not with the liturgical concept itself but with the words used for the congregational act of thanksgiving, the words of the traditional Kyrie and Gloria. It is useless to speculate here about Calvin's distaste for the words of the Latin mass and the reasons for it. The fact is that he displayed such distaste in more ways than one. For that reason the Kyrie and Gloria would be unacceptable in this place in his *Forme des Prières*. Today we would consider using an appropriate psalm or hymn at this point, but Calvin had far less musical material at his disposal: settings of the Apostles' Creed, the Lord's Prayer, the Nunc Dimittis, and fewer than twenty Psalms. That there were other theological considerations involved here as well is a matter that we shall come to presently. But the liturgical reason for the change is to provide a congregational response of thanksgiving to the Words of Absolution, since Calvin felt unable to use the traditional Kyrie and Gloria as Bucer had done.

It is also clear that Calvin by this time was clearly aware that such a response had to be a musical one. For two years he had lived without music in Geneva; indeed it was one of the liturgical situations against which he had already made his protest in 1537. An act of thanksgiving read by the minister alone, no matter how appropriate, simply does not have the same effect as does something sung by the congregation.[8]

To sum up, the change from the reading of the law by the minister to the singing of it by the congregation was to provide an act of thanksgiving for the whole congregation. We can agree with Lekkerkerker's conclusion that Calvin "thus understood the use of the Law as an act of praise."[9]

If that is the liturgical reason for Calvin's alteration, what about the theological ones? We have seen how what could be called a catechetical use of the law in the liturgy, as with Zwingli, was changed by Bucer to a Lutheran use. Why did Calvin move it to still another position in his service? Granted the need for an act of praise and thanksgiving at this liturgical point, why did he choose the law to serve this purpose?

It is not our purpose here to explore the so-called "third use of the law," which is Calvin's insistence on the continuation of the law in the gospel. The theological explanation of this hallmark of Calvin's ethic belongs elsewhere. Our purpose is to indicate how this theological point found its expression in Calvin's liturgical work.

Even though it postdates Calvin by several years, the Heidelberg Catechism makes the point clear by its very organization. Although the Law is introduced early (Q. 3) as the source of the knowledge of sin and

---

8. In the new *Liturgy of the Reformed Church in America* (New York, 1968), p. 10, the Reading of the Law (or of the summary of the law) takes place after the reading of the Assurance of Pardon. It is read by the minister alone. In spite of repeated efforts to explain why it occurs here—that it is in effect an act of thanksgiving for the forgiveness just announced—this usage has never been generally accepted. We need a joyous musical version of the law to make clear that it is in this way that we are giving thanks for our redemption.

9. *Op. cit.*, p. 186.

misery (cf. also Bucer's liturgy), it is virtually left with that except for the use of the Lord's summary of the law (Q. 4). The real exploration of the law and its meaning is saved until Q. 92, where it is taken up under the general heading of "Man's Gratitude and Obedience—New Life Through the Holy Spirit."

Two points should be made here, each of which bears on our inquiry. The first is the heading of Section III itself—"Of Man's Gratitude and Obedience." The thing to be noted here is the coupling of gratitude and obedience, a central concept in Calvin's thinking. The second is the way in which the law is introduced in Question 91, which reads as follows:

Q. But what are good works?
A. Only those which are done out of true faith, in accordance with the Law of God, and for his glory, and not those based on our own opinion or on the traditions of men.

Then follow twenty-four questions and answers in explanation of the meaning of the law.

In expansion of this, three points can be made briefly.

a. Gratitude means obedience. Calvin had a deep suspicion of any act of thanksgiving that did not issue in a style of life. The words of the well-known Anglican prayer of thanksgiving, written by an English Presbyterian who later conformed to the Church of England, are deeply Calvinistic: "And that we shew forth thy praise, not only with our lips, but in our lives; by giving up ourselves to thy service and by walking before thee in holiness and righteousness all our days."[10]

Anyone can bawl out "Glory to God" in singing a hymn and then go about his business as usual. Really to give glory to God means obedience.

b. Obedience means good works. This was, of course, the point made by the Reformation in response to the accusation that it emphasized faith at the expense of good works. True gratitude for the gift of redemption, it was asserted repeatedly, shows itself publicly in acts of goodness. The Reformation had no patience with that kind of pietism which in its extreme stress on inner sanctification minimized or even ignored outward actions. These were the very necessary fruits of obedience, which was itself the chief sign of gratitude.

c. The standard by which good works are measured is the law. It is at this point that Calvin's insight differed from Luther's. As the Heidelberg Catechism puts it, "good works are done out of true faith in accordance with the Law of God." Possibly Calvin remembered from his own Roman Catholic youth too many "good works" which were merely ecclesiastical

---

10. *Book of Common Prayer*, p. 34.

actions. Possibly he felt threatened by the antinomianism already present in at least some sections of the Reformation movement. Whatever the reason, Calvin could not overlook the fact that obedience and good works have a definite shape and dimension. They are not just anybody's idea of what is pleasant or satisfying. Their shape and dimension have been carefully articulated in the Decalogue and in our Lord's interpretation of it.

Hence what has come to be known as "the third use of the law," an insistence that the life-style of the redeemed has been charted and directed by that same law which can send the unredeemed into despair. For the redeemed, the law is now a joyful duty, the way of obedience. As the Catechism says (Q. 115), this is the way in which the faithful are "renewed in the image of God."

It would be surprising if such a theological insight had not found its way into liturgical expression at Calvin's hands. Having agreed to the necessity for some corporate act of thanksgiving following the Words of Absolution, Calvin could think of no better text than the Decalogue, for here is the way in which the people of God seek to express their grateful obedience for the gift of their redemption in Christ. Calvin's relocation of the law to a position after the Confession and Absolution instead of before it (as in Bucer's service) is simply his liturgical way of stating what he believed the function of the law to be in the total life of the people of God.

We have already noted that in the Strasbourg version the singing of each commandment ended with the refrain, "Kyrie Eleis." Quite possibly, as we have noted, that may have been Calvin's way of recognizing the old liturgical tradition of Kyrie and Gloria in Excelsis, which he was replacing. Certainly there must be some significance in the fact that he left the old petition untranslated.

But reasons of that kind would not have been sufficient for John Calvin. The retention of the Kyrie in his version of the Decalogue was also an indication of his recognition that, important as the law was as an expression of grateful obedience, it was also a form of gratitude that could never be completely or perfectly expressed. "Even the holiest... make only a small beginning in obedience in this life" (Heidelberg Catechism—Q. 114). There is a deep theological reason, therefore, behind the inclusion of a prayer for mercy in the act of gratitude, incongruous as it may at first seem. If the gratitude is to be with the whole life, one must recognize his inability to act it out perfectly. The difference is that for the unbelieving, failure to keep the law is a source of guilt and terror, while for the faithful it is a source of the assurance of mercy and forgiveness.

It is true that when Calvin returned to Geneva in 1542, the new liturgy there to which he agreed did not contain the singing of the law as one of its required items. The reason seems to have been the fact that the congregation in Geneva objected to the use of an Absolution. To them it was a dangerous novelty against which they protested by rising from their knees even before the end of the General Confession.[11] In the Genevan liturgy, therefore, after the Votum and the Confession, a Psalm was sung and the Words of Absolution were omitted.

Even though the use of the law is no longer indicated, it would not be difficult to believe that it was nevertheless sung at this same place on many occasions. The Genevan Psalter also contained a musical setting of the Decalogue, though to a different tune, which had no Kyrie refrain. Since the liturgy indicated that something was to be sung at this point, it is not hard to believe that the Ten Commandments were often used, even though their use was no longer required as in Strasbourg. Perhaps in Calvin's thinking the removal of the Words of Absolution meant that the theological function of the law in the liturgy was no longer as clear as it had been.

The use of the Decalogue as part of the liturgy continued to be an integral part of Dutch custom through the years, though seldom in the same position as indicated by Calvin in his Strasbourg *Forme*. One wonders exactly when it ceased to be sung and began to be read by the minister or, as was often the case in the United States, by a *voorlezer* in a kind of preliminary service. It is interesting to note that the Dutch Psalter continued to carry a metrical version of the Decalogue to the Genevan tune in all of its editions. In fact, when the Reformed Church in the United States began to publish its own Psalters in the eighteenth century, metrical versions of the Decalogue were still to be found in them, though by this time they may well have become an ancient tradition rather than a living usage. Since all historians seem to agree that the eighteenth century was a low point in Reformed musicology generally, a time when most congregations had a very limited repertory of tunes, it may well be that this was the time when something which had been sung by the congregation was given over to the *domine* or the *voorlezer*.

Two very general observations may be made in conclusion. The ethical sensitivities of Calvinists in the sixteenth and seventeenth centuries, sensitivities which found expression in the social as well as the individual

---

11. Lekkerkerker, *op. cit.*, p. 188.

realm, have often been noted by historians. Little note seems to have been taken, however, of the fact that one of the real sources of this ethical sensitivity was the continued liturgical use of the law in Reformed worship. Even though the liturgical scheme employed was not always that of Calvin in Strasbourg, his understanding of the law as a hymn of thanksgiving certainly continued to be strong through preaching and catechetical instruction. If the liturgical repetition of things has any psychological effect at all, the liturgical use of the law Sunday after Sunday must have had an enormous effect in subconsciously or consciously sharpening the consciences of generations of Reformed worshipers.

The second observation is really the negative side of the first. It is well known that in the last century (and well into this century in many places) Reformed worship became assimilated to that of evangelical pietism generally. Even where (as in some Reformed churches in the United States) the reading of the law was still indicated more or less in Calvin's liturgical position, it was made clear that this was done as an optional reading from the Old Testament, for which other Old Testament lessons could be substituted. It is safe to say that evangelicalism of that kind had no use for the law as a hymn of thanksgiving.

The loss of any sense of ethical responsibility socially in American evangelicalism is too well known to require comment. It would, of course, be naive to suppose that such a loss in Reformed circles can be totally explained by the elimination of the law from its Calvinistic place in the liturgy. At the same time, that very elimination was itself an indication of what had happened. Since salvation was now seen as a gift of status to be enjoyed privately, what need was there for the law as a hymn of thanksgiving—or as anything else except possibly as an optional lesson from the Old Testament to be read on occasion?

In planning for significant Reformed liturgy in the future, liturgiologists, one hopes, will not forget Calvin's use of the law in the liturgy. Admittedly, a new metrical version of the Decalogue—even with a Kyrie attached—will not answer the purpose. One cannot really see a contemporary congregation responding with something which is ten or eleven stanzas long! But since confessions and even absolutions are becoming fashionable once again in Reformed worship, we need to remember the tradition which says that grateful response must be more than with the lips. We need to discover new expressions of the old Reformed insight that gratitude means obedience and that obedience has shape—the shape of the law of God.

Theology and the Playful Life

Can life before the face of a holy God be an ultimately playful experience? Can a serious orthodox theology support a playful attitude in this worrisome world? Can play serve as a parable to tell us how to be co-laborers with God? This is my question.

First, I should mention some things about play that I do not mean to be talking about. I am not interested in finding religious justification for the occasional game, the festival amid serious toil and troubles. Nor am I trying to do what Johan Huizenga did in *Homo Ludens* or Josef Pieper did in *Leisure, the Basis of Culture:* I am not looking to man's festivities or to an elitist view of contemplative leisure as the key to understanding or saving culture. Nor do I have anything to say pertinent to the popular business of analyzing almost everything we work at in terms of game-theory. And I am not busy with the analysis of interpersonal transactions, as Eric Berne was in his *Games People Play*.

Even more, I must separate what I want to investigate from some recent "theologies of play" which, as I read them, sound like rebounds from death of God theology.[1] These theologies of play seem to be saying that since there was no place for God to touch down in the serious business of making the world habitable for human beings, and since the world without God has proved to be less than a festival of secularity, perhaps God can be resurrected on the playground. In play we get outside those wearisome secular responsibilities that God vacated. In play we

---

1. E.g. David L. Miller, *Gods and Games* (New York, 1973); Robert Neale, *Play and the Sacred: Toward a Theory of Religion as Play* (New York, 1968); Joseph Campbell, *The Play and the Sacred: A Theory of Religion as Play* (Ann Arbor, 1964); and, in his own less radical way, Harvey Cox, *The Feast of Fools* (Cambridge, Mass., 1971).

Lewis Smedes is Professor of Theology and Ethics at Fuller Theological Seminary, and the author of a work on the theology of man's union with Christ entitled All Things Made New. *He has contributed essays to several theological works and he is an editor of the* Reformed Journal. *In his essay, Smedes examines the ingredients of Calvinist theology, reputed for being the seedbed of a work ethic, to see whether it may also contain the roots of a playful perspective on life and work.*

need not expect God to solve problems, do hard jobs, fill gaps, or rescue us from our troubles. So maybe we can hope for God to come back in the garden, where there is nothing to do but sport about in nonresponsible festivals. Play can be the scene of God's return because play has no hard jobs to be done, no gaps of meaning to fill, and no responsibilities that man come of age may be tempted to slough off on God.

Going still further, some have suggested play as a metaphor to give the final key to life as a joke in the post-God era. The real world is a kind of cosmic joke, and play is the myth that helps us understand and survive it. In the words of Ted Estes: "Play becomes a way of going on in a world in which all reasons for action have evaporated, in which the worth of action itself is questioned...a mode of action freed from the teleological hypothesis."[2] Play is a parable not of hope but of despair— with a flair. We know we are not in Eden, cavorting as though all of life were a pastime, but we can make believe. We have no promised future, which play can hint at. Play is a metaphor for a theology of "as if," and believing, at heart, is making believe. Play is a key to a world of make believe. It is a last-ditch stand at making life palatable, not a hope of Eden's return but a return to childhood by default.

"Theology of play," in this sense, is *not* what I am about. What I am asking is whether evangelical theology, a theology of God's presence not his absence, of meaning not of unmeaning, a theology in which the "teleological hypothesis" has *not* evaporated, can produce an attitude of playfulness toward life and the world. I do not expect an unequivocal answer; the best we may get is a dialectic of yes and no.

I. What is Playfulness?

Playfulness is an attitude, a mood, a state of mind. What sort of attitude? We can perhaps find out by taking a look at play itself. Let me list a few of its components, borrowing them, in some cases, from other people who are experts on play.

1. *Freedom.* Huizenga thought that play had to be voluntary. This seems to be true. A person plays just because he wants to. If he is forced, morally obligated, directed by therapists, or has to play for pay, he is not really playing. We do not play if the play activity is imposed on us. This has limits, of course; something we have to do can *become* play, but it cannot become play until we discover that we want to do it.

But play also has a free side. Play frees us from the rules of ordinary work behavior. In work, things are done in a certain way because doing them that way is efficient, a means toward an end. In play, the rules are

---

2. Quoted by David Miller, *op. cit.,* p. xxv.

random, making sense only if we simply adopt them as part of the game. Why may a batter have no more than three strikes? Why must a basketball player leave the game after five or six fouls? Why should a pawn be allowed to move only one square while the queen can roam the board?

> The mind is prepared to accept the unimagined and incredible, to enter a world where different laws apply, to be relieved of all the weights that bear us down, to be freed, kingly, unfettered, and divine.[3]

Hugo Rahner is right. Play requires freedom. And playfulness is a state of mind that befits freedom; it is a sense of doing what one chooses in a game where ordinary rules of propriety, logic, and productivity can be transcended. Freedom has its limits, of course, even in play; and even play *has* rules, as Jürgen Moltmann reminds the theologians of the cosmic game.[4] A mountain climber is limited by the dynamics of gravity and the shape of his mountain; but that he should go through the trouble he does to climb the mountain at all can be explained only by his decision to declare his freedom from ordinary commonsense rules of caution, comfort, and commerce.

2. *Adventure.* Robert Neale says that adventure is a mark of play.[5] I think he is right. For in play—whether in fantasy or in competition— one always enters an arena of uncertainty. If one knows exactly how everything will turn out, he cannot be playing. In most play there is a risk of losing. You risk a bad hand in bridge, breaking a leg skiing, or being beaten in basketball. If the game is rigged, it cannot really be played. If the fight is fixed, it is not really a fight. To enter the world of play a person must venture something. He may be confident of winning, but if he is certain of winning because his opponent agrees to lose or is prevented by pre-arrangement from winning, he is not really playing. As far as I can tell, play needs adventure in order to be play.

3. *Unproductivity.* Josef Pieper sees unproductivity as a facet of leisure,[6] and this could be extended to play. I do not mean that play cannot be productive of some useful good. I mean that people play regardless of the utility of play. The value of play cannot be measured in terms of its usefulness for making deals or improving international relations. And a person who plays a game specifically in order to accomplish something has to that extent missed something intrinsic to playing. A person

---

3. Hugo Rahner, *Man at Play* (New York, 1967), p. 66.
4. Jürgen Moltmann, *Theology of Play* (New York, 1972), pp. 111ff.
5. *Op. cit.*, p. 78.
6. Josef Pieper, *Leisure, the Basis of Culture* (New York, 1965), pp. 25ff.

may include play of some sort in his agenda because he thinks he will be a healthier or happier person if he plays. But if he plays only to make himself healthier or happier, he will merely be exercising, not playing. Productivity has to be a side issue in play.

We may expect, then, that a person who evaluates life only in terms of productivity will not have a playful attitude toward life.

4. *Pleasure.* It would seem obvious that pleasure is an ingredient in play. The player discovers that what he is doing pleases him, and therefore he thinks it is good. The goodness of play may not be thought of as a moral good nor an instrumental good, but rather an intrinsic good in the sense that it is fitting and proper for a person to do it. (Of course, in any given instance, he may be mistaken in his judgment.) The feeling of pleasure is not measured by comfort or lack of it; play often entails pain. Pleasure does not distinguish play from work, of course, since work can give one the same feeling; when it does, work is very close to play. But without this feeling, play is not play. The player likes what he is doing when he plays, and tends to think he is doing a good thing.

5. *Trans-seriousness.* David Miller says that play is nonserious and therefore ultimately serious.[7] I am not sure what he means by "ultimately serious," but I think he means that the one thing we cannot be fully serious about is a revelation of the ultimately joyful meaning of life. In any case, if play is a parable of life, we must understand something about the relationship between seriousness and nonseriousness. Christian theology surely tells us that life is serious, while play is often understood as a respite from the seriousness of living. I think, however, that play is both serious and nonserious and that the playful attitude will involve a dialectic between seriousness and nonseriousness.

Seriousness refers both to an attitude and to an action. We may interpret what we are doing as being a serious business. We may also be serious in doing something which we believe is not a serious business. A serious thing is one that has important consequences for life. An ultimately serious thing is one that has ultimate consequences for life. But it is quite possible to be serious in an activity whose outcome we know will not make any significant difference beyond that activity.

It is, in fact, easy to be serious in play just because we know that what we are doing in play has no serious consequences. People who imagine that play is serious are tempted not to be serious in playing. They are tempted to stack the deck, so that they will not have to risk losing. Or they refuse to throw themselves seriously into the game so

---

7. *Op. cit.,* pp. 139ff.

that they can pretend they might have won had they really tried. They may also play the game fair and hard, but forfeit playfulness by turning it into so serious a competition that they cannot lose with grace. In any case, to make the game serious chips away the seriousness one ought to have *in* playing.

In order to be playful, one has to be serious in playing the nonserious game. Being serious is being involved, committing oneself to the game, and playing as hard as one can. If a player lacks seriousness, he spoils the play. It is not fun to win against an opponent who does not try to beat you. And if he does not try to beat you, he is not really playing. On the other hand, if he takes winning as a serious business, he also spoils the game by not really playing it as a game that has no important consequences. The dialectic of playful seriousness consists in being seriously involved in something we do not interpret as serious business.

There is no doubt a good deal more to the attitude of playfulness than I have mentioned. But I have said enough for my purpose. The question now is whether playfulness—which involves freedom, adventure, unproductivity, pleasure, and trans-seriousness—is an attitude toward life as a whole which can be theologically supported. Or, to put it another way, does play provide a parable about how to face the task of living? Now parables do not furnish truth; they can only illuminate a truth that comes from another source. So we must ask whether Christian theology tells us a truth about life which play illuminates.

My plan is first to talk about some facets in my own theological tradition which have tended to promote an attitude toward life that is not playful. My theological tradition is the Calvinism that produced an ethos which Max Weber observed as "earnest piety," "sobriety," "industry," "frugality," and a general distaste for festivity, banquets, and trivial play[8]—in short, an ethos better described by the phrase "work ethic" than by playfulness. I want very briefly to examine some of the theological counterpoints to them that do after all support a playful attitude even toward work and industry. Then, secondly, I will examine a few facets of the biblical view of God and man that seem rather directly to support a playful perspective on life.

II. Anti-Playful Theology

1. *The programmed universe.* Calvinists, along with other sorts of Christians, believe that behind the apparent whims and caprices of nature

---

8. Quoted by Ernst Troeltsch, *The Social Teachings of the Christian Churches* (Eng. tr., New York, 1957), p. 89.

and history is a divine plan and purpose. What distinguishes Calvinists is their belief that every shift and turn in every man's life is eternally determined by God's decree. John Calvin put it this way: there is "no erratic power, or action, or motion in creatures; rather, they are governed by God's secret plan in such a way that nothing happens except what is knowingly and willingly decreed by him . . ." (*Inst.*, I.xvi.3). "Nothing takes place by chance . . . [so that] the plans and intentions of men, are so governed by his providence that they are borne by it straight to their appointed end" (*Inst.*, I.xvi.6,8).

Now, if "nothing happens except what is knowingly and willingly decreed" by God, at least two of our ingredients of playfulness are excluded from life—freedom and adventure. If every human decision and event is decreed, there can be no free decision on man's part to participate in the "game of life," and there can be no venture on God's part. There can, of course, be an experience like freedom; but if all our decisions and actions are determined, there can be no genuine freedom. Nor can there be adventure on man's part, in the strictest sense, for while he cannot know the outcome, the outcome is pre-programmed; if he "wins," he experiences something like what a fighter experiences who does not know that his opponent has agreed before the fight to lose.

The difficult question of freedom and determination has been discussed by theologians for ages without a clear resolution; but it does seem clear that an attitude of playfulness toward life is firmly discouraged by a theology which views the world as tightly screwed together by eternal decree. Understood in this light, global and personal histories are lived somewhat like the videotaped rerun of yesterday's football game: the decisions about plays and the final score were all made in the real game of yesterday, even though someone ignorant of the real game may watch today's televising as though it had the drama of a real adventure. But there is, in fact, no adventure, and no real play.

Now it is more important that theology be right than that we find a support in it for the playful life. But we may at least question whether the crass way in which we have put Calvin's view is right. The question most ready at hand is whether all the evil that men do is pre-programmed by God. Must we believe that enormous evils like Auschwitz, to mention only *the* monstrosity of modern times, were "knowingly and willingly decreed" by God? If Auschwitz was not divinely programmed, who knows what lesser evils were done by men's free decision? If evil is not, in every sense, pre-programmed, there is indeed an arena in history for genuine surprise, for genuine decisions, for genuine freedom. This tempers the theology of the programmed universe enough to suggest that there are genuine ingredients of freedom and adventure in history for both God and man.

The reality of divine grace offsets the theology of a programmed universe positively, just as the reality of evil does so negatively. At least we can say that this is so if grace is understood as God's free decision to respond to human sin in a surprisingly benevolent way. Understood in this sense (rather than as an eternal ingredient in God's nature constraining him naturally to elect a certain number of predestined sinners to salvation), the reality of grace pries open a window in the programmed universe.

Grace is experienced as a surprise. No one who experiences grace feels as though it were an inevitable link in a chain forged in eternity by a God constrained either by an arbitrary decree which, once made, had to be obeyed or by some inner necessity in the divine nature which could not, even by him, be freely decided on. Of course, man's feeling of surprise at grace, his feeling that grace is amazing and free could be an illusion. But the core of the gospel suggests that this feeling is not an illusion. Everything I read about grace in the Bible strongly suggests that God freely chose to be gracious, that he was not compelled either by a graceless decree or by an inner necessity within his own nature. If this is true, then the appearance of grace in the world undermines every notion of determinism, whether it be the horizontal determinism of contingent reinforcement (in B.F. Skinner's sense) or the vertical determinism of the divinely programmed universe. Grace opens up a hole in the programmed system, and thus also supports an aspect of playfulness in the universe by showing God's freedom in responding to the contingency of evil in a most adventuresome manner.

Two ingredients of playfulness are thus rescued from the programmed universe of Calvinistic theology—freedom and adventure. The first is supported by man's evident decision to do evil things and by God's revealed decision to be gracious to evildoers. The second is supported by the fact that in God's world an event can take place that truly challenges God to enter the lists against it.

It can be added here that the reality of grace supports the playful view of life at still another point of freedom. We noted early on that part of the freedom of play is the freedom to make rules that do not apply to ordinary life, rules that seem very hard to understand for those not in the game. (Any avid football fan quizzed by an uninitiated wife about football rules has experienced this.) The Pharisees were offended by Paul's preaching of grace on precisely this account. They applied the ordinary rules of fairness and justice to God and therefore could not stomach Paul's notion that God freely justified sinners. Paul's answer was (in Rom. 3:21-26) that God's grace *revealed* his justice. God's playful grace reveals a freedom to act in ways that ordinary moral calculus finds either mystifying or offensive, but which from within appear very right.

2. *The burden of sin.* In the light of Christian theology, sin is very serious. And a person must be serious about his sin. But if one is aware of the objective seriousness of his sin and is himself serious about it, he will be hard pressed to adopt a playful attitude to life. The more he thinks of himself as a sinner before the face of a holy God, the less playful he is likely to be about life, for several reasons.

First, he probably suspects that playfulness is a posture feigned by a person trying to avoid the disturbing fact of his sinfulness. Play tends to make us forget our sins and miseries, along with our other troubles. The more one plays the less serious he is likely to be about a matter that he ought to be most serious about.

Second, in terms of his own temperament, the more serious he is about his sin, the less playful he is likely to feel. The more he feels his burden of guilt, the less free and venturesome he feels. Spiritual depression is not conducive to playfulness. If there is energy, it must be dedicated to the burdensome task of overcoming his sin.

Third, the more serious a person feels about his sin, the less likely he is to enjoy a sense of the goodness of life. It is true that if he can convince himself that sin itself fits neatly into a programmed world, he can also convince himself that sin is, *sub specie aeternitatis*, not a bad thing. But this is precisely not to take sin seriously. And most people who believe in a programmed universe do, in spite of logic, take sin very seriously.

Fourth, the person who recognizes what sin is knows that it has compounded the amount of work to be done in the world. Sin makes the weeds grow, the ground hard to cultivate; sin multiplies hungry stomachs to feed, injustices to overcome, sicknesses to heal, and prisoners to visit. Sin creates lusts to be restrained and makes us vulnerable to attacks from Satan. We do not live in Eden. Therefore, it may seem like the worst complacency to suggest that play can be a parable of the Christian attitude toward life.

The burden of sin, then, undermines the validity of a playful view of life at several points. It reduces the spiritual *élan* that a playful attitude requires. It holds suspect any enthusiastic affirmation that life is good. It casts a shadow over any tendency to view productivity as lower than a top priority. And, perhaps most important, it demands that we take a straightforwardly serious view of life. The picture is confused, it should be said, by the suggestion the very word 'playful' leaves, that a playful view of life is trivial or escapist. But even in our more serious sense of the word 'playful' the burden of sin that theology endorses undermines the playful disposition.

Two things suggest another way of looking at sin and playfulness. One is that sin itself is a culprit for turning playful people into straightforwardly serious workers. Pride, the root sin, set the hod-carriers of Babel to work on their God-defying tower. The same sin set religious people under the law to try like grim graduate students to earn a favorable grade point average with God. The hard-working Pharisees, in their sin, were offended at Jesus for making burdens light and yokes easy. And it was the people who tried to turn the gospel back into a work ethic who aroused Paul's deepest anger. Sin creates the illusion that we must be workers or die forever. It is sinfulness, then, as much as our awareness of it, that prevents us from seeing the light from the parable of play.

The other, more crucial thing, is that grace relativizes the seriousness of sin. Grace prevents us from taking sin with undialectical seriousness. Since God took sin with undialectical seriousness, we may take it only with a trans-serious attitude; that is, we must be serious in dealing with it, but must not take sin itself as ultimately serious. Grace rescues us from sin's ultimate word, from the labor camp into which sin transformed life. It further liberates us from the depressing guilt of sin. Finally, grace creates the possibility that we can look sin in its grisly face and still say, "The living of life is a great good." Grace does not turn the world back into an Eden; it does not lead us into make-believe pleasure domes. But it does give the ultimate word that relativizes the nonplayful effects of sin.

3. *The doctrine of vocation.* The Reformers called the monks out of leisurely contemplation and led them back to work. Calvin in particular called them to accept their station as God-appointed and there do the job God appointed them to do. "Every man's mode of life, therefore, is a kind of station assigned him by the Lord; that he may not be driven about at random..." (*Inst.*, III.x.16). People are redeemed by Christ to fulfil their triadic office of prophet, priest, and king. Office means duty. Duty means work. And work means getting something done. Having an office is not the sad consequence of sin, or merely a survival requirement. It is the privilege given creatures of serving under their Great Taskmaster's eye.

There is, of course, a lot of work to be done. There are secrets of nature to be ferreted out, stupid ideas to be disputed, chaos to be ordered, mouths to be fed, roads to be built, souls to be saved—and a great deal more. This essay is not against work: my point is to ask whether we can have a playful attitude about our work.

The seriousness of our vocation is intensified by the limits of our time. We are only people. Each day is limited by the clock, each year by the calendar, and each life by the tolling of the bells. And within our small time frame, we are limited by a small amount of energy and talent to fill it creatively. Meanwhile, the summons from every direction to help produce more good in the world leaves us without respite. And our inner sense of obligation keeps telling us that we ought to do more than we have done. Every child of God is expected to repeat every night: "Forgive us the good we have left undone." It is very easy for the doctrine of vocation to keep us from being playful.

The answer to the work ethic is that grace has come in the form of the promise of the Kingdom of God. God's future has broken through the compulsions of the work ethic to tell us that God alone can *and will* bring in the Kingdom. The sign of the future does not tell us to stop working and start playing. It tells us that what we cannot do in our lifetimes, or a thousand lifetimes, will be done in God's good time. Furthermore, the promise of the Kingdom is that the life of the children of God is ultimately a life of restored playfulness. "Old men and old women shall again sit in the streets of Jerusalem, each with staff in hand for every age. And the streets of the city shall be full of boys and girls playing in the streets" (Zech. 8:4,5). What this comes to in terms of playfulness is that we are encouraged to take our most serious work with a trans-serious attitude. We ought to be serious in it, but ought not to see it as being an ultimately serious business.

The secret of our serious vocations is that we must be dialectically serious about them. The person who views his work too seriously is likely either to turn off in despair or turn to it with a seriousness that prevents him from being playful about it. The promise of the Kingdom gives us a right to wink at it, take it all with less than final seriousness, and only then throw ourselves into it seriously—as we do in play.

Enough of this dialogue with a few Calvinistic doctrines that have buttressed an unplayful attitude toward life. What I have tried to do is show that smuggled into the theology of undialectical seriousness is a message of grace that invites us to look at our serious and unplayful world with a playful eye. Now let us look into some theological items that more positively and directly affirm playfulness.

III. The Playful God

1. *The unproductive Threesome.* What did God do before he had a world to tend? He was planning hell, it has been impishly suggested, for

people who ask such impertinent questions. But the question is not all that improper. The fathers who gave us the doctrine of the Trinity were really responding to the same question. Their answer was that God the Father was eternally generating the Son and that both collaborated in the generation of the Spirit. And the three of them were simply enjoying being with each other. Three persons with nothing much to do, no time schedule to keep, no superior's orders to obey, no problem of survival, and no creatures to worry about. If in some impossible fantasy we could have looked on, we might have scolded the holy Trinity for wasting time. But we would have been outsiders, unable to understand the freedom of the Trinity to have their own rules to play by. And we would have been mystified, perhaps, by the enormous pleasure that they seemed to have in what they were doing. I cannot think it wrong to suppose that if anything on earth could be an analogy of the eternal goings-on, it would be children at play.

2. *The adventure of creation.* God created *ex nihilo*. In other words, he did not have to do it. There was no messy mass to be cleaned up. No rough stuff that demanded to be shaped and formed. The world did not flow like lava from his depths of being, out of some gurgling inner necessity. He did not need a world for his own survival. He took no orders from above. He was free to create or not to create. He did it out of his own good pleasure, for the divine fun of it. Freedom is a condition of playfulness, and the Creator whose image we are was very free indeed.

Was there not also a touch of adventure here? God made a person—not a puppet—for himself. If he had manipulated his creatures as B. F. Skinner does his pigeons, there would be no playfulness to his creation, but God is not "game playing" in his serious play. God had a real world on his hands, with real persons, capable of making good and bad decisions, and thereafter real adventure. There had to be a possibility of things going badly, even a theoretical possibility of losing the real game of fellowship he had in mind. But God was not so insecure about himself as to decline the venture.

3. *The contest of providence.* "You meant it for evil, but God meant it for good." The story of Joseph—a paradigm of providence—is the story of a playful God. Joseph's brothers were serious only in a straightforward, nondialectical way. A less venturesome God would have nipped the whole cruel game in the bud—no playing around. He enters the contest, and plays it according to the rules of the decision-honoring struggle. He plays harder when his partners switch sides and become his opponents. But he is "playing" in the real sense; the game is for real and God accepts its rules. This is evident in the joy he takes at winning: "he will laugh" when he has them in derision (Ps. 2).

There are hints that biblical writers see a playful streak in the Lord of history. Consider Leviathan, the mythical monster in the uncontrolled, threatening sea. What is Leviathan doing in God's world? Where did he come from and why? Listen to the surprising vision of a playful God: "So is this great and wide sea, wherein are creeping things innumerable. . . . There is Leviathan, whom thou hast made to sport therein" (Ps. 104:25, 26). Some translations read: "whom thou hast made to play with." There is a playful thought. The shadow of chaos, the symbol of the destructive urges of the world, myth of life's untamed threat . . . Leviathan—God's playmate. There is also another side, the picture of the end-game, and we should note it. In the end, God does Leviathan in. "In that day, the Lord will punish Leviathan, the fleeing serpent, and he will slay the dragon that is in the sea" (Isa. 27:1).

That God will slay the dragon is not a foregone conclusion secured by fixing the contest in advance. The struggle is not "game-playing" in the make-believe sense. That God will slay the dragon is a hope; and hope is a trust in God as the superior player. Christian hope is not a belief that God never ventured into a real struggle. A fixed fight is not a fight; a programmed struggle is not a struggle. But a real struggle is one entered into as an adventure, and it is a playful struggle if one enters it freely. The way of providence suggests that God did enter a real struggle as a venture and entered it freely. The response of faith is a trust that God will win the serious game he plays. But this faith, which is faith in God and not a belief that the whole struggle is rigged, saves us from taking the struggle as an ultimately serious thing—for we "know" that God will win.

IV. Man, God's Playful Image

1. *Glorifying God.* Our creation and election, we are told, are to the "praise of the glory of his grace" (Eph. 1:6). The end of man, we learn from the catechism, is to glorify God and to enjoy him forever. In its most basic terms, man's failure is his refusal to give God the glory and glorifying the creature instead (Rom. 1:25).

Now, one condition for glorifying the excellence of the Creator is that his excellence be manifest. Where is it to be seen? Why, says the sometimes anti-playful Calvin, *all around us.* Little things and big things alike throw a floodlight on their Maker's splendid features. Doxologies are not only for the elite who are competent for contemplative visions: "even the common folk and the most untutored cannot be unaware of the excellence of the divine art. . . . they cannot open their eyes without being compelled to witness it" (*Inst.*, I.v.2). But even here, God is playfully disguising his glory, hiding it behind insects and lizards, as well as letting it shine more plainly from comets and suns. And we are told, as it were, to stand still, be receptively unproductive, and be awed by what we see. We are guests in the theater, and are privileged to know the star.

The act of God-glorifying is not very productive. We do not get great things done on earth by applauding God. This may be why some Calvinists are not sympathetic with a worship that accents God-applauding. Authentic praise, they tend to say, comes from the labors of our hands; God is praised by the good work done by stewards of his creation. There is no denying this, of course. But the biblical examples tend to correspond favorably to the summons of the Psalmist: "Praise him with trumpet sound; ... with lute and harp! Praise him with timbrel and dance; ... with strings and pipe! Praise him with sounding cymbals . . . with loud clashing cymbals" (Ps. 150:3-5).

It took me a long time to like the notion of being a God-glorifier. I didn't like a God who created human beings just to hear their applause. I had a juvenile fantasy of a narcissistic deity, liking what he saw in the mirror, but hungry for rave reviews. The Lord later gave me better insights into the playfulness of being a God-glorifier. One learns theology in many ways. For instance, I went to a concert not long ago to hear a great violinist perform. It was a splendid concert. Afterwards, we in the audience did our own "playing"; we applauded and applauded and applauded. The violinist bowed and left the stage. We would bring him back by applauding and yelling "Bravo!" He would come back, obviously enjoying every decibel, and then retire again. Then we would bring him back with our doxology. He *let* us play with him. As this game was going on, we were all taken out of ourselves, in a kind of ecstasy, in a game we all played together. And I thought: glorifying God can be a wonderful game to play.

2. *The sexual playmates.* There are few things more serious, more playful—and harder work—than the play involved in sex. It meets all the criteria of play. It is adventuresome; it involves enormous risk because it requires such complete trust. It is free; if it is forced, as in seduction, or when done out of duty, as in obeying the command to populate, it is no longer play. In a real sense it is unproductive; nothing comes of it that will result very directly in the feeding of hungry stomachs or the building of better bridges. It is trans-serious; you must be serious *in* it, but not too serious· *about* it. And it is such an impulsive, spontaneous, irrational game that nobody except the people who play it will understand its own special rules.

Sexual play, it is true, does not fit the leisure ideal of spiritual contemplation. It seems to violate the law of self-discipline and rationality necessary to philosophical leisure. Augustine, who gave high priority to contemplative leisure, was sure that the Christian was meant to struggle *against* the sexual impulse; and the more playful it was, the worse it was, because it was the more likely to handicap our ascent into leisurely contemplation of God. Intense desires for this game and intense pleasure from playing it were for him the marks of a fallen nature. Innocent Adam would never have been excited by Eve, and the two of them could not have walked with God in the cool of the day and then made spontaneous love in his presence at night. If sex were to be tolerated in the Christian life, it had to stop being a game and become work. It had to be done only out of a sense of duty, to bring more souls into the world. Sexuality, in fallen man, was impulsive, spontaneous, volcanic, free, and purposeless— and none of these conditions fits with rational delight in the beauty of the Lord.

But the writer of Genesis has other ideas. He traces the playfulness of sexuality back to creation in God's own image. God made humankind male and female—male and female in all their bodiliness. Sexuality was not a divine afterthought, an improvised device for begetting the human race. Sexual drives were not demonic lust percolating up from some subhuman abyss to ensnare virgin souls. Body-persons have a sexual side to them that is wildly irrational, splendidly spontaneous, and beautifully playful.

The sexual component of our nature testifies that man was meant to find the most meaningful human communion in a playful relationship. In mutual trust and loving commitment, sexual activity is to be a playful festivity. It attests that human being is closest to fulfilling itself in a game. To be in God's image, then, includes being sexual, and sexuality is a profound call to play.

3. *The Sabbath-keeper.* The Sabbath is a sign that God has written over man: "Destined for Playfulness." It is God's own day, given to man in the midst of his work to remind him that festival and celebration, not sweat and toil, are the final truth about man. The Sabbath is the "Lord's Day," dedicated to the faith-fact that "death is swallowed up in victory" and work is swallowed up in play. The Sabbath, to be sure, is in counterpoint to labor. There *"remains* a rest for the people of God" (Heb. 4:1); the time of rest is not yet wholly come. But, in the Sabbath, in the festival of victory, we experience a taste of the banquet that is the end of man. Sabbath unties the knot that shackles us to production and goals and achievements, even though it does not relieve us of them entirely. Monday still follows Sunday, but Monday's seriousness is relativized by the memory of Sunday's playfulness.

The meeting of God with man, of man with God, is holy play, *sacer ludens*.... For this reason, the game points beyond itself, downward to the simple, ordinary rhythm of life; upward to the highest forms of existence.... Play is the requisite for those forms of existence which strive toward a communion with the other, and finally for a meeting with God.[9]

In the festival of worship, something goes on that is akin to child's play. Does it not follow that child's play tells us something about both the Sabbath and that "eternal rest" which it signifies?

The Sabbath exists in dialectic with a world of seriousness. The festival was open to the worst kind of distortion when it was removed from the dialectical tension with the effects of sin in the world. The festival was corrupted in Israel because the Sabbath players perverted the real work of the world on the other days. The poor were defrauded; the weak oppressed; and both were robbed of a truly playful existence. The Sabbath pointed to a new world "wherein justice dwells" along with banquets and festivals. But the overly serious Sabbath-keepers forgot that the symbol of the future was meant to stimulate men to bring something of the playful future into the working present. This is why the prophets said: "Close down the temples and cancel the festivities. Your Sabbaths are a bad smell in God's nostrils." They were an offense because, in a world of sin and imperfection, those who keep the Sabbath must keep it in dialectic with the real work given to God's children, and the real work included making life more playful for those whose poverty and weakness prevented them from playing. But even here, the real work could be done playfully in view of the Sabbath promise that it was God who would complete it.

4. *Man in grace.* Now we must try to get a lot of things together within the concept of grace. What it will come to is this: in order to see the meaning of life in playful terms we must see it in grace-given terms.

Without grace, everything becomes either despairingly serious or playfully illusionary. It is burdensome to be serious without grace, for then one has to be serious without relief. But then, too, without grace, playfulness becomes an escape from seriousness. This is why it is futile to make play a parable for a life mood unless it is a parable to illuminate the reality of a free grace that alone transforms a bitterly serious life into a life of playful hope. Play as the metaphor or myth that illumines life *on its own* is escape from reality. But within grace play can be a parable of life's transserious meaning.

---

9. G. van der Leeuw, *Sacred and Profane Beauty: The Holy in Art* (New York, 1963), pp. 111ff.

Even the cross of Christ—a most unplay-like event—fits into a theology of playfulness. The cross shows God's seriousness about human affairs. Human need was a serious business for God. So the dialectic stops at the cross: God had a serious attitude about what he took to be a serious matter. Moltmann was right when he called a limit to the theology of play here, at Calvary:

> The Cross of Christ remains an offense, and Auschwitz remains Auschwitz—until the dead rise and all begin to dance because everything has become new. Until then there will be laughter underneath tears and tears within laughter. Remain a dialectician of play and don't become an enthusiast.[10]

There was nothing good about the cross; Christ had no pleasure in the pain he suffered there. Yet, even the cross has at least one aspect of playfulness: adventure. The cross was not a rigged contest. The sweat of Gethsemane did not come from a man who knew the fight was fixed.

And, since the resurrection, the cross invites us to a trans-serious attitude about life. We are serious players; but, since Calvary, we know the game we play no longer has ultimately serious consequences. We can be "dialecticians of play" because of God's one undialectical act. Our trans-serious attitude is what the Bible calls hope. But hope is not inside information that the game is predetermined. Therefore we can be playful only as we work. There are injustices to be undone. There are burdens to be lifted. There are stomachs to be filled. There are oppressed persons to be liberated. There are souls to be saved. But even here, it must all be done in a properly playful mood. The revolutionary thinks the world must be transformed tomorrow—by him—and is doomed to despair because he is undialectically serious about his work. The playful cop-out thinks the world can be a Xanadu tomorrow; he is undialectically serious about play—and is doomed to a tranquilized existence. The captive of the work ethic uses play only as an intermezzo in his life of work. Under the cross and in hope of resurrection, the Christian has a hopeful invitation to be playful *in* his serious work.

Looking ahead to being a dancer in the joy of freedom, celebrating with applause the glory of God, he enters life now with the mood of a player. I am not talking about the right to celebrate now and then—though that, too, is a Sabbath gift. I am not talking about turning the Christian mood into triviality and serendipity. I am not talking about play as a metaphor for an ultimately meaningless life. I am saying that the

---

10. *Op. cit.,* p. 112.

theology of the grace-full God can make a player out of a person in those senses I listed at the beginning. Grace opens a window to a world that transcends routine cause and effect, transcends the moral calculus of work and merit. Grace transforms the notion of a rationally rigged universe, with God as the winner of a fixed contest that was never really a contest, transforms it into an adventure of God that gives believers a *hope* that he will be the winner, and that we sinful losers will share his victory. Grace makes it possible to feel that struggle and pain, even in their most horrible forms, are part of a world that is good and pleasant to play and work in. Grace judges that the worth of life is not calculated by productivity, that it has a worth independent of how much we accomplish.

The playful mood is, like true leisure, a state of mind. It is not a justification of longer vacations and more golf games. It is an invitation to look hard at and throw ourselves seriously into what is, under grace, no longer an ultimately serious contest.

Human Variables and Natural Law

ARTHUR F. HOLMES

Ideas are like animals. We are told that in the course of history animals have undergone change by adapting to changing environments. The appearance of some animals changes seasonally or in the face of danger. Ideas likewise tend to change shape in different contexts or under attack; consequently, as someone has said, philosophical theories remain alive long after their brains have supposedly been knocked out.

The concept of natural law is a case in point. The idea that universal moral obligations inhere in and may be rationally derived from the essential nature of man has appeared variously in the social philosophies of pagan Rome, medieval Europe and the modern Enlightenment. It has taken both Aristotelian and Stoic forms, and it is discussed today by both analysts and phenomenologists. Philosophers defend it and denounce it. Theologians bless it and condemn it. Lately the French sociologist and lay theologian Jacques Ellul has reiterated their objections.

Previously I have examined some largely philosophical criticisms of Locke's concept of natural law and tried to indicate possible directions for a new formulation.[1] For this occasion I want to respond to some objections Ellul and other theologians raise to natural law theory in general, objections that I shall refer to collectively as the argument from human variables. First I shall summarize some of the reasons Christians have for still considering so well-worn an idea as natural law; second comes a statement of the theologians' objections and a preliminary examination intended to sift out some confusions and focus the real problem. I shall respond by simply reformulating the idea of natural law in the contemporary lan-

---

1. "The Concept of Natural Law," *Christian Scholar's Review*, 2 (1972), 195-208.

Arthur F. Holmes is Professor of Philosophy at Wheaton College in Illinois. For years a leader among American evangelical philosophers through his direction of the annual Wheaton Philosophy Conference, Professor Holmes has lectured widely and published several books and numerous essays. In his contribution to this volume Holmes reexamines the traditional but controversial natural law theory of ethics, proposing both a formulation and a line of defense for this theory against recent criticisms enunciated by Jacques Ellul and others.

guage of ethical principles, general moral rules, and cases. I do not claim that this is the only defensible version of a natural law ethic, nor that mine is the only way to distinguish principles, rules, and cases, only that it is plausible and that it offers a workable and defensible framework for a Christian ethic.

I. Why Consider Natural Law?

The most obvious reason Christians might give for adopting a natural law theory at all is that Paul seems to teach in Romans 1 and 2 that, just as the whole creation bears witness to the Creator, the inner nature of man bears witness to the Creator's moral law. Paul accordingly speaks of natural and unnatural sex, of natural and unnatural affection, and of practices men know by virtue of the nature of things to be wrong.

This passage has at times been taken to support the Platonic and Augustinian doctrine of innate moral ideas. I shall only say that such an interpretation appears forced and that the doctrine of innate ideas seems to be an *ad hoc* hypothesis that fails for lack of substantial evidence. Whatever else the apostle had in mind, he says little about the structure of moral reasoning by which men discern right from wrong, whether it is intuitive or inferential (except that in Rom. 1:32 the aorist participle *epignontes* suggests that men learned from past experience of God's judgment, without indicating what experience is involved or how the conclusion is derived). Yet Paul is explicit that nature's witness in moral matters is sufficiently discernible to hold all men justly responsible.

Evidently human nature bears witness to the moral law of God because of what man is by creation and his unique place in the order of creation. In other words, the objective basis of moral knowledge is man's nature as a creature in God's image, but the method of reasoning whereby that basis yields us moral knowledge is not explicit. The Christian will therefore be attracted to ethical theories that base obligation in the nature of things, but he has no precommitment to any one theory of moral reasoning. We shall return several times to this distinction.

As to the objective basis, the doctrine of creation teaches that the order of creation and man's unique place in it are ordained by God. This is recognized not only by such natural law theorists as Thomas Aquinas and John Locke but also by those who respect but reject the classical formulations. Emil Brunner speaks of orders of creation; Herman Dooyeweerd of law spheres. Even Ellul, an outright opponent, observes that social institutions such as marriage do not depend directly on man's will or on historical circumstances but are created by God independently of man's assent. They strive for goals which men cannot readily define in advance.[2]

The theist confesses that everything in creation has value, for God originally pronounced it all good. Everything has its place and purpose in relation to the will of God. In this sense man's moral obligation, first to God and then to others, is inherent in the very creaturely nature of this existence. If God is creator of all and all men are created in the same image of God, a proper understanding of human nature may afford some basis for moral judgments that are universally binding. Some such objective basis has, of course, been sought by ethicists ever since Plato groped for a realm of universals to offset the relativism of the Sophists. The early church quickly recognized that Plato's quest is ultimately fulfilled in what the Scriptures declare about the divine Logos of all creation. The idea of a universal moral order, accordingly, merges with the Christian doctrine that creation reveals the Creator's eternal decrees; and Christian ideas of natural law developed. This law is at the same time both the law of nature and the law of God. Since it depends not on man's will and pleasure but on God's, positive human laws are at best fallible historical applications of ideal possibilities inherent in the created order, for which men by nature, though perhaps unknowingly, yearn. In this sense, natural law is "written in the heart." Ellul, for all his opposition to natural law, speaks of a common sense of justice and claims that a fundamentally common content underlies historically variable legislation[3]—an extravagant claim were it not for the doctrine of creation.

II. Red Herrings and the Real Problem

If the idea of natural law appears so compatible with Christian doctrine, why are some theologians among its most spirited opponents? What are some of their objections? Some of them are pseudo-objections, red herrings that, detracting from the real problem, must be distinguished. I start with a box of red herrings. Ellul states:

1. Law is not a self-sufficient and independent reality, but only a part of human reality and of the universe considered in their relationship to God. Natural law, however, revolves around the idea of an independent law, considered on its own merits.
2. There is no law inherent in human nature, since God alone creates law. The law must be revealed law and cannot be natural law.

---

2. *The Theological Foundations of Law* (New York, 1969), pp. 76-79.
3. *Ibid.*, p. 30.

3. Law is not a product of human reason, but only of God's activity in the world. Reason is confined to organizing and ordering. It is neither a source nor standard for justice or for law.[4]

This kind of objection may well apply to a Cicero or a Rousseau, but not to those like Aquinas and Locke who explicitly identify natural law with the law of God revealed in his creation. In theistic versions of the theory, no claim is made that natural law is independent of the Creator-creation relationship, or that natural law is uncreated, or that human reason is its source or standard. The claim is rather the contrary, that natural law is dependent and created, that human reason merely apprehends and organizes what God reveals in his creation, and that God's will is the source of natural law and his wisdom the ultimate standard.

Ellul may well be thinking of natural law on the analogy of scientific law, so that from the human standpoint it is no more than a descriptive generalization devoid of normative power. But the Christian who takes that positivist view of science should nonetheless recognize that he is ultimately dealing with God's creation and its objective order. Otherwise he confuses the ontological question of the ground and source of the observable order with the epistemological question of how what we perceive can be normative for all creation. As we observed earlier, Paul indicates less about the epistemological than about the ontological question.

Once we make this distinction, however, the epistemological problem comes to the fore. Does the observable order effectively reveal anything of the moral law of God to human understanding? Here Ellul equivocates. On the one hand he seems to deny to human reason any general revelation that is intelligible; on the other hand he seems to affirm that men are endowed with a common sense of justice that produces universally similar laws and institutions. If he attributes this universality to the leveling of historical processes and cultural interaction, he must still decide whether such an effect is itself a means of revealing an ideal order or whether it is ethically insignificant. As it is, he not only leaves the epistemological question largely unanswered, but he also confuses it with the ontological question by talking as if any law inherent in human nature cannot be both dependent (ontologically) on God and at the same time dependent (epistemologically) on human reason.

Laying aside those red herrings, let us get back to the real scent. The problem is the argument from human variables, to the effect that natural law's supposedly universal features of human existence, if they exist at all, elude discovery in a maze of human variables. There are religious vari-

4. *Ibid.*, p. 68.

ables, for human nature varies with man's relationship to God; there are philosophical variables, for our views of human nature and of morality are system-dependent interpretations woven into the fabric of different philosophical positions; and there are historical variables, for the content of a natural law ethic seems to change with economic and social conditions.[5] If natural law is relative to these variables, how can it purport to be rooted in universal aspects of human existence and to reveal a law of God that is normative for all?

1. Among theologians, *religious variables* are the most frequently and fully discussed. The problem is not simply epistemological, as if man's relation to God alters only his knowing and not his being. Ellul asks why, if man can by nature know, can he not also do what he knows? If he can know why does he need the revelation of law? If he can do why does he need the grace of God? But this seems like another red herring: a Christian ethic that adopts the idea of natural law does not regard that law as the only source of moral knowledge to the exclusion of biblical teaching; and according to Romans 1 and 2 man does not even know what he *could* know from nature, and he fails to do even what he does actually know. Hence he needs both the revealed law and the grace of God. Why is this? Why is it that man's knowing and doing are both so deeply affected?

Ellul maintains that the natural order of our being has been changed by sin into a natural disorder, and he goes so far as to assert that we have no reason to believe God preserved any attribute of Adam.[6] I cannot think he means exactly what he says. Adam's attributes may all be impaired in fallen man, but our physical, rational, and personal qualities still preserve at least some traces of their original dignity and order. No attribute of man, no area of his life, no single order of his created being, is wholly immune from perversion, but neither is any attribute, area, or order of his being wholly perverted from all trace of its intended purpose. Depravity is total in its extent, not in its intensity. Natural law may thus be obscured, but it is not wholly illusory.

At this point Ellul drops yet another red herring in our path. He claims that natural law is a kind of *gnosis* akin to natural theology.[7] I shall bypass this one with the remark that we must distinguish natural religion, which is plainly apostate, from natural theology, which, with careful safe-

---

5. These variables are cited among Helmut Thielicke's objections to natural law, *Theological Ethics* (Eng. tr., Philadelphia, 1966), I, ch. 21; and in Reinhold Niebuhr's *Man's Nature and His Communities* (New York, 1965), as well as by Ellul, *op. cit.*, ch. 2.
6. *Op. cit.*, p. 61.
7. *Ibid.*, pp. 10, 62.

guards, need not be. Likewise, we should distinguish an ethic built entirely on natural law and not at all on biblical moral teaching (which would admittedly be heretical, but which Aquinas himself denied), from an ethic in which natural law plays some but not an exclusive part.

The real problem in the argument from religious variables is that human nature is not constant but changes with man's relationship to God in sin or grace. The natural inclinations of fallen man are not what they were in the order of creation, and these inclinations are further changed by God's grace. Two ethical concepts highlight the change: love and freedom.

Various attempts have been made to relate love to natural law. Lactantius conceived the law of love as itself a law of nature, rooted in the universal brotherhood of mankind within the family of God's children; yet this not only misses the effect of sin and grace, it also echoes Stoic rather than biblical conceptions of the unity of mankind. Aquinas regarded love as an additional virtue to those based on natural law, a superadditum of grace. Grace simply adds to nature, and love to justice. Augustine saw things differently: love transforms the nature of justice itself from what it was—for instance in Cicero's ideal republic based on his conception of natural law—to what it should be in the Kingdom of God. Grace has a pervasively redeeming effect on man's nature in restoring him to his created order. Joseph Fletcher and others have embraced a wholly agapistic ethic in which love entirely replaces the justice of natural law as the ruling principle of Christian ethics; and they tend to interpret love more in Buber's existential terms than in terms of biblical morality.

Is love then a part of natural law, or an addition to natural law, or a pervasive redemption of natural law, or a replacement for natural law? Existential theologians tend to the last of these options; Ellul is not explicit but seems to opt for some combination of the last two, that is, for Augustine's redemptive theme combined with a dialectical antithesis between nature's present laws and the law of love.

His position becomes more evident when we consider his conception of Christian freedom. Augustine leads us to expect that freedom restores man to the order of creation: *non posse non peccare* becomes *posse peccare et posse non peccare*. But Ellul stresses dialectical antithesis rather than redemptive restoration. Human history is an order of necessity: in politics and law events are determined by economic and social and emotional forces. Violence is governed by the laws of its own inner necessity: violence breeds violence, and so forth.[8] But the Christian is freed to transcend those necessities and to act in love. He has different ends from those

---

8. See his *Violence* (New York, 1969), chs. 3, 4.

of the world and different conceptions of how to act. Accordingly, a dialectic exists in which the Christian stands over against the world, rather than concurring in the existing necessities of natural law. He is free. His nature differs from that of the world around him. What basis is there here for universal moral law?

But Ellul confuses the issue by focusing on man's present existential predicament. He equivocates on the terms "nature" and "natural law" by applying them only to man's present predicament and not, as in natural law theory, to the possibilities still inherent in human nature by virtue of the creative work as well as the restoring grace of God. Augustine seems to me to avoid this confusion.

Once these red herrings have been cleared away, the argument from religious variables becomes less ontological than epistemological. For the Augustinian it cannot be that grace does not tend to restore man to his created nature, nor that love does not tend to transform man's justice by conforming his knowing and doing and being to what the Kingdom of God requires. The argument is rather that the present perverted and mixed condition of man contributes nothing to any reasoned understanding of universal natural law. And this is the argument to which I shall shortly respond.

2. *Philosophical variables* present a less confusing picture. Everybody knows that philosophers, Christian philosophers included, disagree among themselves as to the nature of man and of morality. Even granted a natural law approach, philosophical variables are divisive, for we find Stoics and Aristotelians, rationalists and romanticists, analysts and phenomenologists all involved. There is no one idea of what justice is by nature: Aristotle differs from Locke who differs again from Mill and from John Rawls. Nor is there one idea of what man is by nature: Aquinas differs from Kant who differs from both B. F. Skinner and Gordon Allport. If the specialists disagree so about man and justice, how can we hope for the universal approach of a natural law ethic?

First a confusion must be unraveled. A natural law ethic need not claim that universal agreement as to its basis or its content is possible, comfortable as that might be, nor that it is necessary as a basis for joint action. No one ethical theory has ever met with unanimity, nor in a pluralistic society is it likely to find the breadth of support we would sometimes like for mental comfort and easy action. I do not even think it desirable. Universal agreement can too easily breed uniformity, repress creativity and freedom of thought, and generate totalitarian controls. It is just as well for men that truth must be approached by rational and not by democratic processes. Our present concern is rather with the truth of an ethical theory than with its popularity, important as the latter may be for some kinds of social action.

Philosophical disagreement may confuse the theologian and cause him to back off. Instead, it should be an opportunity to criticize and improve his thinking, not a call to surrender. Unfortunately, Ellul constantly backs off from philosophical disputes without apparently recognizing that by surrendering natural law he has already taken philosophical positions. With or without a natural law ethic, the moral theologian cannot avoid philosophy. He may defer the matter to his philosopher-friends, but he may neither prejudge the outcome nor regard it as arbitrary.

It is frequently affirmed by philosophers that concepts are system-dependent, arguments are person-relative, and logically demonstrable conclusions of a substantial sort are rare. I have argued elsewhere for a "perspectival" view of philosophy, in which an underlying religious or quasi-religious world-view creates the distinctive unifying features of a philosophical position.[9] But none of this makes philosophy arbitrary, merely subjective, or wholly relative. We still have access to objective controls that limit the range of viable options and help us weigh alternatives. Philosophical ideas are held responsible to the range of experience they purport to cover (the criterion of empirical adequacy), and must cohere consistently and unifiedly in the overall body of our reasonably assured beliefs (the criterion of rational coherence). Argument and evidence are still the order of the day.

What then of the argument from philosophical variables? It is not that there are no concepts of man with which to work but that there are too many. What is needed is not an abandonment of all such concepts (for the critic would make more philosophical decisions in the process), but either an extremely plausible one or an approach that minimizes and mediates at least some of the disagreements involved. The argument from philosophical variables becomes a request for some such alternative.

3. *Historical variables.* Social and economic and political conditions undoubtedly influence both the ideas we have about life and liberty and property and marriage and government, and the objective shape they assume in our social institutions. Does this mean that Aquinas' teaching about the natural law of self-preservation and therefore about defensive war is historically relative? Or that Locke's views on property are so shaped by seventeenth-century capitalism that we need no longer heed his call

---

9. *Christian Philosophy in the Twentieth Century* (Nutley, N. J., 1969), chs. 5, 6; and *Faith Seeks Understanding* (Grand Rapids, 1971), ch. 2.

to limit wealth to what can appropriately be used? Or that perhaps the time has come when we can adopt a new morality in regard to sex and open styles of marriage?

According to Ellul the Old Testament statutes are not normative for today, but depended on historical, social, and economic conditions. Natural law as a juridical system was an event in the past history of law to which we cannot return now that different conditions prevail. The specifics of law and politics are not matters of morality in which Christians and non-Christians can work together on the basis of natural law. Human law is pragmatic: it is man's way of organizing his activity under existing conditions. It does not embody any natural law or eternal law of God, but can only be judged on basic issues by the prophetic word. At best it is an empty symbol of God's justice.[10] Human laws and concepts of law are all of them products of history, and as such they are neither unchanging nor rooted in universal law.

Running through Ellul's work one finds the continuing influence of his early Marxism.[11] This is one case in point, the belief that our institutions and morals are not shaped rationally by our ideas but rather by the economic and social conditions of the time. It appears that for sinful man matter (more precisely the material conditions of his existence) rules spirit (thought and culture) rather than *vice versa*. In that sense Ellul still favors the materialistic over the idealist view of man and society. He refuses to endorse the idealism of either Plato or Aquinas or the Age of Reason in expecting man's reason to rule. Ideas do not shape history; history shapes ideas. Man's hope is not in his ideas but in the liberating grace of God.

To debate this claim would take another essay and still more; yet I am not prepared to grant it for the sake of an argument from historical variables, any more than I am prepared to regard other forms of behavioristic determinism as true of all men but liberated Christians. The Christian insists that man is indeed a bodily being and that the material conditions of his existence are extremely significant in understanding why he thinks and acts as he does, but at the same time man is more than the sum and product of physical forces. One does not have to be an idealist to ascribe more influence to ideas and more freedom to fallen man than Ellul seems to allow. As a sociologist he may choose to regard man operationally in deterministic terms, but an operational assumption of neces-

---

10. *Theological Foundations of Law*, chs. 3, 4; *The False Presence of the Kingdom* (New York, 1972), p. 164, *et passim*.
11. See for instance John Wilkinson's Introduction to his translation of Ellul's *The Technological Society* (New York, 1964).

sity cannot be allowed to decide metaphysical questions about mind and matter or freedom and determinism. Again he appears to confuse the metaphysical (what man is) with the epistemological (the limits of scientific knowledge).

What then of the argument from historical variables? We can at least admit its relevance in a moderated form to Christian thought. To the extent that man's morals and institutions are shaped by and change with social and economic conditions, will it not be impossible to see through them to an underlying natural order that should prevail whatever the prevailing conditions at any time or place?

These are the human variables which argue against the idea of natural law. If man's nature varies according to his condition in sin or grace, if the idea of natural law is itself system-dependent, if man's ideas and laws vary with changing historical conditions, can we still claim that inherent in human nature are universal moral obligations which may be rationally ascertained? The real problem, it turns out, is the age-old one of ethical relativism to which our theologians see no solution in the idea of natural law but only in a purely revelational ethic. They just push the problem further back, for then they must overcome the religious relativism that prevails today in company with ethical relativism. I prefer to respond to relativism wherever it arises, and in ethics today we have a ready-made framework that has developed with precisely this problem in mind.

III. *Principles, Rules, and Cases*

Contemporary ethical theory focuses less on natural law than on the relationship between ethical principles, general rules, and particular cases. Thus Kant's categorical imperative is seen as a universal deontological principle on which depend the hypothetical imperatives one adopts as general rules in certain kinds of situation. Mill's utility principle analogously has become the basis for teleological moral rules about such things as property rights and civil liberty. William Frankena has developed a mixed theory combining the deontological with the teleological approach in the two principles of justice and love, while Fletcher adopts the principle of love only, dropping all general rules, and applying it directly to particular cases of a moral act.

In this general context, I offer a series of proposals for responding to the argument from human variables against natural law.

1. Natural law is an ethical principle analogous to those of Kant or Mill or Fletcher. Ethical principles may be regarded as formal rather than constitutive ideas, in the sense that they do not tell us anything specific that we ought or ought not to do, but rather identify the kind of reason-

ing which is believed to underlie whatever specific moral advice may be given. In the statement 'adultery is wrong,' for example, the predicate needs explanation before we see what else is intended than simply "Don't do it!" But with that explanation we can understand what kind of reasons might be given for disapproving adultery. For Kant, 'wrong' means it would violate one's sense of duty; for Mill, the consequences would militate against the maximum good of the maximum number of people in any way involved; for Fletcher, adultery in the particular situation in question would not be an act of love. Each man's principle gives ethical meaning to the statement; it indicates the kind of reasoning thought appropriate in ethics; but it does not by itself and without other input produce a rule about adultery or any other general moral rule or action decision.

In the case of the natural law principle, adultery is said to be wrong when we think back to the sexual nature of man as created and ordained by God. It violates the moral law of God, both that revealed in Scripture and that revealed, if less explicitly, in the nature of distinctively human sexuality. Therefore, in order to know that adultery is wrong on a natural law basis, we must also understand something about man's sexual nature in the order of creation, just as for Mill one must understand the empirical consequences of adultery or for Fletcher one must examine the motives and ends in the particular situation as well as the expected consequences.

2. Natural law is equivalent to the principle of justice understood more in a deontological than in a utilitarian or agapistic fashion. All men, by virtue of their common human nature rather than by virtue of human law, social role, or political status, have the right to equal respect as human persons. The principle may be given a first expression as follows:

P_1. If X and Y and Z are human persons, then they equally have whatever rights and duties derive from their common humanity.

At the level of principle, no attempt is made to specify what particular rights and duties there may be: this awaits the formation of general rules. The point is rather that whatever rights and duties are inherent in the nature of human existence belong equally to all human persons. Not all our rights are fundamentally *human* rights, and not all our duties stem from *natural* law; we may enjoy additional legal rights and have obligations arising from other social roles and contracts. But these may be regarded as case rules rather than general moral rules.

3. Rights, duties, and freedom are all interrelated. If my students, by virtue of their tuition payments and other aspects of the educational con-

tract, have the right to instruction, then as a party to that contract I have the duty to help provide instruction. If as a human person I have the God-given right to life, then you have the God-given duty to respect my life and safety. Moreover, if I as a human person have the right to life then I should be free from attack on my life and safety. Rights, duties and freedoms are correlative things implicit in the natural law of justice.

P₂. If X and Y are human persons so that X and Y have a certain human right, then Y has a corresponding moral duty to accord to X that right, and reciprocally X has the same duty to Y.

P₃. If X and Y are human persons so that X and Y have a certain human right, then Y has a corresponding moral duty to accord to X the freedom to exercise that right, and reciprocally X has the same duty to Y.

As a result, natural law and the principle of justice are concerned with the equitable ordering of outward relationships between people and largely with the social dimensions of ethics; they are therefore foundational to legal and political theory. How the principle of love relates to natural law is not yet evident; but if the concept of natural law is tantamount to the principle of justice then natural law must relate to love in much the same way as justice relates to love.

4. As in the Augustinian tradition, love has a pervasive and redeeming effect on the concept and pursuit of justice. Emil Brunner points out that while justice concerns outward relationships between persons in society, love concerns the inward aspect of human relationships.[12] Justice, then, has primarily to do with reasonably equitable distribution, while love is a whole-personal concern that moves a man not only to seek justice for others, to secure their rights and their freedoms, but also at times to waive his own rights and freedoms in giving to others in need beyond what is simply their due. Love captures the inner spirit of the moral law, natural law included, in that it respects human persons for what they are by nature. Both love and justice (and natural law) are people-oriented, therefore neither grudging nor legalistic. Morality is a matter of the heart, of intention as well as the act.

5. Philosophical variables appear because concepts are system-dependent, and because the principles of justice and love depend on the concept that human persons have value. Some ethicists are content to regard the value of persons as axiomatic, at least in our culture. Others might argue that since persons by definition are valuing beings who value being treat-

---

12. See *Justice and the Social Order* (New York, 1945), Part I.

ed as the human persons they are, it follows that to be logically consistent they must value the same treatment for other persons who themselves value being treated that way. For the Christian, such arguments are supportive but insufficient. And philosophical idealism misleads us when it claims that because spirit is ultimately real therefore persons are inherently valuable, for this forgets that the crucial distinction between divine and human persons is also the distinction between God and his creatures. Rather, the value of human persons stems from the fact that God is a valuing being who especially values persons he creates in his own image, and that he therefore acts for their redemption. But for all these philosophical variables, value is still accorded to human persons on all sorts of bases, so that at the level of principles we may still agree on the formal characteristics of justice and perhaps to a lesser extent of love. This has the effect of minimizing philosophical variables.

6. The same effect occurs if we content ourselves initially with a phenomenological description of the nature of man in terms of the universal areas of activity that structure his existence. Brunner speaks of them as "orders of creation"; Dooyeweerd as "law spheres"; they give rise to Ellul's common institutions. They include sexual and family relationships, physical life and safety, property and economic relationships, law and government. Each area is part of the created order of human existence, and each has appropriate activities and institutions which we value because they are extensions of human personality.

Because these areas are native to man they are perverted by sin. In every area, human behavior and institutions diverge in act and intention from the created order. But this also means that each area is subject to the law of God, thence also to natural law, and that we are expected to bring both justice and love redemptively to bear. If then we are to discern in fallen man anything of a universal natural law it will be by examining these universal areas of his existence.

7. In each area human persons have their rights, so that general moral rules arise to promulgate the corresponding duties—some regarding sex and the family, some regarding life and safety, some regarding property, some regarding government, and so forth. The second table of the Decalogue poses some such general rules in the form of imperatives.

As institutions arise in one or another area, human rights become "shared rights"; and the corresponding duties and rules become shared duties and rules for institutional participation. The family, for instance, like the civil society makes claims on both its own members and other persons; family membership brings me rights and duties that I share with my fellow-members. We often act corporately as well as individually. We cultivate "togetherness" and value "privacy." We exercise and protect our shared rights and liberties; we formulate rules to protect them and to enforce our corresponding duties.

General rules in at least some areas of life are *prima facie* and not exceptionless obligations. In the area of physical life and safety, the right to life begets rules against killing whether intentionally or by negligence. But there may be exceptions. Some arise in special cases. For instance, Exodus 20–23 makes exceptions to the general rule "Thou shalt not kill" in the cases of capital punishment and self-defense, and places accidental manslaughter on a different level of culpability from murder. Yet even these cases are hedged about by case rules to keep exceptions from becoming general rules and therefore abuses. Other exceptions arise from the moral dilemmas posed in complex situations where general rules conflict. For instance, a rule about obeying civil government conflicts with a rule about killing, so that unless the government exempts an individual he himself will have to decide which rule now admits of an exception. Other exceptions arise when an individual forfeits or waives a right. A convicted criminal forfeits certain liberties; a man who sacrifices his life to save a drowning child waives his right to physical life and safety; yet a man may not waive that right through suicide. The widow who gave her mite waived the right to property, but the general rule is still that a man should provide for his own household.

8. While general rules apply to the universal areas of human existence, variations arise in particular historical cases. The more individual the cases we consider and the more specific the rules become, the greater the historical variables.

Changes in case rules may occur for various reasons. One is that social institutions change. For instance, while adultery is morally wrong in a polygamous as well as a monogamous society, a transition from the partly polygamous society of the Old Testament patriarchs to the more monogamous society of the New Testament involves a change in the particular rules governing sexual and family relationships.

Another reason is that technological and human resources change. Modern military technology has called into question the moral rules constituting the just war theory. The population explosion introduces additional reasons for practicing birth control. Capital punishment seems to me no longer justifiable now that we have other means of protecting society and possibly rehabilitating the criminal and there is no statistical evidence that it really deters from violence.

Another reason for change is that human understanding grows. For many years Christian rulers practiced a double standard in war with respect to Christians and pagans, until Francisco da Vitoria argued that all men by nature have the right to equal treatment, so that the same rules of just cause and limited means and so forth apply to Indian and Spaniard, to pagan and Christian alike.

Case rules and positive laws are historically variable. The most general moral rules for the universal areas of human existence are not historically variable, despite occasional exceptions. The less general the rule and the more it directly addresses particular situations, the more subject it is to historical change. The most general rules are approximations, appropriate to the discernible requirements of human nature and of all history, to the justice that should structure and the love that should permeate human relations. Case rules also are approximations, appropriate to the requirements of certain kinds of people in particular situations in history, to justice and to love.

The nature of the moral reasoning involved may become more evident by considering an example.

Why is adultery wrong? What about a general rule here? Each of the preceding eight observations is relevant. The reasoning involved holds no surprises.

(1) Natural law is a formal principle that tells us to look at the inherent nature of things rather than at desires and consequences alone, although no conclusion can be derived without additional input concerning the sexual area of man's created existence.

(2) The natural law principle affirms that human persons should be treated with justice and equity as human persons, not "used," in the sexual or in other areas.

(3) Sexual freedom is not unconditional but is correlative to sexual rights and duties.

(4) Sexual acts should be governed by both justice and love, that is, by an outward structure of rules as well as by a whole-personal concern to give of oneself rather than to get.

(5) The Christian especially will regard sex as sacred, but a Christian view of sex is not arbitrary; it is open to empirical and rational support.

(6) Others have argued on both biblical and extra-biblical grounds that human sexual intercourse has two functions, the unitive and the reproductive. Adultery places the sex act outside of the reproductive sphere of marriage;[13] in addition it normally limits the unitive function of sex to selective physical and emotional aspects of personality. It is thus not a

---

13. Paul Ramsey distinguishes between keeping sex within the reproductive sphere and making every sex act a reproductive act. See his *Fabricated Man* (New Haven, 1970), ch. 1.

whole-personal union, and those involved have no "shared" sexual rights as they would within marriage. Thus natural law reasoning concludes that adultery is wrong because it takes from the human sex act both its unitive and its reproductive significance. It is contrary to the nature of human sexuality in the created order.

(7) The general rule about adultery admits of differing applications in different historical cases. 'Adultery is wrong' may well be exceptionless, unlike the Old Testament rule about killing. Yet it cannot be translated into 'all extramarital sex is wrong,' for that would hold guilty the rape victim along with the rapist. The term 'adultery' excludes such a victim on the ground that the sin of adultery involves an adulterous intention as well as an extramarital sexual act. Nor can the rule prohibiting adultery be immediately translated as 'concubinage is wrong,' for in the Old Testament a concubine was party to "shared sexual rights" (cf. Exod. 21:7-10), and therefore part of the legally accepted order of marriage. Whether institutionalized concubinage and polygamy and "group marriages" are wrong on grounds other than adultery, as for instance that like adultery they violate the created order in the sexual area, is another question to be decided independently. It may be a case of (8) above, where the case rules and institutional structure should remain monogamous because of our present understanding of human persons, of sex, and of marriage. But that only raises further questions, like whether one can legislate monogamy (as distinct from advocating it), especially if human understanding of the alternatives is divided and if variant marriage practices become socially accepted.

Other examples could be given of moral reasoning on a natural law principle; indeed, the literature is replete with examples in the area of killing (war and capital punishment) and political obligation (civil disobedience), although less so in the economic area (wealth and poverty). But enough has already been said to respond to arguments from human variables.

The argument from religious variables we found strewn with red herrings and beset by a view of grace more existential than Augustinian. It reduced to the claim that man's perverted condition reveals nothing intelligible about universal natural law, and in the sexual area at least this claim seems false. The argument from philosophical variables was marked by confusion and inhibition. In effect it requested a way of minimizing those differences, and this we have proposed by pointing to agreement that is possible in defining formal principles and universal areas of human existence. Thereafter philosophical as well as theological reasoning must operate in formulating and applying moral rules. There is no royal road to philosophical agreement. The argument from historical variables came loaded with the deterministic assumptions of quasi-Marxist sociology. In practice these variables appear most at a level where they can be accommodated as exceptions to general rules or changes due to changing cases. Defensible if not demonstrable moral rules are indeed derivable.

The problems of permanence and change and of finding the one amidst the many in ethics are not easily dispelled. But it does seem desirable to locate human variables within a framework of principles, rules, and cases rather than smearing them promiscuously across all of ethics. Ellul and his friends overlook these distinctions and in doing so abandon too quickly not only the idea of natural law but also other philosophical dimensions of Christian ethics.

Natural Law in Aquinas and Calvin

ALLEN VERHEY

The concept of natural law and its use in Christian ethical reflection has a long history, filled with controversy and confusion, which continues among philosophers and theologians to this day. Henry Stob's thought has always been ambivalent toward the concept of natural law, appreciating the attempt to demonstrate universal subjection to the moral law and universal awareness of it, but concerned with tendencies toward a dualism of nature and grace, toward moral pride, and toward unattentiveness to revelation and to the natural misapprehension of God's law.[1]

William Frankena has eliminated at least some of the confusion about the meaning of 'natural law' with his suggestion that

we should put down as a natural law man anyone who does at least the following: (1) He subscribes to moral principles such as MNO. (2) He holds (a) that we are justified in accepting them, directly or indirectly, by truths known by our natural faculties (though not necessarily by logical deduction); (b) that they justifiably ascribe rights and obligations to all men as such, independently of their offices, agreements, laws, or whatever; and (c) that they may therefore serve as a standard by which to judge all human institutions, rules, and actions.[2]

---

1. See the mimeographed syllabus for Calvin Theological Seminary course 512, "Basic Christian Ethics," pp. 98-114. Perhaps Prof. Stob's most appreciative comments on natural law are found in his 1974 Jaymes P. Morgan, Jr., lectures at Fuller Theological Seminary. Cf. the lecture on "Justice," *Calvin Theological Journal*, 9, 2 (Nov. 1974). Apropos the comparison between the two thinkers treated in what follows, cf. also Henry Stob, "Calvin and Aquinas," *Reformed Journal*, 24, 5 (May-June 1974), 17-20.
2. "On Defining and Defending Natural Law," in S. Hook (ed.), *Law and Philosophy* (New York, 1964), p. 209. 'MNO' refers to differing moral principles, specifically, to love, equity, and the right to life, liberty, and security (p. 202); the point, however, is that while natural lawyers may subscribe to different moral prin-

---

Allen Verhey, in a piece complementary to Holmes', addresses himself to a segment of the natural law tradition in ethics. Thomas Aquinas and John Calvin were both natural law ethicists, but Calvin's version, says Verhey, is the more defensible. Verhey, a Lecturer in Ethics at Calvin Theological Seminary, is completing a dissertation on the use of Scripture in moral argument.

Thomas Aquinas and John Calvin were such natural law men. If the contemporary Christian community intends to "rehabilitate" natural law (as some have suggested),[3] the sanctified reflection of these two giants surely demands some careful attention. Because both have natural law *doctrines*, that is, because both approach the concept of natural law as theologians, the natural law doctrines of these two men are close enough to be the subject of simultaneous analysis and comparison.[4]

1. *The law is dependent.* Both Thomas and Calvin see the natural law as dependent on a reality of meaning and value built into the world by God's purposeful creating and sustaining power. For both men, the purposes of God precede and shape what is. Moreover, for both the wisdom of God establishes the purposes of God. They are not merely a matter of arbitrary will. While Thomas emphasizes the creating power of God[5] or constitutive grace, and Calvin emphasizes the sustaining power of God[6] or restraining grace, neither theologian neglects either concept. For both theo-

ciples, they all subscribe to moral principles and make similar claims about their justifiability, status, and normativity.
3. Especially Ian T. Ramsey, "Toward a Rehabilitation of Natural Law," in I. T. Ramsey (ed.), *Christian Ethics and Contemporary Philosophy* (New York, 1966); and J. Macquarrie, "Rethinking Natural Law," in *Three Issues in Ethics* (New York, 1970).
4. On natural law in Aquinas, see R. A. Armstrong, *Primary and Secondary Precepts in Thomistic Natural Law Teaching* (The Hague, 1966); A. P. D'Entreves, "Thomas Aquinas," in I. Kramnick (ed.), *Essays in the History of Political Thought* (Englewood Cliffs, N. J., 1969); J. G. Milhaven, "Moral Absolutes and Thomas Aquinas," in C. Curran (ed.), *Absolutes in Moral Theology?* (Washington, 1968); D. J. O'Connor, *Aquinas and Natural Law* (London, 1967); M. Strasser, "St. Thomas on Natural Law," in E. A. Smith (ed.), *Church-State Relations in Ecumenical Perspective* (Pittsburgh, 1966).
   On natural law in Calvin see J. Bohatec, *Calvin und das Recht* (Graz, 1934); A. C. Cochrane, "Natural Law in Calvin," in E. A. Smith, *loc. cit.*; D. Little, "Calvin and the Prospects for a Christian Theory of Natural Law," in G. H. Outka and P. Ramsey (eds.), *Norm and Context in Christian Ethics* (New York, 1968). A. Lang, "Reformation and Natural Law," in W. P. Armstrong (ed.), *Calvin and the Reformation* (New York, 1909) deserves to be mentioned because of its contention that the concept of natural law was simply part of the Reformer's tradition which really had no place in Reformed thought after the decisive break with the nature-grace scheme of Roman Catholicism. On the other hand, S. H. Rae, "Calvin, Natural Law, and Contemporary Ethics: A Brief Note," *Reformed Theological Review*, 30, 1 (Jan.-Apr. 1971) has called for a reexamination of Calvin's natural law doctrine in the hope of finding "the basis of an authentically Christian moral philosophy which may at the same time appeal to the rationality of the non-Christian" (16).
5. *ST* I.II q 91 a 1,2; q 93 a 3; q 93 a 1: ". . . the ideal of divine wisdom considered as moving all things to their appropriate end has the quality of law."
6. *Inst.*, III.xiv.2; II.ii.17: "We ought to ascribe what is left in us to God's kindness. For if he had not spared us, our fall would have entailed the destruction of our whole nature." Cf. also II.viii.13; I.xvii.1.

logians the law has its being finally in the mind and grace of God.

2. *The law is instrumental.* For both Thomas and Calvin the law leads to grace, but it does so in significantly different ways. In Thomas the law leads to the good life, happiness, which has its own authenticity and integrity; but that authenticity within the capacities of human nature expects and awaits the grace of God to transform happiness into beatitude (*ST* I.II q 62 a 1, 3). In Calvin the law leads to a confrontation with the righteousness of God. Although there is a political use, it is particularly the condemning function of the law which crashes men to their knees in repentance and trust in God.[7] Calvin's political use of the law is more sympathetic to the basic motif of Aquinas; Calvin says that the law is meant "to restrain them from so slackening the reins on the lust of the flesh as to fall clean away from all pursuit of righteousness" (*Inst.,* II.vii. 11). But that very quotation reveals the significance of their difference. Thomas's natural law claims to lead to the fulness of the good life minus only the theological virtues. Calvin's natural law claims only to protect the boundaries of human nature, beyond which the image of God is lost entirely. Thomas provides ends to be sought by man. Calvin provides limits to the actions of men seeking their own ends. In both, however, the law is instrumental to grace. It is this instrumentality which demands a doctrine of *natural* law. Since it is instrumental to grace, it must be accessible to those outside of grace.

3. *There is universal subjection to the natural law.* This is essentially a corollary of Thesis 1 for both men. Because the purposes of God set being and meaning in the creation, to be subject to law is the essential and irrevocable condition of man. Just because he is a man, a creature, he sits under the rule and command of God. God and the law that depends on him are inescapable. But again there is a significant difference between the two theologians. Thomas contends that the purposes of God are immanent as inner principles of motion in everything that moves. Man is in a special category because as a rational and free being he alone is able to be a participant by way of knowledge and choice (*ST* I.II q 91 a 2). Calvin, on the other hand, seems interested only in Thomas's special category (*Inst.,* II.ii.18,22). While Thomas has the natural (rational) law of man's rational nature plus the natural (involuntary) law of immanent principles of motion, Calvin has only the natural (rational) law of man's rational nature.

---

7. *Inst.,* II.ii.21; II.vii.6: "While it shows God's righteousness, . . . it warns, informs, convicts, and lastly condemns, every man of his own unrighteousness"; II.vii.8; II.viii.3; cf. Calvin's comments on conscience, III.xix.15; IV.x.3.

4. *There is universal awareness of the natural law.* This is clearly the critical thesis. Both theologians want to avoid allowing their theological doctrines of natural law to diminish its status as *natural* law. This concern is forced on them by their thesis that the law is instrumental to grace. The law is a presupposition for the gospel, and not simply a result of the gospel. It is here that the really hard question arises for both men: the epistemological question.[8] If they admit (and they not only admit but contend) that the law is dependent on God for its being, can they also contend that an awareness of the law is independent of the knowledge of God?

St. Thomas admits that man's intelligence has been darkened by the fall so that man does not see the eternal law as it is in itself except in the beatific vision. Nevertheless, every rational creature knows it in a measure at least. "All men know the truth to a certain extent, at least as to the common principles of the natural law; . . . and in this respect are more or less cognizant of the eternal law" (*ST* I.II q 93 a 2). That is Thomas's claim that all men know. But how do they know?

The first principle of the natural law, according to Thomas, is that the good is to be sought and done, the evil avoided (*ST* I.II q 94 a 2). Reason knows this first principle by simple analysis of the word "good." With this first analytical principle there is as yet no determination of what "good" means synthetically, no determination of which particular ends are to be sought. But with this basic recognition of himself as purposive and of his obligation to seek an end proper to himself, man continues to reflect upon himself, "so that whatever the practical reason naturally apprehends as man's good belongs to the precepts of the natural law." Because "good has the nature of an end," Thomas looks for those things to which man has "a natural inclination," an involuntary drive, an immanent entelechy. These the reason apprehends as being good and, therefore, to be sought. Man shares with all living beings a natural inclination to preserve the self. Reason apprehends this inclination as being good and promulgates the precept to preserve the elemental requirements of human life. But man is more than that, and that life which must be preserved must be ordered toward a higher inclination.[9] Man shares with the animals a natural inclination to propagate and rear offspring. Reason apprehends this inclination as good and promulgates the precept to bear and

---

8. Kai Nielsen raises "the epistemological difficulties which surround such conceptions"; "The Myth of Natural Law," in S. Hook (ed.), *Law and Philosophy*, p. 123.
9. "The order of the precepts of the natural law is according to the order of natural inclinations" (*ST* I.II q 94 a 2).

educate children.[10] But more than that, man is rational and social. He has a natural inclination, peculiar to himself, to seek truth and avoid ignorance, especially with respect to the social life of man and to his knowledge of God. He has both a social inclination and a religious inclination. Reason apprehends these inclinations of man and promulgates the precepts to seek the truth and avoid error, to live in society with other men, and to worship God (ST I.II q 94 a 2). Reason continues to reflect on these primary derivations from the first principle and makes secondary and tertiary derivations which stand in greater danger of being mistaken.[11] According to Thomas, then, the natural law is known essentially by reason apprehending the fundamental natural (involuntary) inclinations of men.

Calvin, too, claims that there is universal awareness of the natural law. He says that "the frailty of the human mind is surely proved: even while it seems to follow the way [equity] it limps and staggers. Yet the fact remains that some seed of political order has been implanted in all men. And this is ample proof that in the arrangement of this life no man is without the light of reason" (Inst., II.ii.13). This quotation focuses both the stronger sense of sin in Calvin and his claim that the law, nonetheless, is known by reason. But how does Calvin attempt to justify this claim?

The image of God in man is, in Calvin's thought, both relational and structural.[12] Structurally, it is found in the human faculties of understanding and will (Inst., I.xv.7). Relationally, the image is the right ordering of these faculties: understanding rightly ordered is "true knowledge," will rightly ordered is "true righteousness," and understanding and will together in integrity constitute "true holiness" (Inst., I.xv.4). The relational image all men have lost in the fall, but the structural image remains (cf.

---

10. See the discussion of this by Bernard Lonergan, "Finality, Love, Marriage," in F. E. Crowe (ed.), Collection: Papers by Bernard Lonergan, S. J. (New York: 1967). Lonergan's essay is a contemporary account of Thomas's natural law teaching on this point.
11. ST I.II q 94 a 4. An example of a secondary derivation in Aquinas is his justification of monogamy on the basis of the precept to rear and care for children, SCG III.124; cf. ST suppl 65.1, and Calvin, Inst., II.ii.23, where the Reformer makes a similar point that in the concrete application of general principles there is a greater danger of being mistaken.
12. Inst., I.xv.4: "Nevertheless, it seems that we do not have a full definition of 'image' if we do not see more plainly those faculties in which man excels, and in which he ought to be thought the reflection of God's glory. That, indeed, can be nowhere better recognized than from the restoration of his corrupted nature. . . . God's image was not totally annihilated and destroyed in him [Adam]. . . . The end of regeneration is that Christ should reform us to God's image."

note 12 above). Men have lost true knowledge, true righteousness, and true holiness, but all men have and exercise understanding and will. All men, to fill in Calvin's definitions of 'understanding' and 'will,' "distinguish between objects as each seems worthy of approval or disapproval" and "choose and follow what the understanding pronounces good" (*Inst.*, I.xv.7). Because of sin the understanding is darkened, the will is bound, and the relationship between the two is broken; still, men make distinctions and seek ends.

Since reason, therefore, by which man distinguishes between good and evil, and by which he understands and judges, is a natural gift, it could not be completely wiped out; but it was partly weakened and partly corrupted, so that its misshapen ruins appear.... Similarly the will, because it is inseparable from man's nature, did not perish, but was so bound to wicked desires that it cannot strive after the right (*Inst.*, II.ii.12).

Still, the understanding and its efforts "do not become so worthless as to have no effect" (*Inst.*, II.ii.13), especially with respect to what Calvin calls "earthy things." Because the loss of true knowledge, righteousness, and holiness creates radical differences in the ends sought by men, we cannot expect men to agree about an end or a set of ends; we cannot expect men to agree about the "good." But because "man is by nature a social animal,"[13] the differing ends come into unavoidable conflict, and man cannot help being aware of this conflict and the demand it makes for

---

13. *Inst.*, II.ii.13. The quotation continues: "he tends through natural instinct to foster and preserve society. Consequently, we observe that there exist in all men's minds universal impressions of a certain civic fair dealing and order. Hence no man is to be found who does not understand that every sort of human organization must be regulated by laws, and who does not comprehend the principles of those laws. Hence arises that unvarying consent of all nations and of individual mortals with regard to laws. For their seeds have, without teacher or lawgiver, been implanted in all men." This passage has sometimes been taken as the key to Calvin's natural law concept, but it is open to various interpretations. The "natural instinct to foster and preserve society" sounds very much like St. Thomas. And it ought to be noted that Calvin does sometimes talk about created ends (e.g., III.x.2; III.xix.8), but the in-created *telos* in those cases belongs not to man himself but to food, clothing, wine, etc. The "unvarying consent of all nations and of individual mortals" might lead one to look to *consensus gentium* as the basis for Calvin's natural law. Again, it ought to be noted that there are attempts within Calvin to establish sets of empirical generalizations as the basis for obligation (cf. IV.xx.16). David Little's essay "Calvin and the Prospects for a Christian Theory of Natural Law" focuses on this motif in Calvin. My own reconstruction would emphasize "certain civic fair dealing" in the quotation above. While Calvin's treatment of natural law is not altogether consistent and while I admit that my own analysis is a reconstruction of Calvin's teaching and like all reconstruction may contain some construction as well, I think it is the most faithful to Calvin.

"civic fair dealing and order." Within the conflict of ends each must acknowledge the other as the structural image of God, as one endowed with reason and will, as distinguishing for himself and choosing what is "good." This structural image of God, even though it is turned toward evil, is not without its intrinsic value. "We are not to consider that men merit of themselves, but to look upon the image of God *in all men*, to which we all owe honor and love" (*Inst.*, II.vii.6).[14] Because a man claims his own dignity on the basis of this structural image, he may not refuse to acknowledge the other's claim to the same dignity on the same basis. Therefore, the law which is demanded because the man-in-society is the man-in-sin and which is vindicated because the man-in-society is the image of God, is not any of the diverse conceptions of "good" but "the original conception of equity" (*Inst.*, II.ii.13). It it the principle of equity which Calvin identifies with the natural law (cf. *Inst.*, IV.xx.16).

All men have the structural image of God. All men sin. Those are clearly theological claims. But rendered into an epistemology of natural law they mean that men choose values and act on them, and that when these values and acts collide, men cannot expect the claims they make for themselves on the basis of their rational moral agency to be acknowledged unless they honor the same claim made on the same basis by the other. The most rudimentary of principles of rationality, consistency, and impartiality toward the evidence thus establishes an impartiality toward persons, a basic (or presumptive) equality. All men, then, are able to know and can be expected to know their obligation to limit the wilful seeking of their own ends according to the equal freedom of all others to seek their ends. This boundary of equity is recognized by all men (*Inst.*, II.ii. 13). While this is not yet the full measure of concern for the neighbor's good that neighbor love is, neither is it unconnected with that love.

Calvin's treatment of the second table of the decalogue is illustrative. The basic ethical principle, I suggest, is equity. Equity validates certain fixed points, the commandments of the second table. From those fixed points it is possible to move rationally according to the principles of synecdoche, contraries, and intention[15] to what is required of a full neighbor love. The clearest example is Calvin's treatment of the sixth commandment, "Thou shalt not kill" (*Inst.*, II.viii.39-40). The commandment

---

14. Italics added. Cf. *Comm.* on Gal. 5:14: "The image of God ought to be particularly regarded as a sacred bond of union; but, for that very reason no distinction is made here between friend and foe, nor can the wickedness of men set aside the right of nature."

15. *Inst.*, II.viii.8-10, where Calvin introduces, defends, and illustrates these three inference licenses. He uses them in the discussion of each commandment.

"rests upon a twofold basis: man is the image of God, and our flesh." Calvin makes it clear that he is referring to the *structural* image of God here when he says, "We shall *elsewhere* discuss how this exhortation is to be derived from the redemption and grace of Christ." Man is to be respected as the image of God, as having understanding and will. We ought not, for the sake of our ends, deprive another man of his right to distinguish and choose his own "good." Murder, then, as it deprives a man of that rightful equity, is never a legitimate means to achieve any "good." "Thou shalt not murder" is thus a fixed point; it establishes a boundary for discretionary behavior.

Calvin then moves in argument from that fixed point established by equity to claims concerning the good, from proscription of means to prescription of ends, from deontology to teleology. He licenses these moves in argument by the principles of synecdoche, contraries, and intention. If the part is the prohibition of murder, the principle of synecdoche allows the claim that the whole is the prohibition of all plotting and even wishing anything against the safety of the neighbor. The contrary is also true: if we are to ward off what is harmful, then we ought to seek whatever is to the neighbor's peace and well-being. The intention of this fixed point is to protect human life; "hence each man ought to concern himself with the safety of all." In this way Calvin moves from duty to the good. Finally, here—and in each commandment—the disposition to love the neighbor is established. And thus neighbor love can be included within natural law.[16]

It is noteworthy that in Calvin—as in Thomas—the decalogue was given because, although the natural law should suffice, the intelligence of man is sometimes dull, sometimes malicious. God gave the decalogue that men might have a check on their reasoning and for ready reference for those with busy hands or slow minds.[17]

---

16. Calvin is concerned theologically to demonstrate the unitary character of the law: the law of God is one, but known in different ways (cf. *Inst.*, II.viii.1; IV.xx. 16; *Comm.* on Deut. 10:12). Calvin seems here to be concerned with one of the motifs of Thomas (see our Thesis 2 above: "The law is instrumental to grace"): that the law itself frees one for the voluntary performance of the law when one sees the point of it. To see the point of equity frees one for love. If that is the case here, then Calvin might seem to lose "theological control" since theologically the law is powerless in Calvin. It is only Christ who frees. But perhaps we need only say that Christ can free through his Spirit working with and through the law even where his name is not known.

17. *Inst.*, II.viii.1: "it is necessary both for our dullness and for our arrogance." Cf. *ST* I.II q 91 a 4. In both Calvin and Aquinas the decalogue is distinguished from the rest of the Old Testament legislation as that from which the rest derives, of which the rest is an application "with regard to the condition of times, place, and nation" (*Inst.*, IV.xx.16).

5. *The natural law is normative for social ethics and political obligation.*
Thomas and Calvin share this thesis with all great natural law ethicists.
They differ significantly, of course, in their theories of political obligation
precisely because of their disagreement about natural law.

For St. Thomas political obligation is justified by that social inclination of man. "Man is by nature a political and social animal."[18] When
reason apprehends this inclination of man for social life, it promulgates
the precept of political obligation. Societies ought to be formed because
they are necessary for the development of man's potentialities. But more
than that, the social nature of man warrants the emphatic assertion of a
complete integration of the individual into the life of the community.
"All men being a part of the city, they cannot be truly good unless they
adapt themselves to the common good" (*ST* I.II. q 90 a 3 ad 3; cf. q 92 a
1 ad 3). Since every man is a part of a political community, his "good"
must be defined in terms of the common good. The progression of natural
inclinations orders other goods to the social good. In this progression of
ends, Thomas is clearly working out an "organic" conception of the state:
the individual is subordinate to the corporate entity, and all individual
ends must be ordered to its end. If, however, this looks too much like Leviathan,[19] it is necessary to look only a little more deeply. This common
good is, according to Thomas, that

> in the first place the community must be united in peaceful unity.
> In the second place the community, thus united, must be directed
> towards well-doing.... Thirdly, and finally, it is necessary that there
> be, through the ruler's sagacity, a sufficiency of those material goods
> which are indispensable to well-being (*On Princely Government* XV).

And with respect to the "unity" that is called for, it must be further observed that "this is only a unity of order and not an unconditional unity.
Consequently the parts which form it can have a sphere of action which
is distinct from that of the whole" (*Commentary on the Nic. Ethics* I.i.).

Moreover, the natural law which licenses political authority also limits
it. If a law "is at variance with natural law, it will not be law, but spoilt
law" (*ST* I.II q 95 a 2; cf. q 92 a 1 ad 4). Positive law, then, can be
either just or unjust. A law is unjust by its end, origin, or form; accordingly, a law is unjust if it seeks the private end of the ruler, if it exceeds
the power of the magistrate, if it imposes inequitable burdens for the com-

---

18. *ST* I.II q 95 a 4; q 96 a 4; *On Princely Government* I.i and frequently. This
leading idea Thomas takes over from Aristotle.
19. Cf. the criticism of N. Wolterstorff, "Contemporary Christian Views of the
State: Some Major Issues," *Christian Scholar's Review*, 3,4 (1974), 314-16.

mon good. "Such laws do not, in consequence, oblige in conscience, except, on occasion, to avoid scandal or disorder" (*ST* I.II q 96 a 4). A law is also unjust if it contradicts divine law. In the former cases there is warrant for resistance unless the result of resistance is a greater evil than obedience to these unjust enactments. In the latter case, men *must* resist.

This introduces the problem of the relation of church and state. While Thomas does not want these two collapsed, and indeed confines the state to judgments on external actions (*ST* I.II q 100 a 9), and while in Thomas political authority has a value of its own as an expression of a rational and natural order,[20] still, according to the progression of ends, the state ought to be subordinate to the church. It must accept the scheme of a hierarchical, graded society according to the progression of ends and rationally accept its subordinate place. Government does not take the responsibility for this religious end because it is not attainable by natural human virtue, but there is a natural human inclination, which can only be fulfilled by the grace of God. Therefore, the church exists out of the grace of God toward man's desire and the state recognizes naturally its subordination to this higher order.[21]

Calvin also considered the social nature of man to be the basis of political obligation, but in a fundamentally different way.[22] Each man bears the structural image of God; each must be free to discern and seek the "good." But all men bear that image, and so all men must have an equal freedom. That means that in society laws are needed in order to insure

---

20. Because of this Thomas can see genuine good in the governments of infidels (contrast Augustine); *ST* II.II q 10 a 10: "So the distinction between the faithful and the infidel, considered in itself, does not invalidate the government and dominion of infidels over the faithful."

21. *On Princely Government* XIV: "Now the man who lives virtuously is destined to a higher end, which consists . . . in the enjoyment of God: and the final object of human association can be no different from that of the individual man. Thus the final aim of social life will be . . . to attain to the enjoyment of God. If, indeed, it were possible to attain this object by natural human virtue, it would, in consequence, be the duty of kings to guide men to this end. . . . But the enjoyment of God is an aim which cannot be attained by human virtue alone, but only through divine grace. . . . The ministry of this kingdom is entrusted not to the rulers of this earth but to priests, so that temporal affairs may remain distinct from those spiritual. . . . So the authorities have never hesitated to place themselves at the service of the altar." Cf. *ST* II.II q 60 a 6. For an account of contemporary Roman Catholic arguments for religious freedom see J. C. Murray, "Religious Freedom," in J. C. Murray (ed.), *Freedom and Man* (New York, 1965).

22. *Inst.*, IV.x.5: "Human laws, whether made by magistrate or by church, even though they have to be observed (I speak of good and just laws), still do not of themselves bind the conscience. For all obligation to observe laws looks to the general purpose, but does not consist in the thing enjoined."

that one man will not use his freedom against another man's equal freedom.[23] Calvin says,

> No kind of government is more happy than one where freedom is regulated with becoming moderation and is properly established on a durable basis (*Inst.*, IV.xx.8).[24]

The exercise of political power is licensed by the duty to protect and preserve that freedom, and it is limited to that duty.

> Indeed, the magistrates ought to apply themselves with the highest diligence to prevent the freedom (whose guardians they have been appointed) from being in any respect diminished, far less violated (*Inst.*, IV.xx.8).

The freedom of each demands that the freedom of all be limited, but it must be limited as little as possible, only in a measure, namely the measure of equity.

> Equity alone must be the goal and rule and limit of all laws. Whatever laws shall be framed to that rule, directed to that goal, bound by that limit, there is no reason we should disapprove of them (*Inst.*, IV.xx.16).

Calvin's political theory, then, is based on the principles of freedom and equity.[25] These, in turn, are based on natural law, as we have seen. Together they demand order and provide the boundaries enabling civic righteousness. These are the criteria for the justness of law and the legitimate use of power.[26]

---

23. Cf. Calvin's treatment of Christian freedom (*Inst.*, III.xix.12; IV.x.32), where the restraint placed on the exercise of freedom is not the equity due the neighbor but the Christian love due the neighbor.

24. Cf. also *Comm.* on Gen. 39:2; Jer. 38:25f.; I Cor. 10:29; and the judgment on the legitimacy and limitations of ecclesiastical legislation (*Inst.*, IV.x.1): Calvin rejects church laws which "tyrannously oppress conscience"; he demands that "spiritual freedom . . . remain unimpaired"; he accuses Roman Catholic decrees of usurping "unlimited and barbarous empire" over souls; "thus the freedom given by him to the consciences of believers is utterly oppressed and cast down." But if natural law limits church authority, it also licenses it: "We see that some form of organization is necessary in all human society to foster the common peace and maintain concord" (IV.x.27). The final license and limit to authority is, of course, the word of God (IV.x.8,30). But Calvin does not see this as contradictory to the place he has given natural law, for both are dependent on God.

25. Calvin rejects as "perilous and seditious" the notion of a theocracy established on the political system of Moses (IV.xx.14).

26. These principles are operative when Calvin favors a mixed constitution. The democratic element is justified because "if one asserts himself unfairly, there may [i.e., needs to] be a number of censors and masters to restrain his willfulness" (IV.xx.8). These principles license the power of the state to wage war and limit

It must be admitted that Calvin does not apply these principles with equal rigor or even consistency.[27] Church-state relations are a good example. On the one hand, he clearly wants to separate church and state. There are two kingdoms—one spiritual and internal, to which belongs piety; the other political and external, to which belongs "the duties of humanity and citizenship which must be maintained among men" (*Inst.*, III.xix.15). These two "must always be examined separately; and while one is being considered, we must call away and turn aside the mind from thinking about the other."[28] On the other hand, it is part of the duty of the state, Calvin says, "to cherish and protect the outward worship of God, to defend sound doctrine of piety and the position of the Church" (*Inst.*, IV.xx.2; cf. IV.xx.9). Moreover, it ought to prevent idolatry, sacrilege, blasphemies, and other public offenses against religion. The best interpretation of this confusion is that Calvin believed it the duty of the state to protect the freedom of Christians. "It [the state] provides that a public manifestation" of religion may exist among Christians" (*Inst.*, IV.xx.3). But this is a liberty which seems to belong to the Christian religion alone —and at that point Calvin's own principle of equity must correct Calvin's thought.

*   *   *

The natural law doctrines of both Calvin and Aquinas are powerful and intriguing. Calvin's alone, however, seems to me to be persuasive. Con-

---

that power by criteria like just cause, last resort, and just conduct (IV.xx.11,12). They license and limit the power of the state to exact taxes (IV.xx.13). Calvin does not conclude that unjust laws or unjust magistrates may be disobeyed (IV.xx.22-29; but cf. IV.xx.31: "if they command anything against him, let it go unesteemed"). He does, however, both approve and urge the protection of the freedom and equity of the citizens by the "lesser magistrates" (IV.xx.31). Calvin calls it their duty to restrain the "willfulness of kings." If they refuse this duty they "betray the freedom of the people." Something like the category of "legitimate authority" is clearly at work in Calvin's treatment of revolution. Throughout these sections Calvin uses Scripture not as proof, but as example. The basic principles are, I think, freedom and equity; the basic proscriptions, anarchy and tyranny.

27. There may be a number of factors contributing to this inconsistency. Among them would certainly be Calvin's too-mechanical view of God's providence (cf. IV.xx.8,25). The charge of sedition against Calvin ("Prefatory Address," "Reply to Sadolet") may have affected him; see Paul Woolley, "Calvin and Toleration," in John H. Bratt (ed.), *The Heritage of John Calvin* (Grand Rapids, 1973), for an analysis of this inconsistency and an historical explanation for it. There can be no doubt that Calvin feared anarchy more than tyranny; cf. *Comm.* on I Pet. 2:14. But there can also be no doubt that followers of Calvin like Christopher Goodman, the Huguenot who called himself Junius Brutus, John Lilburne, and others were faithful to Calvin in their defense of liberty and equity against tyranny.

28. Cf. *Inst.*, IV.xi.3: "The church does not assume what is proper to the magistrate; nor can the magistrate execute what is carried out by the church."

trary to St. Thomas, I fail to see how the involuntary inclinations of man can obligate him morally. They are submoral; and, while decisions must be made *about* them—in controlling them, for example—I do not see how they can be normative for those decisions. Judging from my own "involuntary inclinations," I find no generally trustworthy guidance in them. Instead, they need to be "reined" by reflection and decision about the right and the good.[29] To allow 'good' to be defined by these involuntary drives is, I think, to commit the naturalistic fallacy. If someone were to expose the naturalistic fallacy by asking, "But are the involuntary inclinations *good?*", a perfectly legitimate question,[30] Thomas is forced to fall back on either intuition or the providence of God. And both of those— in different ways—give up the case for rational apprehension of the natural law.

Calvin, on the other hand, has shown both that and how men are obliged by their own rationality to certain minimal duties. The case does not rest on certain natural (involuntary) inclinations, nor are the primary precepts claims about goals or purposes. Men do, of course, have aims and goals. And in Calvin *that* they have these ends, rather than *what* ends they have, is the basis of natural law. As image-bearers of God, men reflect on, choose, and act on ends. In the contexts of sin and society, these ends come into conflict. In the conflict situation men make claims for themselves on the basis of their rational moral agency. They cannot expect that claim to be honored unless they are willing to honor the same claim when it is made on the same basis by another. Thus equity is established, and equity in turn validates certain minimal duties.

---

29. Cf. *Inst.*, II.ii.26. St. Thomas might counter that I am talking about the law in the "fomes" (*ST* I.II q 91 a 6). But that changes nothing. If "fomes" is an involuntary inclination, why is it not allowed to direct the moral life as well? The answer to that cannot be in any one of the natural inclinations but can be in man's reason, in the natural law considered as something else than involuntary drives.

30. Cf. the "open question argument" in G. E. Moore, *Principia Ethica* (Cambridge, 1965), pp. 15f.

Christian Perspective on Private Property

CARL F. H. HENRY

Controversy over private property has split the twentieth-century world in two. In the name of economic justice, the free world advocates private property; in the name of economic justice the Communist world rejects it. Both the Communist revolution and Western political adjustments have blunted the free world's convictions about private property. The whole realm of property now staggers under problems, compromises, and uncertainties. In many lands nationalization has become largely a matter of public indifference, and common ownership of property is hardly a live political issue.

In lands of fairly advanced economic development reduction of vast disparities of wealth and poverty has lessened some of the explosive potential of the property debate. But private property remains a politically volatile issue where great masses of people are hungry, as in rural India. The use of property (what ownership exists *for*) has become as fundamental an issue as ownership itself.

Although private property is a major social concern of this century, free world literature treats the theme cavalierly; indeed, it often neglects it entirely. United States Information Agency libraries around the world are so lacking in constructive volumes on this subject that to prepare any respectable defense of private property from their resources would be almost impossible. The same complaint can be made against many public libraries in the Anglo-Saxon world. Meanwhile, Communist spokesmen constantly affirm the illegitimacy of private property. Since alien views thrive in a climate of indifference, the free world is especially obliged to engage earnestly in this debate. This duty of studying the property issue is doubly incumbent on any society that not only considers private property indispensable to a just social order, but also—contrary to the Communist rejection of supernatural sanctions—presumes to find a basis for

Carl Henry, presently lecturer-at-large for World Vision International, was for twelve years the editor of Christianity Today. *He has written and edited numerous volumes of evangelical theology and ethics. In his essay Henry vigorously argues the biblical basis for the moral right of private property, cautioning, however, that a Christian perspective on property rights must be tempered by a Christian concern for human need.*

ownership in man's God-given rights. In a time when the problem of property constitutes a pressing question of social morality, this generation must face the issue with new boldness and energy, and in a manner that soundly probes its spiritual and theological implications.

The scriptural revelation of man's nature and destiny sets the theme of property—like all other human concerns—in the larger context of God's purpose in creation and redemption. In the Bible God's sanction of private property stands in a framework that proclaims divine right above human rights; and only on this basis do human rights become inalienable. While the biblical view of rights and responsibilities may not be the only answer short of a planned society, it is nonetheless the only view long enough and wide enough to escape internal instability and external demolition.

In thus speaking of the biblical view of property I am not unmindful of several facts, notably the fluctuations of ecclesiastical opinion. Roman Catholic theologians and canonists have viewed private property as justified. Several encyclicals of Leo XIII strongly insist on the necessity and justice of private ownership, and the encyclical *Rerum Novarum* expressly condemns as unjust the socialist design to abolish private property. The Roman Church condemned as heretical Anabaptists and other sectarians who renounced private property and charged the Catholic Church—a holder of vast properties—with worldly-mindedness. In its support of private property the medieval church largely perpetuated rather than transformed the pagan Roman view of absolute property rights—of which we shall speak later—although recognizing the existence of personal abuses. Yet, consistently with the notion of some early church fathers that private property springs from avarice, the church from the fourth century onward from time to time also espoused community possessions and elimination of private property as normative; during the Inquisition, moreover, the Roman Church disregarded the right of personal property of the offender or his posterity.

In our own day church bodies of several denominations have acquired such extensive properties not directly related to their distinctive ministries that municipal planners and churchmen alike warn increasingly that this accumulation of tax-favored or tax-free properties may invite ultimate expropriation. The problem is compounded by church construction of large buildings, presumably erected for spiritual ministries, which stand unused much of the week.

Not in practice only, but in the realm of theory also, the Christian witness is compromised. Modern ecclesiastical and ecumenical pronouncements on economic matters often reflect the influence of socialist theory. Already in 1887 the episcopate of the Anglican churches throughout the world, in the Lambeth Conference, appealed to the clergy to emphasize "how much of what is good and true in Socialism is to be found in the precepts of Christ." In erstwhile Christian lands now dominated by Communist forces, the morality of private ownership is no longer the common teaching of the churches. Textbooks on Christian social ethics generally give little thought to the theme of ownership, though German scholars more than others show awareness of the subject. Spokesmen for Anglo-Saxon church bodies frequently approve welfare legislation, yet neglect the exposition of scripturally revealed principles bearing on property rights as well as other social concerns. Many American clergymen shun the theme of private ownership in their pulpits, except when exhorting members to larger contributions. Even evangelical Protestants seldom express Christian conscience on this important issue, except by the occasional adoption of resolutions at annual conferences.

The socialist removal of certain functions of ownership from the determination of property owners and institution of compulsory charity were aimed in part to overcome the misuse or abuse of property. This possibility is encouraged whenever the use of property is undisciplined by ethical and spiritual considerations. Any doctrine of property devoid of biblical legitimation will inevitably license immoral practices. When man as a sinful creature fashions and justifies the right of property in isolation from divine prerogatives, he no longer properly balances rights and responsibilities, but will compromise the one in protecting the other. Unjustifiable excesses will incur the penalty of unjust restrictions as well-intentioned but misguided reformers seek to erase social wrongs by their techniques of compulsion. Recent modern history has certainly taught that unless the present system of property is spiritually molded in the light of Christian principle, its alteration will be arbitrarily demanded by non-Christian speculation. In the case of Communism, the stifling device of government correction and regulation promoted unjust demands in the name of justice: the wealthy were deprived of their goods, but the poor have hardly found utopia.

To view the subject of private property from the standpoint of biblical revelation is therefore imperative, not simply in order to anchor the Christian community firmly to the biblical view of life, but also to apprise the human race of the norm or criterion by which mankind will be divinely judged in regard to property relationships. Neglect of the scriptural view created a climate in which even some secular theorists could misrepresent as authentically biblical speculative views of property which lacked true scriptural sensitivity. Think, for example, of the ease with which some writers have conjoined the words "Christian socialism." Or consider their description of the author of Luke's Gospel as "the socialist among the evangelists."[1] A German socialist insisted that if Jesus were on earth he would affiliate with the Social Democrats. Early in this century A. Kalthoff depicted Christianity as a socio-economic movement and Jesus as the ideal hero of a communistic proletarian revolution.[2] Such perverse attachment of Communist and socialist speculations to Christian motifs and their arbitrary misrepresentation as the proper climax of Reformation thought, ought to spur the Western world to probe anew the biblical treatment of property.

Property rights must indeed be viewed in relationship to the whole social system in which they stand; they cannot long be preserved apart from other social ingredients. Nor can the social environment escape fundamental alteration when property rights are in jeopardy. But the property question must not be assessed simply within socio-economic horizons. The subject arises within the context of the broad religious and cultural crisis facing the world today. It must, therefore, be considered in the larger realm of both theological and anthropological realities. In fact, biblical religion deals with the property question not simply as an isolated economic concern, but rather in the context of the will of God. F. C. Grant's reminder is timely that "it is less than ever possible, nowadays, to represent early Christianity as a revolutionary social (or social-economic) movement. . . . It is clear that Christianity was from the very beginning a purely religious movement. . . ."[3] But this central spiritual vision did not mean that Christianity was, therefore, indifferent to human rights and duties; rather, as pure religion it summoned every human activity under the rule of God. Judeo-Christian revelation lifts the discussion of property above the merely horizontal perspective of an abstract antagonism between individual and society; instead, its perspective is vertical, stressing the practical responsibility of all men to their Creator and under God to one another. The clash of individual and group interests, in which contemporary theory abstractly locates economic conflict, is thus challenged by an even more fundamental dimension of relationships, subjecting individual and social behavior alike to divine judgment.

In such a setting the absolute contrast between individual right and social right disappears: all human rights are for the individual and every individual right is also a human right. The transcendent Creator stands

1. H. Holstzmann in *Protestantische Kirchenzeit*, No. 45 (1894).
2. A. Kalthoff, *Das Christusproblem: Grundlinien zu einer Sozialtheologie* (Leipzig, 1902).
3. F. C. Grant, in W. D. Davies and D. Daube (eds.), *The Background of the New Testament and Its Eschatology* (Cambridge, 1956), p. 101.

above all as the ultimate source, sanction, and support of enduring rights; and on earth every man and all things are seen as God's own—God's creatures and his creation. In a word, God is their absolute owner, and man's possessions are a contingent and limited entrustment.

Here the contrast of the biblical with the ancient pagan view of property is immediately apparent. The Roman or Justinian view derives ownership from natural right; it defines ownership as the individual's unconditional and exclusive power over property. It implies an owner's right to use property as he pleases (even to spoil or destroy it), irrespective of the will of others, and to do so continually. This view, preserved well into the Middle Ages, still remains the silent presupposition of much of the free world's common practice today.

The biblical view, as we shall see, differs in important respects from this pagan view. But it is its contrary rather than its contradictory. Sometimes the contrast between the Judeo-Christian and Roman views has been stated so sharply as to create sympathy for the Communist rejection of private property; but no scriptural basis exists for this arbitrary alternative. The Judeo-Christian revelation is clearly on the side of private property. While it provides no *carte blanche* for a secular capitalistic civilization, the biblical view does not assail private property *per se*, but assumes its legitimacy and reinforces its propriety as a social institution.

1. Jehovah gave the Promised Land to the Hebrews, and their right to it was not forfeited by either poverty or slavery. This assignment of a land to the Hebrews implies the propriety of private property. The universal right of private property cannot be deduced from this alone, in view of the temporary nature of the Old Testament economy. The New Testament church is not assigned possession of one sector of land as was Israel, but is set as a light among all nations; by its practice of justice and benevolence the church is to demonstrate that the community of faith waits for unlimited possession of the earth in righteousness and mercy.

2. The Mosaic law implies that private property is legitimate and not sinful. It confers the highest sanctity on the principle of private ownership and reinforces the inviolability of property. The Eighth Commandment teaches that it is sinful to take what belongs to another, and the Tenth Commandment that it is sinful even to covet what belongs to another. This right of ownership is presupposed in the details as well as in the broad outlines of the whole Mosaic legislation, and by its application throughout Scripture.

The commandment "Thou shalt not steal" prohibits the removal of another's property, and its fraudulent retention, or injury to it through indifference or carelessness. One must pay in full for neglect that results in the loss of another's livestock (Exod. 21:33ff.), and restitution twofold, fourfold and fivefold is stipulated as compensation for stolen animals (21:37ff.). The Mosaic Law had as part of its educational purpose to reinforce respect for propery rights, and penalized the thief progressively according to whether he retained stolen property in his possession (and had the capacity to restore it) or had sold or destroyed it. If a thief is apprehended, but cannot make restitution, he must earn compensation by labor (22:4). Injury to another's property through neglect is also to be compensated (22:5f.).

3. The teaching of Jesus and of the apostles does not condemn private property but presupposes and reinforces its legitimacy. The New Testament reaffirms the Decalogue (Matt. 19:18f.; Rom. 13:9ff.), and the teaching and practice of the New Testament Christians assume the legitimacy of private property. Jesus and his disciples had a common fund to meet their expenses (John 13:14), but the disciples retained ownership of the boats and nets to which they returned after the crucifixion (John 21:3ff.). Jesus' headquarters at Capernaum seems to have been the house which Peter retained as a private dwelling (Mark 1:29; 2:1), even as Mary, Martha, and Lazarus, whom Jesus loved, had their own home in Bethany (Luke 10:38ff.; John 12:1ff.). The assumption that private ownership is wrong makes havoc of Jesus' appeal to men's rights over their property to illustrate their duty to God (cf. Luke 19:12; Matt. 21:33).

The so-called communist passages of the New Testament are misnamed, for they disclose no kinship with Marxian dogma. That some of the early Christian believers in special circumstances voluntarily shared their possessions is clear enough (Acts 2:44f.; 4:32ff.). But the notion that wealth is sinful and poverty meritorious is no more to be found in the Gospels than elsewhere in the Bible. Although Jesus' sayings about the rich and poor appear in Luke's Gospel in their most uncompromising form (cf. Luke 6:20; Matt. 5:3), these passages cannot, contrary to some interpreters, be fairly considered to be hostile to wealth and partial to poverty. Andrew N. Bogle long ago stressed that in the Acts of the Apostles no inference about so-called communist activities of the primitive church is permissible beyond Luke's explicit statements.[4] The facts remain that the practice of community of goods by the Jerusalem church did not survive perpetually; that it was not observed universally; that Paul neither instructed churches he founded to practice such community of goods, nor condemned them for their failure to do so; that even believers who shared

---

4. A. N. Bogle, "Property," in Hastings' *Dictionary of the Gospels.*

possessions *sold* their houses and lands; and that in the local situation where community of goods was observed, Peter specifically reinforced the right of private property in his rebuke to Ananias: "While it remained, was it not thine own? And after it was sold, was it not in thine own power?" (Acts 5:4). The scriptural criticism of the use of property and wealth affords no license for the drawing of socialist or communist conclusions.

Yet, while the Judeo-Christian revelation does not repudiate private property, it does not therefore endorse every version and justification of private property. The Bible associates ownership with conditions of righteousness that confer moral goodness on man's holding and use of possessions; it does not approach the subject of private property from a merely legal point of view. The Bible has an eye to ownership that is both legally right and morally good. Against any derivation and protection of property rights based exclusively on politico-economic positions, whether conservative or liberal, Christian theology has a dual responsibility; it must show that the Communist rejection of private property misunderstands God's purpose for human society, and it must show that God's ordination of things can be equally dimmed and distorted where human rights are promoted in a strictly secular manner. Although some proponents of the pagan Roman view also appeal to rational and moral principles to reinforce a constructive use of property, the Judeo-Christian view holds man spiritually accountable to God for the use of his possessions. In the pagan Roman view unless man's control of property is sovereign, its possession is not private. This theory is tenable if man is a part of God (as classic Roman philosophy assumed) or if no God exists (as modern secularism presupposes). But if God is sovereign and man is his subject, the Creator may allow man certain rights over against other men in respect to some property, while simultaneously asserting his own right over all men and all property.

In view of the modern temptation to perpetuate the tradition of private property solely on a nontheological basis, we must emphasize that capitalism, just as much as Communism or socialism, can minimize the will of God in respect to property. Insofar as civil law is concerned, however, the biblical view presupposes and reinforces man's legal right of ownership which, in respect to human society, is only virtually and not absolutely absolute. Private property is a legal right and when acquired has, as President James Madison put it, "a right to protection as a social right."[5] Although man is not sovereign owner, the use of his possessions

---

5. *Letters and Other Writings of James Madison* (Philadelphia, 1865), IV, 51.

is suspended on his personal decision. When the Roman emphasis on sovereign individual possession is viewed in the context of the state, rather than in the context of the supernatural world, it has much in common with the biblical view. The Old Testament narrative of Ahab's effort to acquire Naboth's vineyard near the royal palace (I Kings 21:1ff.) is pointedly relevant. When Naboth declined the king's proposals for purchase or exchange of land, Jezebel had Naboth falsely accused and stoned to death. Elijah pronounced doom on the tyrant, and Jezebel's death was viewed as a divine punishment (II Kings 9:25f.). Private property implies man's formal right to use and enjoy his possessions as he pleases subject only to restrictions imposed by agreement or covenant or by law. The scriptural view of man's spiritual accountability presupposes his formal legal freedom to use possessions as he determines.

This distinction between what is legally right on the one hand, and what is spiritually and ethically good on the other, is inherent in any view that preserves the realities of moral freedom. While a man has no spiritual ground for not believing in God, he does have the legal right to be an atheist; while he has no moral basis for selfish use of private property, he has a legal right to use his possessions that way. Man's property right in respect to God is never absolute or indefeasible, but always derivative and conditional. In respect to the state and society, however, man's property right has formal divine sanction even if his use of property subverts God's spiritual intention. The moral use of property confers goodness on its possessor, but it does not confer the legal right of ownership. It is not man's legal and moral right to properly acquired property that is to be questioned but rather his moral use of it.

Therefore it is important not to contrast legal right and moral right absolutely, but to emphasize their partial coincidence. Christian theology distinguishes both the order that the state requires as justice and the benevolence that the church spiritually demands from the order that society tolerates out of custom or approves in terms of ideology. The church has no mandate to impose spiritual imperatives on an unregenerate society. But the church is obliged to proclaim those revealed principles which government must promote and men must observe for the sake of a just society; social custom, tending to assign finality to the mood of the masses, needs always to be challenged by revealed morality. The state has no rightful authority to modify the divine principles of social justice, including individual freedom to do the will of God. From the viewpoint of biblical ethics the rejection of private property involves the rejection of a divinely sanctioned ideal, an arbitrary restriction of human freedom, and an ideological frustration of the possibilities of a just social order.

Justice in respect to the possession of property is found neither through the church's ordering of society or the state's ordering of society in a manner that dissolves individual freedom and moral responsibility; it is found rather in promoting and preserving the divine order of work, ownership, and possessions that God has ordained for mankind.

Yet a Christian ethic of property must not be divorced from biblical teaching as a whole. Scripture nowhere approves private property as a possession that stands wholly at man's free disposition independent of moral and spiritual obligations.[6] Always and everywhere ownership implies responsible possession under God and subjection to the just claim of one's neighbors.

In respect to politico-economic philosophy the Bible establishes no approved code of detailed legislation, but instead supplies principles by which to resolve particular problems. The Bible, for example, proposes no ideal "regulation" of property by governmental control of human affairs, nor does it dictate quantitative limits in respect to ownership. But it does stipulate principles for the moral use of property, so that ownership is both protected and limited by divine commandment.

a. All land is intended for appropriate use, primarily that of meeting man's common needs. It is intended first of all for those who work it, not for those who do not work it. The normal pattern of existence in the Old Testament is that of the peasant farmer family united by the soil and its care. But today only a fraction of the populace could be supported by agricultural pursuits. A fundamental fact of capitalism is the dependence of great masses of people on land and assets that belong to others. Hence, one must distinguish an order of priority between, on the one hand, property that is necessary for survival, property that is necessary for true freedom, property that is held as a service, and property that is accumulated for profits, and, on the other hand, property that is aggrandized for power and property that cancels the liberty of others. In the latter area there exists a special responsibility for protecting the possibility of regular industry, meaningful labor, and personal freedom for dependent workers. The worst of all solutions is state control of power in a planned society; less objectionable is legislative constraint on the free use of power in a democratic society; preferable is voluntary use of economic power in a morally responsible way in a spiritually sensitive society.

---

6. The Evangelical Revival renewed the lagging sense of the stewardship of possessions: "It viewed property not so much in the light of the Decalogue as in the far more searching light of the Gospel of the Cross, and of the sacred obligations it imposes on the Christian conscience"; H. G. Wood, in L. T. Hobhouse *et al.* (eds.), *Property: Its Duties and Rights* (London, 1913), p. 165.

b. The inheritance of possessions is a socially cohesive factor. Where inheritance ceases the family ceases. Since all possession comes by attainment or gift, inheritance is not wrong but desirable. What is wrong is its misuse to promote a life without service.

c. The Old Testament both guaranteed and restricted permanent ownership (Lev. 25:23) by invoking the Year of Jubilee, which was binding on every man in the Hebrew theocracy. The land was not to be sold "in perpetuity" because God is its ultimate owner and because the people are "strangers and sojourners" (Lev. 25:8ff.). In the Jubilee year property reverted to its original owners (Lev. 25:10) and all slaves were to be set free (even as God had rescued the entire community from slavery in Egypt); it was a time of recovery of "liberty throughout the land." In addition, the land was to lie fallow as in the sabbatical year. Today some of the objectives of Jubilee are attained in other ways. Since the Industrial Revolution, scientific farming, for example, has achieved renewal of the land without sabbatical rest. An agricultural society, whose possessions are mainly in the form of land, could implement an actual return to possessions in a fixed year only with great difficulty. In an age of trade, commerce, and capitalistic enterprise, when property is diversified, it could hardly be carried out at all. But its spirit and intention—to protect the poor from enslavement—are not wholly out of reach. The Old Testament prophets denounced unlimited acquisition, retention, and perpetuation of property holdings as choking the vitality and depressing the life of others who were thereby precluded from acquiring property (Isa. 5:8). Today the amassing of properties is discouraged by estate taxes which in effect return a part of their value to the common pool. Modern economic theory often tends wrongly to think of wealth as a fixed quantity, like land; its problem, then, is to keep wealth divided among a great number of people. But this notion is naive: a generation ago there was no property, as there is today, in television, jet planes, space missiles, and so on. The space age has opened up a new and controversial sphere of property rights, that of air rights. There is a striking difference, moreover, between the Old Testament restrictions, which had a divine sanction in the life of the community, and modern legal restrictions, which differ from country to country and which often seem intended to abridge rather than to preserve the right of property and fail to promote individual sensitivity and responsibility.

d. When it comes to determining the most appropriate use of the land, the answer (short of a planned society which operates on the basis of objectionable criteria) must be sought in the purposes for which the land is used, including that of economic return.

e. Since God wills government, the state may be a property holder. But the state is not to be *the* property holder, since only God is sovereign owner and lord of all. Insofar as civic legislation does not conflict with divine authority, the lawful authority of government is to be supported. In the absence of voluntary discipline and as an expression of the corporate conscience of the community, government may be called on to legislate restraints on undesirable uses of property. But the state dare not insulate itself against criticism which aims at limiting its activity to preserving universal justice and restraining it from legislating the special interests of any one class to the detriment of another. The penalties of government limitation of human rights are greater than is generally assumed, and are not worth the risk. The exercise of freedom without moral and spiritual maturity soon sets up a demand for legal restraints, including restrictions on rights and liberty. Preventing the misuse of private property contrary to public order and the general welfare is indeed the duty of the state, but that is not its first duty; acknowledging and maintaining private property are the state's prior responsibility. Private property, moreover, is not an institution to be authorized by the state but an inalienable right divinely conferred on mankind.

f. In early times a segment of the apostolic community practiced the sharing of possessions in compassionate responsiveness to each other's needs. Thus, these people demonstrated their belief both in the value of persons amid property and in the priority of stewardship over selfishness in the life of faith. Their voluntary detachment from possessions misled some early church fathers into the theory that private property resulted from avarice.

As noted above, legal ownership, from the biblical point of view, is spiritually and morally vindicated by the use of possessions in the service of God and man. There is no basis for the viewpoint of the religious socialists, however, that when ownership stands under God's judgment it becomes a matter of legal indifference. While the Bible approves government preservation of justice and restraint of injustice, it does not encourage such government manipulation of human life and property that compulsion replaces liberty. The error of the socialist thesis is twofold: first, its "acceleration of the eschatological" (that is, its ambition to establish a utopian society in the present) fails to recognize that human life in the present fallen age exists under political and economic systems that are not identical with the Kingdom of God; second, it arbitrarily ascribes socialistic features to this Kingdom.

That Christianity is to challenge the social order creatively is true enough; there is, however, no biblical basis for defining that challenge in terms of an attack on either the right or the form of private ownership.

PART II

Essays in Christian Philosophy and Theology

.

Adventure in Verification

O. K. BOUWSMA

Get into perspective, how it is with us. And let us use for this purpose a variation on the fantasy of Kafka. We live in a city, and it's up-to-date. So, of course, there are telephones. People in the city talk to each other over the telephone. They order groceries, gossip, spread the news, find out what time it is, call the police, and so on. But there are a number of people in the city who use the telephone for a quite different purpose. And to some of the other people in the town this is a great mystery. They sometimes ask, "Who are you calling?", and the reply is, "We are calling the President or the King."

"And what do you say to him?"

"We thank him for daily bread. We thank him for all sorts of things, sunshine, for instance. And we ask for help and ask him too to bear with us, and so on. We carry on a regular conversation."

"And does he speak to you too?"

"Of course. He gives us orders, makes us promises, exhorts us, encourages us when we falter. He is kind. Sometimes he calls. That can be frightening too."

It happens now and then that one of these people will ask, "And could I listen in?", but then when he does he hears nothing, not even a busy buzz. It sounds to him more like a disconnected phone. After that he is at first still more puzzled. It even occurs to him that the trouble lies in his ears. He soon gets over that. He goes on asking questions. Has so-and-so ever seen the President? The answer to that is that, of course, he hasn't, that no man has ever seen the President, none of these people who make calls has seen the President. The fact is that the President is invisible.

The man shakes his head: "An invisible President! And how then did

O. K. Bouwsma is presently Professor of Philosophy at the University of Texas, after a distinguished career in the Philosophy Department at the University of Nebraska. He is a past president of the American Philosophical Association, Western Division, and author of numerous essays in philosophical journals. In his contribution to this volume Dr. Bouwsma scrutinizes—in his characteristically puckish manner—the claim that theological propositions, to be acceptable, must be verified by the procedures of empirical science.

you ever get involved in this? Speaking over the telephone and having regular conversations with an invisible President?"

To this the reply is not so ready. How did he get involved in this? He finally manages to say that at home such calls were a regular part of their daily life, as daily as bread. In emergencies there were special calls.

But hadn't it ever occurred to him that the whole thing might be a hoax? An invisible President? No, it never had, though of course he had heard such talk. He had never paid any attention to it, and it had never affected his devotion to the telephone.

Now consider this situation. There are people living in the city. There are mountains nearby and one especially high mountain. When these people are about to make an expedition, sailing ships to Yort, over the wine-dark sea, they sacrifice an ox to Zeus, and they implore Zeus to keep the wind in their sails and to direct their darts and arrows to their targets. There are others in the company of Zeus, such as Athena and Apollo. These gods have their favorites, and they play out their rivalries by playing their favorites against one another, particularly on the battlefield. Sometimes Athena sends a cloud to enshroud Achilles in order that when he is in peril Hector may not be able to find him. There are other occasions when the people take alarm and look towards that high mountain. This happens when disaster strikes, as for instance when a dragon roars outside the city or when pestilence or flood or famine overwhelms the populace. "What have we done?" they exclaim. For disaster is a sure sign of guilt. The priest may assure them that it is Zeus that is angry, for there is an unclean thing in the city, no doubt a man afflicted with *hubris*. They seek him out, send him into exile, and the curse is lifted. And then at a public ceremony they sacrifice another ox. This is the symbol of reconciliation.

Now imagine a stranger who has come to the city, a brother of Xenophanes, and a great-grandfather of Euripides. He hears all this talk about Zeus and Athena and the quarrels and the curses and the roasting of the ox, and naturally he doesn't understand it. "Zeus?" he asks. "In Melos and in Athens we too have suffered disasters but we know nothing of Zeus." And then in awed tones they tell the brother of Xenophanes about Zeus and the whole company of the gods who take so much interest in what human beings do and in their expeditions. He listens but says nothing. When they have finished he asks, "And did you say that they live on Mount Olympus and drink nectar and eat ambrosia and that their blood is ichor?" He is obviously fascinated. Still, it seems that he does not believe a word of it. He is determined, however, to find out for himself. "And," he asks, "have you ever been on Mt. Olympus?"

They exclaim at this, "Of course not! No man in his senses would approach Mt. Olympus. Such a man could not live." They are horrified. A human being peeping through the shrubbery and prowling the heights of Olympus!

He is, however, not the least discomfited by this. He has already determined, like Prometheus, to make the ascent, expecting to find nothing on the heights of Mt. Olympus but a cover of scrub oak and a scattering of mountain goats nibbling on the high ridges.

And now what do you think happened?

He climbed the mountain one moonlit night. Actually it was, as mountain climbing goes, not difficult. It was nothing compared to Everest or even Rainier. He made it easily. When he got to the top, however, he was surprised. The whole of the mountain top was fringed with a jungle-growth of shrubs, trees, and vines which were impenetrable. He could neither climb over nor get through. It made him apprehensive. "Surely," he said to himself, "this was planted to keep prowlers out." And he began, for the first time—finding himself near believing—to wonder which of the gods was the gardener. It surprised him. There was, however, nothing to do now but go back down into the city to get his hatchet. He was, however, considerably sobered by that wall of greenery, and he made his second ascent with fear. It would be a frightening thing if he were to come upon strong and fierce men on the other side of the wall whose secret place he was breaking into. And what if there were giants there? He did not expect even now to find Zeus and the company of immortals. He went about cutting his way through the brambles and vines with a fast-beating heart. What if ...? What if ...?

At last, working through seven days and seven nights he cut his way through the wall. Even then there was just enough room for him to struggle through, and the branches closed round the opening. He saw no one, no man, no giant, no god. At least he thought he did not. And he thought he too was seen by no man, no giant, no god. This gave him courage. Before him stood a palace of white marble, not as large as the Pentagon, but still a large and sumptuous edifice, in a style now known as Olympiad. If (as he supposed) there were no Zeus and no Apollo, etc., here, at least the architecture was a worthwhile surprise. He broke through the brush about dawn, looked about him and decided that the better part of valor and verification would be to wait and then to explore under cover of darkness. So he retreated again into the wall. It would be too bad, after all his work, to be sent tumbling down the mountain by an angry guard perhaps twice his own size. He forgot to bring his Greek opera glasses. So he waited. Someone has said that a good part of verification is waiting.

Darkness seemed to be late that night. But it finally came. He could make out lights coming on down in the city below. Here and there a candle burned, the candle of some sculptor working overtime; and in an open plain to the right a man was running with a torch upraised, no doubt practicing for a race. Torch races were very common in those days. He saw a few lights on boats and reflected in the water, a pretty sight, and a new thing in the Piraeus, just having come in with a new ordinance recently instituted by the Eleven or the Thirty-Two or somebody else. The moon had waned by this time so that when darkness came it was very dark. It was no fun crouching there among the brambles. He was scratched, too. But suddenly the whole mountain was ablaze with light and the whole palace glowed. He was amazed and enchanted. It was beautiful! For a moment he was overwhelmed with the splendor and he forgot why he had come. Fountains played and there was music. He closed his eyes and opened them again to see the lights afresh and to swoon again in the soft Lydian airs. He would no doubt have remained in this way fixed and transported (a state possible only on Olympus and hence called the Olympian trance) had not an unexpected thing happened. The lights went out, the fountains stopped playing, and the music ceased. He peered into the darkness. He heard an owl. And then, happily, the lights of the palace shone through the high windows set back among the pillars. It was lovely, a palace fit for the gods if there should be any here. He tried to get a better look, brushing aside a stubborn branch, and it whipped him across the face. That brought him to; and he realized that if he were to accomplish his mission, now was the time.

He crept out of the opening, and arranged the branches to conceal it. Then he stood still and surveyed the scene. "If there are inhabitants here," he meditated, "and there must be—why otherwise the lights?—surely they are in the palace or they are having supper on the patio." Why this occurred to him he never could figure out. It must have been an inspiration, as we shall soon see, though there seems at this late date little reason to speak so extravagantly about a subordinate hypothesis such as this. And then he began to move. You cannot have verification in a situation like this without moving. He approached the grand stairway built of the earliest Pleistocene marble, and felt it with his fingers. It was smooth as glacia-lacustrine. He marveled. "How did they ever get that up here?" he asked himself. Then suddenly, looking up towards the top of the stairs, he saw on the other side of the great open doors, made of solid gold, each weighing two tons, a chandelier such as he had never seen before, "a heaven-tree of stars," gleaming in the vaulted ceiling and lighting the grand hall that shone with counter-gleaming. He walked through the doorway. He saw no one, not even a Nubian slave. That would not have surprised him. He tiptoed about. He heard no one. It was very still. He looked about him and caught his reflection in a mirror. The hall was lined with mirrors. "The creatures that inhabit this place must be very beautiful," he said, "otherwise why should they have so many mirrors?" It never occurred to him that human beings of some fantastically higher sort or noble giants or exalted gods would spend time before such mirrors primping or arranging the folds of gorgeous mantles woven of the finest Penelope cloth. And he was right. He leaped before the mirrors to stir them with leaping fire.

Suddenly he stopped. Had he seen a great shadow move across the wall? No, there was nothing. He took out his silver flute and played five notes. A unicorn passed by, looked in and shook its head. "That's strange," he said. But no sound of voice or musical instrument responded to his five notes. He called just a call as schoolboys do in his native city, the Abdera shrill. Once again there was no answer. The unicorn walked slowly away. "No one here," he said, and he walked back to the doorway to look for the bell. There was no bell. He kicked the door hoping to arouse someone in that way, but you cannot make a noise kicking a golden door. He gave up.

And then it occurred to him: "The Patio! The Patio!" And he bounded down the steps and walked hurriedly around the palace until he came to an ilex tree which stood high above a pool around which, lying on couches and walking or standing, the inhabitants of that great empty palace were now assembled.

He stood now under the ilex tree—and fixed his eyes on the scene below. It was dazzling, so bright. The colors were brighter and the outlines were sharp and clear. He thought of Aldous Huxley and mescaline. And then it suddenly struck him that he could not possibly think of Aldous Huxley and mescaline since neither of these had been invented yet. He looked again, rubbed his eyes, and realized that he now stood on Mt. Olympus and that the air and the times were not the same as those below the mountain. He tried to look into the past and into the future but no more either of past or future flew in. And then he settled down like a good mortal to survey the scene. He tried to calculate the extent of the pool. But as soon as he settled upon some figure such as two and one-half hectares the pool would visibly lengthen or shorten, and he would wait for the pool to make up its mind. It did not. He soon made up his mind that there were built-in frustrations against any spying mortal who might want later to report: "It is exactly so." And he gave up. He tried too to count the gods and goddesses, but here too he failed. Zeus, however, he identified. And that was what he wanted most of all to do.

So the brother of Xenophanes had indeed verified that, as these citizens said, there are, not men, not giants, not Titans, not hemi-demi-semi-gods, but—well, whatever they are—gathered around the pool, laughing and jesting and romping as they never would have done had they known that Xenophaneses or Plato was standing there under the ilex tree. But were they gods—that is, were they immortals? Well, yes. Had he not seen them pass "the bowl of cherries," as they jokingly referred to the nectar bowl? Of course, he had see them then, quaffing and laughing. (By the way, did Plato say that the gods did not laugh or that they did not laugh boisterously or only that in human company they should behave more sedately?) And then, of course, there was the huge table laid out with ambrosia in the form of a most royal wedding cake, layer upon layer, mounted with two figures, one of a swan, sweetly remembered of Zeus, and the other of a heifer, most sweetly remembered of Hera, "of the white arms." It was quite obvious from this who were in command and who designed the cake in this gathering. Xenophaneses was satisfied. Indeed he had spied upon the immortals. For see: who drink nectar and eat ambrosia? Are not these the drink and the food of immortals and not of mortals? Hence, too, the famous Greek fear of eating mushrooms and of drinking any liquid with foam on it, for might not the penalty of such eating and drinking be an immortality which, as Jonathan Swift in a later time reminded us, might not be desirable?

Xenophaneses lingered by the ilex tree. He was now obviously waiting for something to happen. It occurred to him—he had heard of scientific explorations and of the notes King Minos had made at the time that he had gone off on a safari and returned home with an oversized bull which he later housed in the library of Crete, from which he had for this purpose removed all the books; he figured the bull could not read—in any case, it occurred to him to take notes, but the truth of the matter is that he could not write. Besides, he wanted to look. However, it turned out to be a tame affair. Nothing unseemly happened and he became impatient to return to the city. But before he left he took out his hunting-blade, a rather primitive version of our jackknife though for those days a really up-to-date piece of steel with a hinge and shield; and he carved his name on the ilex tree. This, in 1975, is reminiscent, though at this time (some years before Pericles) it could not have been, of that explorer—Perry or Cook—who raised as an extension of the North Pole another pole high above the earth to show passersby who might be slowed up in the snow that (as the saying among scientific explorers goes) Kilroy was here. No doubt Xenophaneses had something of the same sort in mind. He brushed out the chips from his engraving and stood for a moment admiring both his handiwork and his name. It might come in handy should he at some later time come upon unbelievers who, like himself, should ask: "And have you ever been on Olympus?" Then he could say: "Yes, I have" and he could tell them about the ilex tree and about his name there in large letters, in which, as Plato learned, and who knows, perhaps from this very carving, there is a special advantage. They are easier to read. So he left, the tireless gods still around the pool in quiet talk nibbling away at the ambrosia on the table, now leaning like Pisa from too much nibbling on the south side.

He was well satisfied. He had seen for himself. He had verified. "What! No Zeus? Don't be silly. I've been there." And he was not sorry he had gone to all this trouble. His arm still ached from wielding that hatchet. Verification is not easy.

So he returned to the city. It was still dark and the market place was deserted. All the chess tables were empty. He crossed over by way of Ajax Lane to Agamemnon Boulevard and so home. He was in high spirits. Tired as he was (physically, that is) he did not immediately "hit the straw." (This expression which was in common use in those days, quite different from our own "hit the hay," has in recent years been regarded as reflecting the state of the economy of that time, the popularity of straw indicating—it is or was one of the indicators—a dearth of something, most likely a prolonged drought, and so a preponderance of straw over hay.) Instead he took from his bag of books which he had carried all the way from Lesbos, having changed to another boat there, his precious copy of Homer. He read and read until dawn and then he went to sleep. He read now with a new zest. He had never found Homer so interesting. For hadn't he seen some of the chief actors in this history? And in the course of his reading, at one of the most exciting moments, it suddenly occurred to him that while he was standing alongside that ilex tree he had not taken notice of any other names carved in the bark. Surely Homer's must have been there. Still Homer might not have carried a knife. Blind as he was he might have had little use for a knife. Still Xenophaneses wished he had looked. And he wondered. Had there been interviews? How did Homer find out all these things? Did the gods keep archives and did Homer have privileged access? The palace was very large and there was room surely for many volumes. How he longed to know whether Homer too, perhaps before he was blind, had climbed Olympus and fought his way through that wall, that green wall, hawthorn and ivy and creepers and wild plum and barberry immensus. Tomorrow he would think of it again. He had acquired a taste for verification.

When Xenophaneses woke the next morning he was excited. He had seen Zeus and the company of immortals. And now he glanced at the book alongside the straw and remembered some of the things he had read concerning what they had done. He remembered too how when he had gone up the mountain he would hardly have conceded "Well, maybe" and when he had come down he had said "It is so"—and he hungered for "It is so." But as his expedition to Mt. Olympus showed, it was not an easy "It is so" he wanted. He would pay with cuts and bruises if need be. And in spite of his respect for the authority of Homer—it was in the air in Athens—he kept asking such questions as "And did Zeus do that?"; "And did Zeus say that?" And, as he said later in discussing such matters with his philosophical friends, one detail that continued to haunt him was that Zeus was only ten feet tall. It was past noon in Athens as he lay on his straw, thinking—and he remembered now, too, that some one of the few golden men would at some future time say that thinking is the soul in conversation with himself—and listening to the clamor of metal chipping marble on the hill just above his modest diggings. And he got up.

First he ate breakfast, "a grand spread of loaves and cakes on fresh leaves," with wine of course. He also ate "olives and cheese and a country stew of roots and vegetables." There was also a bowl of figs and acorns. The "peas and beans" man was late today. He ate with relish. You can't expect to do the work of verification without eating well. He had tried that once in Melos and found out nothing except that you have to eat to verify. "No mastication, no verification," as he said with an acorn in his mouth. When he had finished his breakfast he pulled out the stump he sat on, set it against the wall, and took up his writing board and his copy of Homer. He had work to do. He was to be the author of a verified theology. First, he had to assemble what he described as theological propositions. After that would come verification. So he set out to do what any intelligent man of that century or the twentieth would do. He culled from the first book of Homer a list of sentences which, as he supposed, would furnish a test of the possibilities. He was in high spirits. Hadn't he climbed Olympus and seen for himself?

And here now is a list of the sentences he culled. Most of them, as you might expect, are sentences about Zeus.

"And so the counsel of Zeus wrought out its accomplishment."

"Now may the gods that dwell in the mansions of Olympus grant you to lay waste the city of Priam, and to fare happily homeward."

"So spake he in prayer and Phoebus Apollo heard him and came down from the peak of Olympus wroth at heart, bearing on his shoulders his bow and covered quiver...."

"...for in his mind did goddess Hera of the white arms put the thought...."

"... seeing that a dream too is of Zeus."

"... by his soothsaying that Phoebus Apollo bestowed on him."

"... if ever Zeus grant us to sack some well-walled town of Troy."

"I have others by my side that should do me honor, and above all Zeus, lord of counsel."

"Athena came to him from heaven, sent forth of the white-armed goddess, Hera, whose heart loved both alike and had care for them."

"Whosoever obeyeth the gods, to him they hearken gladly."

"... even they that by Zeus' commands watch over the traditions."

"... seeing that no common honor pertaineth to a sceptred king to whom Zeus apportioneth glory."

"... even Zeus that thundereth on high."

"... to Zeus whose joy is in the thunder."

"For Zeus went yesterday to Okeanos, unto the noble Ethiopians for a feast."

"Father Zeus ... do honor to my son; ... grant thou victory to the Trojans; ... do my son honor and exalt him with recompense."

"But Zeus, the Cloud-Gatherer, said no word to her and sat long time in silence."

"Then Zeus, the cloud-gatherer, sore troubled, spake to her: Verily it is a sorry matter if thou wilt set me at variance with Hera whene'er she provoketh me with taunting words."

"Kronion spake and bowed his dark brow, and the ambrosial locks waved from the King's immortal head; and he made great Olympus quake."

"Then the father of gods and men made answer to her: 'Hera, think not thou to know all my sayings; hard they are for thee, even though thou art my wife.' "

"Most dread, son of Kronos ..."

"... the Olympian, lord of lightning."

"And laughter unquenchable arose amid the blessed gods to see Hephaestus bustling through the palace."

After he had made his list he sat back on the stump, his back against the wall—he had heard that a verificator should ponder the possibilities for verification in a relaxed position, thereby allowing the mind a maximum of inflation—and he read through the list. Some of them he found exceedingly fascinating such as these: "for in his mind did goddess Hera of the white arms put the thought . . ."; and "seeing that a dream too is of Zeus"; and "by his soothsaying that Phoebus Apollo bestowed on him." He pondered over these. It would be difficult. It would not do to make a general inquiry. He would first of all need to settle upon a certain thought, a certain dream, and a certain (it had better be famous) case of soothsaying—in the event he wanted later to publish his results in the Pantheon Press. Finding the certain thought, etc., could be done though it would be more work. And then what? He had climbed Olympus once and he could do it again. The path was still open. And he thought of himself leaping down those marble steps inlaid with gold, from the ilex tree to the poolside, tapping the goddess Hera of the white arms on the shoulder, at least two feet above him, and saying: "Your Majesty, would you verify for me a little matter that you know all about? Mortals are mortal but they are very curious." He thought he would find the goddess Hera helpful and easy to talk to. Then he would get it settled about Hera's putting a thought into someone's mind. He did not think he could verify that short of asking Hera herself. If she wouldn't tell, he wouldn't find out. It never occurred to him that he would not be welcome. "The poor innocent babe!" He would more likely be whisked off on a cloud, quicker than he could say "Your Majesty," and dropped like rain alongside some little boat in the Piraeus—or cast head first into the pool and come up somewhere in the Aegean. When, however, he came now to think of himself approaching Phoebus Apollo to ask him about the most recent phenomenon of soothsaying, and wanting to know whether he, Phoebus Apollo, "Your Honor," was responsible, he suddenly thought of that bow and covered quiver full of arrows, and he felt a hot stinging in his well-rounded thigh. Five minutes later, recovered, he thought of himself walking down those marble steps on tiptoe, bowing and paying his respects as he went, and stopping before the throne, and addressing Zeus, as though Zeus were some genial lover of science and founder of the Institute for Less Mystery, "I hope I am not interrupting anything important but concerning dreams now, could you give us the authentic lowdown?" He hadn't even planned on a nod from the throne before speaking, which shows at once that he did not go to parochial school or, as they were called in those days, the Olympics. But he soon recovered. He remembered the line: "To Zeus whose joy is in the thunder" and he frowned as he thought of "The Cloud-gatherer," "his dark brow" and the "ambrosial locks." He was overwhelmed. He would try something easier first, something on the fringe. The most interesting things would have to come later.

(Years after this at a meeting of the P.L.B., the Panhellenic Learning Bust, an annual affair at which the feasters eat each other's work, he confided to fellow-ravishers that at the time he was considering his confrontations with the Makers of Fact or the News, on Mt. Olympus, the difficulty that bothered him most was not the matter of protocol but that of language. It wasn't that, as he anticipated, they, the interviewed divinities, would not understand him—they are adept in understanding 426 languages—but that he would not understand them. For it seemed to him likely that they would speak to him in the language to which they were accustomed—the oldest language spoken anywhere, in fact, the original language. He had as a matter of fact undertaken the study of the language which among mortals is said to approximate it most nearly, namely Frisian, but about that time there was an earthquake and he gave it up. Apart from our interest in the subject-matter of the fragment, it shows us something of the character of the meetings of the well-learned long ago).

As I hinted earlier, after due consideration, Xenophaneses decided that, however much he would like to know some things, he did not think that, young as he was, it would be wise to risk the lightning on Mt. Olympus. The ilex tree was as far as he would go. For the present he was resigned to investigate matters on what he modestly referred to as "the fringes." The two sentences which struck him then as easily amenable to what he lovingly described as "scientific method" were these: "For Zeus went yesterday to Okeanos, unto the noble Ethiopians for a feast"; and "Kronion spake and bowed his dark brow, and the ambrosial locks waved from the King's immortal head; and he made great Olympus quake." It amazed him that Zeus "made great Olympus quake." And this he set about to investigate first.

It was well known in the city that there were occasions on which great Olympus quaked. There had been at least two of these during the last thirty years. On one occasion on which some people who remembered said that the mountain had shuddered in what they said were quite distinct tantrums or traumas—there were a series of these—a great bundle of shrubbery had come down the mountainside and buried a horse that, frightened as it then was, came dragging a mound of blueberry bushes into the marketplace. That quake was remembered thereafter as the Blueberry Quake. On another occasion after an unusual tremor, about half an hour after the tremor, what the natives described as a huge dishpan with the initial 'H' engraved on the rim came tumbling and banging and bouncing down the rocky slope. That half-hour interval had often been referred to as a measure of the height of Olympus. But the letter 'H', which I have already said was taken to be an initial, had aroused more speculation. Was it, as some said, "H stands for Hera," from whose kitchen it had no doubt been hurtle-turtled, or as others said, "H stands for Hephaestus" whose handiwork it certainly was. At any rate these details still fresh in the popular memory were enough to convince Xenophaneses that indeed great Olympus did quake. There were in those days no public records, no seismographs. In fact weather reports and weather forecasts as we know them, including reports of quakes and tidal waves, did not come into the Athenian press until about 600 B.C. It was, however, said that at the time of the last quake the water splashed so high along the board walk on the waterfront near the fishmarket that women shopping there were drenched and some lost their fish.

So that there had been quakes was well authenticated. Xenophaneses wished that tomorrow there might be another quake but there would, as he well knew, have been no point to that. The question was as to whether Zeus made the quake—and concerning this the people whom he met in the gymnasium where he went to interview citizens were not of much help. Some said "Of course, Zeus did" but when Xenophaneses pressed them a bit they said "We've always known that" or "Tiresias told my father." Only one of them said that he had read it in Homer. It seems that what they called their scriptures were not much read; not, of course, that it would have been any help to Xenophaneses. Others said "Zeus? Why should Zeus make the mountain quake? He has other things to do, such as pure thinking." One young man was not very nice and snorted, and began "Zeus, if there is a Zeus, but there is no Zeus," and Xenophaneses, who was now thirty-five years old, an older man, really laid him out and called him a whippersnapper and rebuked him for such irresponsible talk. "Go," he said, "and climb Olympus and look down from the ilex tree before you throw in your fifty cents that isn't worth two." (This expression "your fifty cents that isn't worth two" had come in recently with the new coinage in which the drachma was withdrawn. The reform, however, did not last and so the expression also went out.) Without the expense of verification he never could or would have spoken with such authority. Rumor has it that that young man later joined Xenophaneses in his investigations and was responsible for several of the experimental devices which played so important a role in the advance of theological science.

When Xenophaneses sought more detail among those who said "Of course, Zeus did," asking how Zeus did this, there were, as he came to see, two factions. There were those who said that Zeus did this by waving his ambrosial locks. These called themselves the orthodox adelphics. The other group, of a more rationalist bent, did not, as they said, understand how Zeus could do this by waving his ambrosial locks. They were careful to insist that Zeus did indeed wave his ambrosial locks. They did not want to deny that. But they said that Zeus made great Olympus shake by stamping his foot. One can readily see in this suggestion anticipations of that later controversy among theoreticians as to whether a cause causing one can cause an effect without said cause being in juxta-contact with the what in which the caused effect inheres. Xenophaneses was inclined to the stamp-foot view, a view also more popular among the younger citizens. What surprised him, however, most of all was that no one among those he asked, held the view, later publicized by Archimedes in a lecture written on a wall, to the effect that Zeus had made great Olympus shake not by waving his ambrosial locks nor by stamping his foot but by the use of a lever. Archimedes, as we now know, never did climb Olympus and this may account for what we cannot help regarding as an anthropomorphism.

Xenophaneses, at the end of a month, was convinced that, if he were to investigate this matter and once and for all settle the issue, he would have to ascend Olympus once more. But when? Naturally, it would be best to do this on the day or night before the quake in order to be in a position to observe Zeus, especially during the five minutes just preceding the quake. He would watch then to see whether Zeus shook his ambrosial locks and then . . . or stamped his foot and then . . . or whether he sank his crowbar into the side of the mountain and shook it and then . . . or something else. What if Zeus only coughed, would Xenophaneses be ready for the quake and make the proper connections? He thought of that and hoped he would be ready. He made his preparations and waited for the day before the day of the next quake. Which day was that? For that information he consulted the astrologers. They all agreed. It would be the sixth of the seventh. On the fifth of the seventh he ascended the mountain and took his place under the ilex tree. Five minutes before the quake—his hourglass had sprung a leak—he took out his knife to smooth out an irregularity in the carving of his name in the bark of the tree. And while he was busy the quake came, and he was knocked off his feet and fell face forward in a bed of ripe strawberries. He had missed. There would not be another quake in fifteen years.

He went down the mountain disappointed. Along the way he flung the hourglass from him and it was shattered on a stone. "You're an anachronism anyhow," he shouted after it. He forgot that on Olympus there are no anachronisms. When he got home he wrote an account of his adventure, in order that the future of verification might not lose the benefit of his effort. His own adventure he described as one of weak verification due to sand—quicksand, too quick for the hourglass. It never occurred to him that not quicksand but vanity was the condition which led to his having his eyes fixed on his own good name in the bark of the tree when they should have been fixed on Zeus who made Great Olympus shake, not by waving his ambrosial locks, nor by stamping his foot, nor by a crowbar, nor by a cough but in his own sweet way.

Xenophaneses was tired. He rested the next day, it was the seventh of the seventh and he always rested on the seventh. On the eighth of the seventh he went fishing. He had no luck. He didn't mind. He watched the minnows. For hours not a theological proposition went through his mind. But on the 14th of the 7th, after 102 nibbles, there it was: "For Zeus went yesterday to Okeanos, unto the noble Ethiopians for a feast." Now did he, Zeus, do that? He would find out. He would vindicate Homer. And he did. He first sent letters to the Ras Selah who invited him to visit him in the city of Addis Ali Baba, saying that indeed Zeus had visited us, noble Ethiopians, and would he like to inspect the banquet hall where Zeus (on a public relations jaunt) and the chieftains had feasted for a fortnight and perhaps had eaten more than was good for their figures. The hall had been preserved in memory of that occasion and there was still a mound outside the silver door in the rear where the leavings of the feast had been carried in order to tempt the flies away from the tables while Ras Selah and the chieftains—horsemen and hurlers of the spear who put on a show for their guest—and the Grand Thunderer and Cloud-Gatherer sat down to drink dark red wine. He went. And this time he kept to his business. His business? Verification. He saw the hall and he saw the mound.

*   *   *

Afterthoughts

The proof for the existence of God clicked at 3:00 in the afternoon, and at 4:00 of the same afternoon he went out and sold all his goods—"for he had great possessions"—and gave the money to the poor. His wife, who lost all her jewels, blamed the proof. That shows how dangerous proofs are. God snares a man in a tangle of words on paper (to God by way of geometry), and then the man loses his shirt ("thy cloak also"). God takes from a man his automobile, his easy chair, his house, and so on. A man must be careful. A proof can ruin a man; climbing a mountain is safe. Or playing with matches.

*   *   *

The ontological proof for the existence of God is like the proof for the existence of the elephant from the premise that there is something that has weight.

*   *   *

The man who is impelled to prove the existence of God is like the princess who was locked in the tower (ivory) and ordered to spin gold out of straw. Everyone knows there is straw enough, some straw is very fancy straw, and may look like gold. All the same, spinning gold out of straw is quite a stunt.

Aquinas on Anselm

ALVIN PLANTINGA

Twenty-some years ago I had the pleasure of taking two courses from Henry Stob: a course in medieval philosophy in the fall semester and one in the philosophy of St. Thomas Aquinas in the spring. As one might expect, these were fine courses. Professor Stob's lively and enthusiastic grasp of the great medieval philosophers and his insights into the profound topics they explored served us as inspiration and example; most of us who took his courses acquired a permanent interest in the subject. This paper is a continuation of one of the many discussions precipitated by our class sessions.

In *Summa Theologica* I q 2 a 2, Aquinas addresses himself to Anselm's ontological argument. He states it thus:

> Further, those things are said to be self-evident which are known as soon as the terms are known, which the Philosopher says is true of the first principles of demonstration. Thus, when the nature of a whole and part is known, it is at once recognized that every whole is greater than its part. But as soon as the signification of the name *God* is understood, it is at once seen that God exists. For by this name is signified that thing than which nothing greater can be conceived. But that which exists actually and mentally is greater than that which exists only mentally. Therefore, since as soon as the name *God* is understood it exists mentally, it also follows that it exists actually. Therefore the proposition *God exists* is self evident.

This presentation of the ontological argument displays a striking feature. The argument is clearly the one Anselm sets out in *Proslogion 2* (and after setting out the same argument in the *Summa Contra Gentiles*,

---

Alvin Plantings is Professor of Philosophy at Calvin College. The essay that follows treats a celebrated piece of natural theology, the ontological argument for the existence of God, propounded originally by St. Anselm in the eleventh century. Plantinga considers some initially puzzling features of Aquinas' treatment of this argument, and concludes that on two important points Aquinas' contribution to the subject was not only relevant but also correct. Plantinga's work in the philosophy of religion and ontology has brought him international recognition. His most recent book is
The Nature of Necessity.

Aquinas develops, in the next paragraph, what is clearly Anselm's *Proslogion* 3 argument—the one Charles Hartshorne calls the modal argument). Yet Aquinas does not ascribe this argument to Anselm, or even so much as mention the latter by name. Moreover, as Aquinas takes the argument, it is an attempt to show, not that God exists, but that his existence is self-evident and in no need of demonstration. Anselm, however, does not speak of self-evidence in this connection:

It is one thing for an object to be in the understanding, and another to understand that the object exists. When a painter first conceives of what he will afterwards perform, he has it in his understanding, but he does not yet understand it to be, because he has not yet performed it. But after he has made the painting, he both has it in his understanding, and he understands that it exists, because he has made it.

Hence, even the fool is convinced that something exists in the understanding, at least, than which nothing greater can be conceived. For, when he hears of this, he understands it. And whatever is understood, exists in the understanding. And assuredly that, than which nothing greater can be conceived, cannot exist in the understanding alone. For, suppose it exists in the understanding alone: then it can be conceived to exist in reality; which is greater.

Therefore, if that, than which nothing greater can be conceived, exists in the understanding alone, the very being, than which nothing greater can be conceived, is one, than which a greater can be conceived. But obviously this is impossible. Hence there is no doubt that there exists a being, than which nothing greater can be conceived, and it exists both in the understanding and in reality (*Proslogion* 2).

Here there is no mention of self-evidence; and, far from claiming that God's existence needs no demonstration, Anselm seems to be giving just such a demonstration. Why then does Aquinas treat the argument as an attempt to show that God's existence is self-evident? How does self-evidence get into the picture?

In terms of the overall structure of the *Summa Theologica* the answer is easy to see. Aquinas begins by asking whether, in addition to natural science broadly conceived, anything else is required. The answer, of course, is that Sacred Doctrine or Divine Science is. This science is revealed by God, who is its subject matter: "The subject matter of a science is that of which it principally treats. But in this science the treatment is mainly about God; for it is called theology, as treating of God. Therefore God is the subject matter of this science" (*ST* I q 1 a 7). After concluding that this Divine Science is argumentative—that arguments are appropriate to it—Aquinas turns to our knowledge of the *existence* of its subject matter. Here he takes up the suggestion that the existence of God is self-evident and in no need of demonstration; it is at this point that he examines Anselm's argument.

When we turn to Aquinas' reply to that argument, more questions arise. He begins by distinguishing two kinds of self-evidence:

> I answer that, A thing can be self-evident in either of two ways; on the one hand, self-evident in itself, though not to us; on the other, self-evident in itself, and to us. A proposition is self-evident because the predicate is included in the essence of the subject; e.g., *Man is an animal,* for animal is contained in the essence of man. If, therefore, the essence of the predicate and subject be known to all, the proposition will be self-evident to all; as is clear with regard to the first principles of demonstration, the terms of which are certain common notions that no one is ignorant of, such as being and non-being, whole and part, and the like. If, however, there are some to whom the essence of the predicate and subject is unknown, the proposition will be self-evident in itself, but not to those who do not know the meaning of the predicate and subject of the proposition. Therefore, it happens, as Boethius says, that there are some notions of the mind which are common and self-evident only to the learned, as that incorporeal substances are not in space. Therefore I say that this proposition, God exists, of itself is self-evident, for the predicate is the same as the subject, because God is His own existence as will be hereafter shown. Now because we do not know the essence of God, the proposition is not self-evident to us, but needs to be demonstrated by things that are more known to us, though less known in their nature—namely, by His effects (*ST* I q 2 a 6).

Later we shall look at this distinction in more detail; for the moment we may be satisfied with the following rough approximation:

> A proposition *p* is self-evident in itself if and only if its subject term includes its predicate term

and

> *p* is self-evident to us if and only if we understand it and thereby see that it is true.

Aquinas then turns specifically to the argument:

Reply Obj. 2: . . . granted that everyone understands that by this name *God* is signified something than which nothing greater can be thought, nevertheless, it does not therefore follow that he understands that what the name signifies exists actually, but only that it exists mentally. Nor can it be argued that it actually exists, unless it be admitted that there actually exists something than which nothing greater can be thought; and this precisely is not admitted by those who hold that God does not exist.

Precisely how shall we understand this response to Anselm's argument? "Nor can it be argued," says Aquinas, "that it actually exists, unless it be admitted that there exists something than which no greater can be thought; and this, precisely, is not admitted by those who hold that God does not exist." How is this a refutation of Anselm's argument? Is it more than an unsupported declaration that the argument is unsuccessful? Anselm seems to have an easy retort: "It can indeed be argued, and the fact is I've just argued it." Here, then, is a crucial question: How, exactly, does Aquinas' reply bear on Anselm's argument? What *is* Aquinas' reply? Is it a good one? Secondly, Aquinas claims, as we have seen, that God's existence is self-evident in itself. How does this claim comport with his rejection of Anselm's argument? Furthermore, God's existence, though self-evident in itself, is not, according to Thomas, self-evident to us; this is because "we do not know the essence of God." But if the essence of God is not known to us, presumably it is not known to Aquinas. How then does he know that God's existence *is* self-evident in itself? And if the essence of God is not known to us, does it not follow that the singular proposition *God exists* is not merely not self-evident to us, but utterly uncomprehended by us? If we are unable to grasp the essence of God, if we do not know what he is, how can we grasp or understand the proposition that he exists?

We have two basic questions, then: (1) does Aquinas have a good reply to the argument Anselm presents? and (2) can he sensibly hold that God's existence is self-evident in itself though not to us? Let us take these up one at a time.

I

We have already seen (above, p. 122) the version of the ontological argument Aquinas gives in the *Summa Theologica;* he states the argument in similar but fuller fashion in the *Summa Contra Gentiles*:

> Those propositions are said to be self-evident that are known immediately upon the knowledge of their terms. Thus, as soon as you know the nature of a whole and the nature of a part, you know immediately that every whole is greater than its part. The proposition *God exists* is of this sort. For by the name God we understand something

than which a greater cannot be thought. This notion is formed in the intellect by one who hears and understands the name God. As a result, God must exist already at least in the intellect. But He cannot exist solely in the intellect, since that which exists both in the intellect and in reality is greater than that which exists in the intellect alone. Now, as the very definition of the name points out, nothing can be greater than God. Consequently, the proposition that God exists is self-evident as being evident from the very meaning of the name God (*SCG* I.10).

Perhaps we can put this argument more explicitly as follows. Suppose we let the term 'God' abbreviate the phrase 'that than which a greater cannot be thought.' Taking

(1) God exists in the understanding but not in reality

as the hypothesis for a *reductio ad absurdum* argument, we can proceed as follows:

(2) What exists both in the intellect and in reality is greater than what exists in the intellect alone (*premiss*).

(3) It is thinkable that there be a thing that exists both in reality and in the intellect (*premiss*).

(4) Therefore it is thinkable that there be a thing that is greater than God.

(5) Therefore it is thinkable that there be a being greater than that than which a greater is not thinkable. ((4), *replacing 'God' by what it abbreviates*).

(6) (5) is false (*premiss*).

(7) Therefore (1) is false ((*1*)-(6), *by reductio ad absurdum*).

But if (1) is false, then if God exists in the understanding (and even the fool will testify that he does), he exists in reality as well.

A slightly different statement of the argument enables us to put Aquinas' objection a bit more briefly. As before, suppose for *reductio* that

(1) God exists in the understanding but not in reality.

Then

(8) For any object x, if x does not exist in reality, then it is thinkable that there be something greater than x.

(9) Therefore it is thinkable that there be something greater than God ((*1*), (*8*)).

(10) Therefore it is thinkable that there be something greater than that than which a greater is not thinkable ((*9*), *replacing 'God' by what it abbreviates*).

This version of the argument then proceeds just as the first.

Now Aquinas presents the argument as an attempt to show that God's existence is self-evident. Furthermore, he clearly construes it as an argument for the conclusion that the proposition *God exists* is self-evident *for us*—"known immediately upon the knowledge of its terms" (*SCG* I.10) or "known as soon as the terms are known" (*ST* I q 2 a 2). But what, then, would be the function of Anselm's argumentation? Why would it be necessary, if the proposition *God exists* were self-evident? Here we can usefully distinguish what we might call indirect from direct self-evidence. Consider an argument form, for example, *modus ponens*:

p; if *p* then *q*; therefore *q*.

Let us speak of *the corresponding conditional* of an argument form as the conditional statement form whose antecedent is the conjunction of the premises of the argument and whose consequent is its conclusion. The corresponding conditional of *modus ponens*, then, is

If *p*, and if *p* then *q*, then *q*.

Now suppose we say that a proposition is directly self-evident to us if it is self-evident to us in Aquinas' sense—that is, if we understand it and understanding it is sufficient for knowing that it is true. Then we can say that a proposition is indirectly self-evident (to us) if it is a consequence of propositions that are directly self-evident, by argument forms (*modus ponens, reductio ad absurdum*, etc.) whose corresponding conditionals are also directly self-evident. And if it is plausible to hold that each of an argument's premises and each of the argument forms it employs is directly self-evident to us, it will be plausible to hold that its conclusion is indirectly self-evident to us. Perhaps it is not unreasonable to take Anselm's premises and argument forms as directly self-evident; so perhaps it is plausible to follow Thomas in viewing his argument as an attempt to show that God's existence is (indirectly) self-evident to us.

But now to the main question: just how does Aquinas mean to refute the argument? What is the objection to it? "Nor," says Aquinas, "can it be argued that there actually exists something than which nothing greater can be thought...." How shall we construe this objection? The *Summa Contra Gentiles* is a bit more explicit:

> What is more, granted that everyone should understand by the name God something than which a greater cannot be thought, it will still not be necessary that there exist in reality something than which a greater cannot be thought. For a thing and the definition of a name are posited in the same way. Now, from the fact that that which is indicated by the name God is conceived by the mind, it does not follow that God exists save only in the intellect. Hence, that than which a greater cannot be thought will likewise not have to exist save only in the intellect. From this it does not follow that there exists in reality something than which a greater cannot be thought. No difficulty, consequently, befalls anyone who posits that God does not exist. For that something greater can be thought than anything given in reality or in the intellect is a difficulty only to him who admits that there is something than which a greater cannot be thought in reality (I.10).

How shall we understand this? Is there really something of substance here, or only the allegation that Anselm's argument is unsound? ". . . a thing and the definition of a name are posited in the same way"; accordingly, "that than which a greater cannot be thought will likewise not have to exist save only in the intellect." Here Aquinas means to claim, I believe, that this argument establishes at most a *connection* between the two properties *being a being than which none greater can be thought* and *existence*. Anselm's argument shows that whatever has the former has the latter; but it does not show that anything has the former. The argument shows that if a thing were such that nothing greater could be thought, then it would indeed exist; it does not show that there is such a thing as a being than which nothing greater can be thought.

We can put Aquinas' point in a way that was not available to him but still does justice, I believe, to his intentions. The argument as we stated it (second version) goes from

> (1) God exists in the understanding but not in reality

and

> (8) For any object *x*, if *x* does not exist in reality, then it is thinkable that there be something greater than *x*

> (9) It is thinkable that there be something greater than God.

On the surface this inference looks appealing, but strictly speaking an intermediary step is required:

(8.5) If God does not exist in reality, then it is thinkable that there be something greater than God.

(8.5), of course, would follow from (8) by the rule of inference logicians call *universal instantiation.* According to this rule, what is true of everything is true of any specific thing you pick; hence from *everything is mortal* one properly infers *Socrates is mortal.* According to (8), everything has the property of being such that if it does not exist, then it is thinkable that there be something greater; (8.5) concludes that God has this property. But universal instantiation can conceal pitfalls. For example, there are no dragons; hence nothing is a dragon; hence everything is a non-dragon; hence Fafner is a non-dragon. Here something has gone wrong at the last step. In the same vein, consider the inference from

every integer has a successor

to

the largest integer has a successor.

Here, too, something has gone amiss.

The difficulty is not hard to locate. By universal instantiation one properly moves from a proposition of the form *everything has P* to one of the form *a has P* where the latter predicates of some specific object *a* the property the former says everything has. But there is no such thing as Fafner; hence there is no object such that the proposition expressed by the sentence 'Fafner is a non-dragon' predicates of that object the property of being a non-dragon. Similarly for the greatest integer; since there is no such thing, there is nothing of which the proposition expressed by the sentence 'the greatest integer has a successor' predicates the property of having a successor. We properly use universal instantiation to go from a universally quantified statement to a proposition predicating the appropriate property of something; but of course we cannot properly appeal to this form of argument to justify the step from a universal proposition to one that fails to predicate a property of anything.

The application to the argument at hand is obvious. We are justified in inferring

(8.5) If God does not exist in reality, then it is thinkable that there be something greater than God

i.e.,

(8.5) God is such that if he does not exist in reality, then it is thinkable that there is something greater than he from (8) only if we already know that there is such a thing as the being than which a greater is not thinkable. Since this is just what the argument purports to establish, it is ungraceful of Anselm to appeal, in the argument, to a form of inference whose proper use presupposes its truth.

To put the matter a bit differently: suppose, says Aquinas, we grant the truth of (8); suppose, that is, we grant that every object is such that if it does not exist in reality, then it is thinkable that there be something greater than it. We cannot straightway conclude that the being than which it is not thinkable that there be a greater is such ihat if *it* did not exist in reality, then it is thinkable that there be something greater than it; for we don't yet know that among the objects there *is* one than which none greater is thinkable. If there is no such object, then clearly we can't employ universal instantiation to conclude that it has the property ascribed to everything by (8). Suppose we accept (8); we can properly add that each object is one than which it is thinkable that there be a greater, provided we do not hold that among the objects there is a being than which it is not thinkable that there be a greater. As Aquinas puts it: "For that something greater can be thought than anything given in reality . . . is a difficulty only to him who admits that there is something than which a greater cannot be thought in reality."

We may imagine Anselm replying as follows. Even if the being than which none greater can be thought does not exist *in reality*, it does exist in the intellect; hence we can think and reason about it. In particular, we can consider the proposition that this being exists in the intellect alone and not in reality; and we can show that this supposition leads to a contradiction. Granted, the conclusion of an argument by universal instantiation must predicate of something the property its premiss says everything has; but that something need not be anything that exists in reality; existence *in intellectu* is sufficient. To hold otherwise is to display a deplorable prejudice in favor of what exists. We could put the matter as follows: Aquinas' objection, in essence, turns on the claim that the universal quantifier '(x)' in a universally quantified proposition must have a range R, a set of objects taken as values of its variable. A proper argument by universal instantiation, then, proceeds from a universally quantified proposition, one that predicates some property P of each member of R, to a proposition that predicates that property of some specific member of R. He adds that we cannot properly hold that the quantifier in (8) includes in its range a being than which none greater can be thought unless we already know that there *is* such a being—which is just the point at issue. And Anselm's retort, we are supposing, is as follows: indeed a quantifier must have a range; but why limit its range to objects that exist in reality? There is no reason why a variable cannot range over objects that exist *in intellectu,* whether or not they exist in reality as well.

If I understand Aquinas right, his answer is that there aren't any things that do not exist; hence, there are no sets some of whose members are nonexistent; and hence no quantifier includes nonexistent members in its range. It is a mistake and a confusion to suppose that in addition to all the things that exist (exist in reality)—persons, houses, numbers, propositions, properties and the like—there are some more things that do not exist in reality but do exist in the intellect. The things that exist are all the things there are. And here I think Aquinas is right.[1] Of course it is sometimes correct to say something like "Nick's Nobel Prize exists only in his mind"; but this is no more than another way of saying that Nick believes he has won a Nobel Prize and in fact has not. And if I say "the being than which none greater can be thought exists in the intellect," what I say should not be construed as the claim that there is a certain object—one that has the property of being the only thing than which it is not thinkable that there be a greater—that lacks the good fortune to exist in reality and has to settle for existence in the understanding as a sort of consolation prize. What I say should instead be taken as or as equivalent to the claim that the property or concept *being the only thing than which none greater is thinkable* has been grasped or apprehended.

Many versions of the ontological argument begin by construing the hypothesis for *reductio,* namely,

(1) God exists in the understanding but not in reality

as a proposition predicating a property of a certain being—a being that at any rate exists in the understanding if not in reality. They then proceed to argue, by way of general principles relating greatness and existence, that this being must exist in reality as well. Aquinas' objection, I believe, is fatal to every version of this sort.

II

Now we turn to our second group of questions. We have seen (above, p. 124) that Aquinas begins his comments on Anselm's argument by

---

1. For the argument on this point, see my *The Nature of Necessity* (New York, 1974), chs. 7, 8.

distinguishing two types of self-evidence: a proposition may be self-evident in itself and it may be self-evident to us. Of course it is hard to see how merely making this distinction could serve to refute Anselm's argument or cast doubt on its conclusion; and in fact Aquinas is here aiming in a different direction altogether. The subject for discussion in Question 2 is the existence of God; and the first query is whether the existence of God is self-evident, and in no need of argument. Aquinas and others held that God is *metaphysically simple*, that he lacks all composition.[2] Hence there is no composition of essence and existence in him; his essence *is* his existence, and each is identical with God himself. Now of course this suggestion raises substantial problems of interpretation; but the immediate question, the question to which Aquinas here turns his attention, is this: does divine simplicity, thus understood, not entail that the proposition *God exists* is self-evident? Thomas's reply is by way of a *distinguo;* this proposition is self-evident in itself, but not to us, who have no apprehension or grasp of the essence of the object denoted by the singular term 'God.' "Now because we do not know the essence of God, the proposition is not self-evident to us, but needs to be demonstrated by things that are more known to us . . . namely, by his effects" (*ST* I q 2 a 1).

But this raises further questions. If the essence of God is not known to us, presumably it is not known to Aquinas. How, then, does he know that it includes or is identical with God's existence? How does he know that the proposition *God exists* is self-evident in itself? And if the essence of God is not known to us, does it not follow that the proposition expressed by the sentence 'God exists' is not merely not self-evident to us, but utterly beyond our comprehension? Presumably the word 'God' is a proper name; if so, it expresses the divine essence.[3] If we are unable to grasp or apprehend that essence, we shall be unable to grasp the property expressed by the subject term of the sentence in question. How then can we grasp the proposition it expresses? Indeed, have we any reason to suppose that it does express a proposition?

Perhaps these questions can be answered. Our first task is to see more clearly how Aquinas understands self-evidence here. The term 'self-evidence' receives two quite different explanations in the relevant passages. Speaking of propositions self-evident to us, he puts it thus: "Those propositions are said to be self-evident that are known immediately upon the knowledge of their terms. Thus, as soon as you know

---

2. Cf. *ST* I q 3; *SCG* I, 16-23; *De Entia et Essentia*, V, 76-83.
3. For a discussion of the connection between proper names and essences, see *The Nature of Necessity*, ch. 7, sect. 3.

the nature of a whole and the nature of a part, you know immediately that every whole is greater than its parts" (*SCG* I.10). While there may be more than one way of construing this explanation, the basic idea is clear: a proposition is self-evident, in this sense, if a grasp or apprehension of it is sufficient for knowledge of its truth; if upon understanding it, one just sees that it is true.[4] The proposition Thomas cites about wholes and parts is of this nature, as are simple arithmetical propositions and the corresponding conditional of *modus ponens*. Of course this notion must be relativized to persons. What is self-evident to you may not be to me. $2 + 1 = 3$ is self-evident to nearly everyone; $15 + 7 = 22$ may be self-evident to some but not everyone; $37 \times 54 = 1998$ might be self-evident to some few with a particularly powerful grasp of integers and their ways, but the rest of us require calculation, some of us needing pencil and paper. Still further, Aquinas clearly holds that a proposition is self-evident to a person only if he does in fact grasp it and consequently sees that it is true; the fact, if it is a fact, that he *would* see that it is true if he *were* to understand it, is not sufficient for its being self-evident to him. This explanation of self-evidence, then, can be stated as follows:

(11) A proposition p is self-evident to a person S if and only if S sees that p is true just by understanding it.

Self-evidence in itself receives a different explanation; "A proposition is self-evident because the predicate is included in the essence of the subject, e.g., *man is an animal,* for animal is contained in the essence of man" (*ST* I q 2 a 1). Here presumably Aquinas is thinking of the essence of an object x as a property P that meets two conditions: first, P is essential to x, in the sense that it is impossible that x should have existed and lacked P, and secondly, one can say what sort of thing x is by citing P. Consider, for example, the property of being self-identical. It is not possible that Socrates should have existed but lacked self-identity; this property, therefore, is essential to him and thus meets the first condition for being an essence of Socrates. On the other hand, it fails to meet the second; since everything has self-identity, one cannot say what kind of thing Socrates is by pointing out that he has it. *Being human,* or *being a rational animal,* however, meets both conditions and thus would be an essence of Socrates. Now perhaps we can state this account of self-evidence as follows:

---

4. *Ibid.,* ch. 1, sect. 1.

(12) p is self-evident in itself if and only if the essence of the subject of p includes the predicate of p,

where a property P includes a property Q if it is not possible that there be an object that has P but lacks Q. But what is it for the essence of the subject of a proposition to include its predicate? The example (*man is an animal*) suggests the following. Suppose for the moment we restrict our attention to universal affirmative propositions; and suppose we think of such propositions—*all men are rational*, for example—as containing a subject property (*humanity*, or *being a man* in this instance) and a predicate property (*rationality*). Then we may say that the essence of the subject includes the predicate if the predicate property is included in the essences of the objects falling under the subject property—if, that is, each of the objects displaying the subject property is such that its essence includes the predicate property.

Although this account is clearly suggested by Aquinas' words, it has some anomalous consequences. For example, the proposition *all bachelors are unmarried* would not be self-evident on this showing, since *being unmarried* is not part of the essence of your typical bachelor. Aquinas himself, like most priests, was a bachelor. *Being unmarried,* however, was not part of his essence; there is falsehood, but not logical impossibility, in the proposition that he was married. So *being unmarried* is not included in the essence of bachelors; accordingly, the proposition *all bachelors are unmarried* is not self-evident in itself under the present explanation of that notion. The same may be said of the proposition *all black cats are black; being black* is not part of the essence of black cats. On the other hand, if all the animals in this room are human beings, the proposition *all the animals in this room are rational* turns out to be self-evident on this account. Worse, singular existentials such as *Socrates exists* turn out self-evident. As we have seen, a property P includes a property Q if it is not possible that there exist an object that has P but lacks Q. But for any property P you pick, it is not possible that there exist an object that has P but lacks existence. *Every* property, then, includes existence; in particular, Socrates' essence does. Thus God's existence will be self-evident on this account, but the same will hold for the rest of us.

These anomalies suggest that Aquinas' meaning lies in a different direction, as do the words he uses further on in the very same passage quoted above:

> If, therefore, the essence of the predicate and the subject be known to all the proposition will be self-evident to all; as is clear with regards to the first principles of demonstration, the terms of which

are certain common notions no one is ignorant of, such as being and non-being, whole and part, and the like. If, however, there are some to whom the essence of the predicate and subject is unknown, the proposition will be self-evident in itself, but not to those who do not know the meaning of the predicate and subject of the proposition (*ST* I q 2 a 1).

These words—the last sentence in particular—suggest that Aquinas sometimes uses the phrases 'essence of the subject' and 'essence of the predicate' interchangeably with 'meaning of the subject term' and 'meaning of the predicate.' If we understand him this way, he seems to be suggesting that a sentence like 'The whole is greater than its parts' expresses a proposition self-evident in itself if the meaning of its predicate term is included in the meaning of its subject term—if, that is, the subject property of that proposition includes its predicate property. So perhaps we can state his explanation more accurately as follows:

(13) Where *p* is a universal affirmative proposition, *p* is self-evident in itself if and only if its subject property includes its predicate property.

Taken this way, the self-evident is a special case of the necessary—i.e., a proposition is self-evident in itself if it is necessary, and universal affirmative in form. This seems to represent Aquinas' intentions; but I suspect that restriction to universal affirmative propositions is just a matter of inadvertence on his part. I should think he would want to regard other necessary propositions—e.g., *if all men are mortal and Socrates is a man, then Socrates is mortal*—as also self-evident in this sense. So I suggest we understand Aquinas as using 'self-evident' in this context to mean the same as 'necessarily true' or 'true in every possible world'. (Of course if we wish to insist on the apparently arbitrary restriction to universal affirmative propositions, we can do so without loss in the present context; the proposition *God exists* is singular and thus counts as universal affirmative.)

Here, then, we have two quite different accounts of self-evidence: on the first self-evidence (to a person *S*) is a matter of a proposition's being such that a grasp or understanding of it is sufficient for knowledge of it (for *S*); on the second a self-evident proposition is necessarily true. Of course there is a link between the two; most or all propositions self-evident in the first sense are also self-evident in the second. Still, they are distinct conceptions; many propositions self-evident in themselves are not self-evident to us. For example, Goldbach's conjecture that every even number greater than 2 is the sum of two primes is either necessarily true or necessarily false. Hence either it or its denial is self-evident in itself; but since it is not known whether this conjecture is true, neither is self-evident to us. And if Aquinas is right, God's existence has just this status; it is self-evident in itself but not to us. It is a necessary truth that God exists, but not one we know just by understanding it; the reason, of course, is that God's essence is unknown to us. But if we have no grasp or apprehension of God's essence, should it not follow that we have no grasp or apprehension of the proposition *God exists?* Should it not follow that this proposition is not merely not self-evident to us, but is totally beyond our grasp, so that we cannot so much as understand it? To put the matter a bit differently: should it not follow that the proposition expressed by the sentence 'God exists' (if indeed that sentence expresses a proposition) is one we can't understand? And if so, how could we *prove* this proposition, as Aquinas thinks we can?

Here Thomas makes an interesting and subtle distinction. He argues that we do not need a knowledge or apprehension of the essence of God to demonstrate his existence: "Now in arguments proving the existence of God, it is not necessary to assume the divine essence or quiddity as the middle term of the demonstration; . . . in place of the quiddity, an effect is taken as the middle term. . . . It is from such effects that the meaning of the name *God* is taken" (*SCG* I.12). And in the *Summa Theologica*: "Now the names given to God are derived from His effects..." (q 2 a 2; see also q 13 a 1).

We can put this point as follows. The name 'God' in the sentence 'God exists' is not a proper name of God and does not serve to express the essence of God.[5] Rather, that word is short for some such definite description as 'the Creator and sustainer of all there is' or perhaps 'the first cause' or 'the unmoved mover.' But none of the properties expressed by these descriptions—*being the unmoved mover*, for example, or *being the uncaused cause*—is identical with or included in God's essence: he could have existed and refrained from creating. We can prove and therefore know the proposition *the first cause exists* (or *there is a unique first cause*) and we can grasp and understand the property *being the first cause;* but this property is one we human beings can apprehend without being able to grasp the essence of God. And hence the proposition expressed by 'God exists' is one that can be grasped by those who have no apprehension of God's essence.

Consider an analogy. I might know that Paul has just referred to exactly one thing. I then grasp or understand the property *being the thing*

---

5. *Ibid.*, ch. 5, sect. 3.

just referred to by Paul; and I know, furthermore, that this property is exemplified by something. But I may have no idea what that thing is—for all I know it could be his wife or a 4 x 4 matrix or the Zwier outside loop. It could be a complicated function I could not so much as grasp without two weeks' preliminary study. In the latter case the description 'the thing that Paul just referred to' denotes a certain object and I know that it does; but the essence of the object it does denote is beyond my comprehension.

Similarly then, says Aquinas, in the case of God. The proposition *God exists* picks out God by a certain description. We can grasp this description and prove that it is not empty, that there is something to which it applies. But a grasp of this description is not sufficient for a grasp of the essence of the thing it denotes; and in fact we have no grasp or apprehension of that essence. Furthermore, this proposition—the one expressed by 'God exists'—is not self-evident in itself. It is not a necessary truth. For it entails that some things have been *moved* or *caused;* and that this is so is a contingent truth. God was under no logical obligation to create anything; had he not created anything, he would not have been first mover nor even a mover at all. So the proposition *God exists* is contingently true and hence not self-evident in itself.

Now of course Aquinas also says that the existence of God *is* self-evident in itself: "for the predicate is the same as the subject, because God in his own existence, as will afterwards be shown" (q 2 a 1). How shall we understand this? Perhaps as follows. Aquinas sets out to demonstrate the existence of God—that is, the existence of a unique unmoved mover and first cause. He then argues that an unmoved mover or first cause must be ontologically simple, without ontological complexity. Hence in such a being there is no composition of essence and existence; God's essence is identical with his existence. God himself, furthermore, is identical with his essence and with his existence. Here, of course, there are some fascinating questions. At the moment we shall have to bypass them; but it is at any rate clear that according to Aquinas the simplicity of God entails that his existence is self-evident in itself.

But how is this consistent with our conclusion that according to Aquinas the proposition *God exists* is contingent and not self-evident in itself? What we must note here is that there may be *several* propositions predicating existence of God. There is, for example, the proposition expressed by the sentence 'God exists'—a proposition equivalent to the claim that there is a unique first mover. But there are others—for example,

(14) The being worshipped by St. Paul exists.

(14) predicates existence of God, since the being worshipped by St. Paul *is* God. But (14) is not equivalent to the proposition expressed by 'God exists,' for the former, unlike the latter, entails that St. Paul worshipped something. Accordingly, there are several nonequivalent propositions predicating existence of God. And among these, if the existence of God is self-evident in itself, is one that *is* necessarily true, true in all possible worlds. This proposition would have the essence of God as its subject property; it singles out God, not by properties inessential to him, such as the property of being worshipped by St. Paul or the property of having created the world, but by his essence. An analogy: it is plausible to suppose that the proposition *the null set exists* is necessarily true. The proposition *the set Paul just mentioned exists*, however, is contingent (since it entails the contingent truth that Paul has just mentioned a set); and this despite the fact that the set Paul just mentioned *is* the null set. So the proposition *the set Paul just mentioned exists* is contingent, despite the necessary existence of the set Paul just mentioned. Among the propositions predicating existence of a necessary being, there will obviously be some that are contingent.

On Aquinas' view, then, there is a necessary proposition predicating existence of God—a proposition whose subject property is God's essence. Since we have no grasp of God's essence, we have no grasp of this proposition; we cannot assert it, deny it, doubt it, or believe it—at least not in any straightforward manner. We know, however, that there *is* such a proposition; furthermore, we can refer to it and we can both believe and know that it is true. Suppose I know that Paul asserted just one true proposition yesterday morning and no false ones (Paul was uncharacteristically laconic). Suppose furthermore that the proposition he asserted was a deep and difficult truth I couldn't understand. Then I can refer to the proposition he asserted yesterday morning and say of it that it is true, although I am not able to grasp or understand it. Yet I have good reason to believe that there is such a proposition and that it is true.

Similarly, then, in the case of God's existence. The proposition expressed by 'God exists'—the proposition we can grasp, apprehend, and prove—is a contingent truth and self-evident neither in itself or to us. There is another proposition predicating existence of God, however— a proposition whose subject property is God's essence. This proposition is necessarily true and hence self-evident in itself. Because God's essence is utterly beyond our ken, however, it is one we cannot grasp or apprehend. This proposition, accordingly, is self-evident in itself but not to us.

We began by asking two questions: does Aquinas have a sound objection to the argument Anselm presents? And can he sensibly hold that God's existence is self-evident in itself but not to us? We can now see, I think, that we must answer both questions affirmatively.

Tillich's Religious Epistemology

DEWEY J. HOITENGA, JR.

God is the problem and the answer, the beginning and the end, the presupposition and the goal of Tillich's thought. The central idea in his religious epistemology is that of the "symbol"; yet he also asserts the truth of a literal, nonsymbolic proposition about the nature of God. The dualism signified by this twofold theory of predication does not quite conceal, however, an underlying monism. Tillich articulates this monism in an idealistic philosophical system and in a theory of religion and culture which can be seen as a secularized Protestant "culture mysticism."

According to Tillich, " 'God' is the answer to the question implied in man's finitude" (*ST*, I, 211).[1] This question is the question of the infinite, and it arises because man can recognize himself as finite. Such a recognition presupposes that he is aware of the nonfinite, in other words, that he "transcends his finitude" (*ST*, I, 231). This self-transcendence has an implication for our knowledge of God, namely, an "inner tension" that Tillich calls man's "ultimate concern." The tension arises because the *concern* requires for Tillich an object which can be "encountered concretely," while *ultimacy* points to what "must transcend every preliminary

---

1. The following abbreviations are used for works of Tillich cited in the text of this essay: *ST* = *Systematic Theology* (Chicago, 1951ff.); *RS* = "The Religious Symbol," *The Journal of Liberal Religion*, 2,1 (Summer 1940); *KB* = "Answer," in C. W. Kegley and R. W. Bretall (eds.), *The Theology of Paul Tillich* (New York, 1952); *TS* = "Theology and Symbolism," in F. E. Johnson (ed.), *Religious Symbolism* (New York, 1955); *RSKG* = "Religious Symbols and Our Knowledge of God," *The Christian Scholar*, 38,3 (Sept. 1955); *PE* = *The Protestant Era* (Chicago, 1948); *RPT* = *The Recovery of the Prophetic Tradition in the Reformation* (Washington, 1955).

Dewey J. Hoitenga, Jr., is Professor of Philosophy at Grand Valley State Colleges, Allendale, Michigan, and a frequent contributor to religious and philosophical publications. In "Tillich's Religious Epistemology" Hoitenga focuses on the much-discussed concept of religious symbol in Tillich's philosophical theology. In attempting to guard against the sin of idolatry, Tillich stresses that religious symbols convey no literal truth about the Holy. Hoitenga argues that Tillich cannot really state his view coherently, and moreover that Tillich's view is not so much Christian as a "secularized culture mysticism."

finite and concrete concern." And "the conflict between the concreteness and the ultimacy of the religious concern is actual whenever God is experienced.... It is the basic problem of every doctrine of God" (*ST*, I, 211).

Further analysis, Tillich suggests, shows that this conflict involves contradiction: "The word 'God' produces a *contradiction* in the consciousness" (*RS*, pp. 27f.). For example, "if one says that God has personality in an eminent, namely, an absolutely perfect sense one must add that this very assertion supplies the negation of personality in God in the sense of 'being a person'" (*KB*, p. 334). Hence the concept of God for Tillich is a dialectical one. "The *via eminentia* . . . needs as its balance the *via negationis*, and the unity of both is the *via symbolica*." Thus, as he says, "the center of my theological doctrine of knowledge is the concept of symbol" (*KB*, p. 333).

A religious symbol, like any symbol, employs "the material of our daily encounter." But it also "points to the ultimate level of being." It is just this dual reference that makes the symbol appropriate to the problem of God which we have described (*TS*, pp. 109f.). The various characteristics of symbols in general, and of religious symbols in particular, are described by Tillich in numerous writings over many years, and the separate descriptions do not always quite coincide. Essentially, however, the characteristics of symbols reduce to two: they relate us, in a way nothing else can, to distinctive "levels of reality"; and they are "socially rooted and socially supported."

First, symbols "point beyond themselves to something else" (*RSKG*, p. 189). This they have in common with signs, but here the similarity ends. "The difference between symbol and sign is the participation in the symbolized reality which characterizes the symbols, and the non-participation in the 'pointed-to' reality which characterizes a sign" (*RSKG*, p. 190).[2] Tillich therefore rejects "negative theories" of the symbol (like Freud's, for example), which "deny that the symbol has an objective reference and attribute to it merely a subjective character." For Tillich, "These theories are especially dangerous for religious symbols, since the latter do not refer to a world of objects, yet they intend to express a reality and not merely the subjective character of a religious individual" (*RS*, p. 16). Symbols thus have a "revelatory" significance: "Every symbol opens up a level of reality for which non-symbolic speaking is inadequate" (*RSKG*, p. 191).

What is the "level of reality" that is opened up, participated in, pointed

---

2. See also *ST*, I, 177; *KB*, p. 335; *TS*, p. 110.

to, by the religious symbol? It is that level of reality designated by such terms as the infinite, the ultimate, the holy; or again, "that which is unconditionally beyond the conceptual sphere . . . the ultimate reality implied in the religious act, the unconditioned transcendent" (*RS*, p. 15). In still other words, it is

> the depth dimension of reality itself, the dimension of reality which is the ground of every other dimension and every other depth, and which, therefore, is not one level besides the others but is the fundamental level, the level below all the other levels, the level of being itself, or the ultimate power of being (*RSKG*, p. 192).

And thus the symbol, by opening up the ultimate through the use of the concrete, is the answer to the "problem of God."

But what will make certain finite, "concrete" materials more adequate in functioning as religious symbols than others? As we have now seen, "religious symbols are double-edged. They are directed toward the infinite which they symbolize *and* toward the finite through which they symbolize it" (*PE*, p. 61). We should therefore expect Tillich to give an account of their adequacy in terms of a double reference: to the nature of the transcendent on the one hand, and the finite on the other.

How does the transcendent, to which the symbolic language of religion points, determine its adequacy as a symbol? Since religious symbols "participate in" and "open up" the transcendent, we might look for some resemblance between the symbolic material and the transcendent; but any such resemblance Tillich explicitly rejects:

> Genuine symbols . . . provide no objective knowledge, but yet a true awareness. . . . The criterion of the truth of a symbol naturally cannot be the comparison of it with the reality to which it refers, just because this reality is absolutely beyond human comprehension. . . . The only criterion that is at all relevant is this, that the unconditioned is clearly grasped in its unconditionedness (*RS*, p. 28).

Again, "that which is signified lies beyond the symbolic material. This is the first and last thing we must say about religious symbolism" (*TS*, p. 116). Or again, "the truth of a symbol is that it drives the mind beyond itself" (*RPT*, p. 3).

According to Tillich, then, the only function which the transcendent has in regard to the adequacy of religious symbols is to determine their formal character as symbols. Their content will need to be explained, as we shall see, exclusively by reference to the finite world of human experience. This skeptical view contrasts with the traditional theistic theory of predication comprehended in the doctrine of *analogia entis*. On the traditional view, the difference between the infinite and the finite indeed qualifies the similarities that exist between them, but does not eliminate them entirely. Tillich's view also contrasts with other "symbolic" theories of recent vintage which maintain that religious symbols can work cognitively through resemblances between them and their religious object.[3]

Tillich's argument for his view is not so much epistemological as religious. If the worshiper in any way identifies the content of a symbol with the transcendent which it symbolizes, he will be in danger of idolatry: "All idolatry is nothing else than the absolutizing of symbols of the Holy, and making them identical with the Holy itself" (*RSKG*, p. 193). And "every religion in its very essence has the idolatrous element.... There is no one who does not try to grasp God according to his capacity, and to shape such a God as he can understand on his own level" (*RPT*, p. 3). Christian theism is as open to this threat as any other religion. "The danger of the personal symbol is only that its symbolic character may be forgotten and that a judgment about the depth and meaning of reality may be transformed into a judgment about a special being beside us or above us" (*PE*, p. 119). We must, according to Tillich, "resist the idolatrous identification of the ground of our being with the God of ordinary theism who is a being existing in addition to other beings. The God of traditional theism is a symbol for the God beyond the God of theism. The God beyond the God of theism is the ground of being and meaning" (*TS*, p. 115).[4]

This seems to ignore the question whether the personal theism of Christianity provides at least a more adequate symbol than those provided in other, nonpersonalist religions. For Tillich's view is that the Unconditioned Transcendent, to which any religiously symbolic language points, plays no part in determining an answer to this question; it determines only that whatever symbol is used must never become an idol. But if skepticism about the specific nature of unconditioned reality is the price to be paid for avoiding idolatry, any worshiper who believes that religion should be informed with reason is faced with an unpleasant dilemma indeed.

Is there any ground for choosing one set of religious symbols over another? In spite of the foregoing, this is an important question for Tillich. For what he takes to be significant about the history of religion is not the opposition of religion to mythology, but the conflict between

---

3. For a recent exposition of the former see E. L. Mascall, *Existence and Analogy* (London, 1949); for examples of the latter, W. M. Urban, *Humanity and Deity* (New York, 1951), and E. Bevan, *Symbolism and Belief* (Boston, 1957).
4. See also *The Courage to Be* (New Haven, 1954), pp. 182-86.

the myths of the respective religions (*RS*, p. 22). This is only another way of saying that there has been a conflict of religious symbols, since Tillich defines myths as "configurations of symbols" (*TS*, p. 115). Is there any standard at all by which we can evaluate this conflict?

We have already seen that Tillich excludes the possibility of any non-symbolic, cognitive reference to the nature of the Unconditioned Transcendent. The only other possible reference is to the concrete, empirical reality of our experience, for this is what provides the material for the symbolic content. Tillich develops this in his doctrine of the "encounter," which seems to be an alternative term for "experience."[5] Religious symbols originate in the same way as symbols generally: "They are always the results of a creative encounter with reality. They are born out of such an encounter; they die if this encounter ceases." Though the special character of symbols as religious is that they "point to the ultimate level of being," yet in order to create them "we must use the material of our daily encounter" (*TS*, pp. 109f.). Thus "religious symbols are created in the course of the historical process of religion," and this involves "a tendency that is two-fold, toward religious transcendence and toward cultural objectification" (*RS*, p. 32).

The second part of this tendency suggests both the origin of the symbolic content of religious language and therefore also the sole standard of its adequacy. Tillich elaborates all of this in a view of the relationship between religion and culture. The "basic thesis" of his philosophy of religion, he says, is that "the sphere of religion in so far as it is expressed in the symbols embraces the whole autonomous culture." There is of course a "difference between the symbolic and the objective character of cultural creations" (*RS*, pp. 21f.). A cultural product is objectively *there* for us, but not as such religiously symbolic. It becomes symbolic when it becomes an expression of our ultimate concern. Tillich's formula is: "Religion is the substance of culture, culture is the expression of religion" (*PE*, p. xvii). This means that religion constitutes the awareness of unconditionedness within experience, while culture supplies the concrete, determinate character of that experience.

What are the implications of all this for the adequacy of specific religious symbols? Tillich says that "symbols cannot be replaced by other

---

5. Tillich claims to reject Schleiermacher's derivation of the "contents of the Christian faith" from experience (*ST*, I, 42). As will be evident from what follows, it is not at all clear that Tillich escapes the impact of the post-Kantian view of experience on modern theology. Consider also his "autobiographical reflection" on Otto's *Idea of the Holy*, which, he says, "determined my method in the philosophy of religion, wherein I started with experiences of the holy and advanced to the idea of God, and not the reverse way" (*KB*, p. 6).

symbols. Every symbol has a special function which is just *it* and cannot be replaced by more or less adequate symbols" (*RSKG*, p. 191). By this Tillich means simply that the truth of religious symbols "is their adequacy to the religious situation in which they are created, and their inadequacy to another situation is their untruth" (p. 196). Thus Tillich's view of the truth of symbols is intimately connected with his view of their origin in human experience. Though Tillich rejects, as we noted above, "negative theories" of religious symbolism, since they deny the reference of such symbolism to the Unconditioned Transcendent, he appreciates such theories to the extent that they have "recognized one aspect of the development of symbols: they have shown that the psychological and social situation is decisive for the selection of symbols in all spheres" (*RS*, p. 16). He goes on to deny what the negative theories affirm, namely, that religious symbols express this situation alone, and arise exclusively from it. But as we have seen, the only sense in which they do not arise from it is that the unconditionedness to which they point is distinct from and transcendent of this empirical situation. As we shall see, however, the unconditioned is, in the final analysis, actually a "qualification" of this situation which gives rise to religion and religious language.

The material which is suitable as a symbol of the Holy, then, is relative to the religious consciousness in any given situation. Tillich's view that "God does not exist"—that it "is as atheistic to affirm the existence of God as it is to deny it" (*ST*, I, 69, 237)—is a good illustration of his point. For the modern religious consciousness has been influenced by idealistic and by positivistic thought, in both of which "existence" is restricted to the finite objects of empirical experience. In such a "situation," then, the term 'existence of God' is no longer appropriate. The same thing is true for the traditional attributes of God such as love, mercy, knowledge, and power. "These attributes of God are taken from experienced qualities we have in ourselves. They cannot be applied to God in the literal sense. If this is done, it leads to an infinite amount of absurdities" (*RS*, p. 194).

To summarize: religious symbols function, for Tillich, by revealing ultimate reality through the finite reality from which their content is drawn. Instead of being a cognitive agent for illuminating the nature of the ultimate, however, the symbolic language of religion instead attests to the great difference between ultimate reality and the finite world. As a result, the word 'God,' Tillich believes, is always ambiguous, until its literal or symbolic meaning is specified:

The word 'God' involves a double meaning: it connotes the unconditioned transcendent, the ultimate, and also an object somehow endowed with qualities and actions. The first is not figurative or symbolic, but is rather in the strictest sense what it is said to be. The second, however, is really symbolic, figurative (RS, p. 27).[6]

This "double meaning" leaves Tillich, in effect, with two Gods which must somehow be brought together: the God of the church and the "God beyond God"; the God who is so real that he can be prayed to and the God who "is not something we can find in the context of reality"; the God who is the "highest being" and the God who "is not a being besides other beings"; the God who as symbol is the object of theology and the God who as literally definable is the object of metaphysics (RS, pp. 193f.; TS, pp. 107f.).

A number of difficulties attend this outcome of Tillich's thought. First of all, there is the distance between the God of religion and the God of metaphysics. The metaphysician alone would seem to be able to articulate, in the language of ontology, what God really, "literally" is; while the man of faith and worship is alone capable of, and restricted to, symbolic language—the highly expressive and evocative, but noncognitive language of religion. To be sure, Tillich tries to regard this as a gain, not a loss for the religious man; for, he says, "the literal is not more but less than the symbolic," since "every symbol opens up a level of reality for which non-symbolic speaking is inadequate" (RSKG, pp. 191, 195). As we have seen, however, religious symbols open up *nothing more* about the nature of God than his infinity, his ultimacy, his unconditionedness. Yet it requires the metaphysician, it seems, both to *see* that this is what the symbols do, and to describe that to which religious symbols point, in the literal statement about the unconditioned transcendent or being-itself. This I take to be what Tillich himself is doing when he writes, for example: "The non-symbolic element in all religious knowledge is the experience of the unconditioned as the boundary, ground, and abyss of everything conditioned."[7] What the religious man has that the metaphysician lacks appears to be the symbolic language and the religious experience that gives rise to it. What the metaphysician has that the religious man lacks is the literal knowledge of what religious language is all about.

How can these two, and the two kinds of languages they produce, be brought together? Tillich has indicated what he believes to be the answer to this question:

---

6. See also RSKG, p. 193.
7. "Reply," *Journal of Liberal Religion*, 2,4 (Spring 1941), 203.

Undoubtedly, it might well be the highest aim of philosophy to find the point where reality speaks simultaneously of itself and of the Unconditioned in an unsymbolic fashion, to find the point where the unsymbolic reality itself becomes a symbol, where the contrast between reality and symbol is suspended (*RS*, pp. 32f.).

It is instructive that the contrast between the literal and the symbolic here envisaged breaks down in Tillich's very efforts to distinguish them. For his efforts at a literal statement about God multiply: from God's unconditioned transcendency Tillich moves on to "being-itself," and then to the "ground of being," the "power of being," and "the power of the ground" (*ST*, I, 235f.). The same thing occurs in his descriptions of God's relationship to the world: from God's being "the ground of being" Tillich moves on to his being "the abyss of everything conditioned," "the depth dimension of reality itself . . . the level below all other levels, the level of being itself" (*RSKG*, p. 192). But all of these can be seen as symbolic expressions that meet Tillich's criteria for such expressions— for they all arise from our experience of finite objects and relationships. Indeed, it could be argued that the very idea of being, which supposedly becomes a *literal* description of God by adding the suffix 'itself,' is really the central *symbol* of Tillich's system.

Yet if it were possible to overcome the difference between literal and symbolic expressions for the nature of God, then, Tillich believes, "the deepest demand of the religious consciousness would be fulfilled: religion would no longer be a separate thing." It would become "an immediate concern with things in so far as they confront us unconditionally, that is, in so far as they stand in the transcendent" (*RS*, pp. 32f.). Religion no longer separate from what? The answer is, culture; and for an understanding of this, we need to refer again to the "basic thesis" of Tillich's philosophy of religion: "Religion is the substance of culture, culture is the expression of religion." A study of the past suggests a direction for the future: "Everything in time and space has become at some time in the history of religion a symbol for the Holy . . . and the key is that everything in reality can impress itself as a symbol for the special relationship of the human mind to its own ultimate ground and meaning" (*RSKG*, pp. 192f.).

This is what I called at the outset a secularized culture mysticism; and it is the vision in Tillich's religious thought which, I believe, is supposed to bridge the gap between the literalism of ontology and the symbolism of religious language. Tillich speaks of a "theonomous culture" as the ideal which avoids both heteronomy and autonomy in human life and thought. It is a culture in which "religious" language would disappear:

"Religious thinking and action represent manifestly what is hidden in secular thinking and acting; they are not something beside the secular or above or against it or a part of it; they are the representative expression of its ground and aim" (*PE*, p. 220; cf. pp. 59, 205).

Christianity, it seems, gets submerged in this larger view of human history; consider the task of a theonomous analysis of culture: "to show that in the depth of every autonomous culture an ultimate concern, something unconditional and holy, is implied." Such an analysis can be performed "without special reference to organized religion, the churches being only a part of the whole picture, but with a decisive reference to the religious element which was and is hidden in all . . . anti-religious and anti-Christian movements. In all of them," Tillich believes, "there is an ultimate, unconditional, and all-determining concern, something absolutely serious and therefore holy, even if expressed in secular terms" (*PE*, pp. 58f.).

In more theological language, what such culture mysticism comes to is described by Tillich as follows:

> The idea is that if God is All in All, there is no more need to speak of God in special symbols and even to use the word God. Speaking of things would mean speaking of the depth in which things are rooted and the heights to which they are elevated. For me the greatest religious utterances are those in which this type of non-symbolic speaking is more or less reached. But they are rather rare and they must be rare, because our real situation is that of distance from God and not of God being all in all (*RS*, p. 33).

These words reveal the crucial assumption of Tillich's thought: that in the last analysis, reality is all one, identical with itself, beyond any ontologically valid finite-infinite distinction. As he puts it in one place: "The Unconditioned is a qualification of the conditioned, of the world and the natural, by which the conditioned is affirmed and denied at the same time."[8] Such metaphysical monism is inevitable in a philosophical theology that fails to accord the Christian doctrine of creation a central place. In the end, there is nothing for Tillich but God and the manifestations of his *own* being; and "if there is a knowledge of God, it is God who knows himself through man" (*ST*, I, 172). This means also that man, finally, is really divine, "before the fall . . . in an essential . . . unity with God" (*ST*, I, 206)—a unity to which he returns by participation in Christ as the "New Being," the appearance of essential Being under, yet tran-

---

8. Review of H. N. Wieman, *The Growth of Religion*, in *The Journal of Religion*, 20 (1940), 69-72.

scending, the conditions of existence. As for the present situation of estrangement, Tillich leaves the explanation of this to the mystery of freedom.

Tillich's thought, like that of the existentialist philosophers and the neo-orthodox theologians, begins with an "infinite qualitative difference" between God and man. Unlike theirs, however, it ends with that difference all but blotted out.

On Having Nothing to Worship:
The Divine Abyss in Paul Tillich
and Richard Rubenstein

KENNETH HAMILTON

I

Carl J. Armbruster has sought, rather oddly, to counter the suggestion that Paul Tillich's description of God is pantheistic. Father Armbruster writes that Tillich has avoided, "successfully it seems," the pitfall of pantheism. "He repeatedly insists that God is not only the ground of being but also the abyss of being which infinitely surpasses finite beings and thus prevents him from being identified with them."[1]

Now this is odd because, far from being anti-pantheistic, Tillich's view of God as both abyss and ground is fully in line with pantheistic theory. A view of God as the Absolute, in denying that God can be *a* being, must equally deny that God can be the sum total of all being*s*. Indeed, monistic theories of God find it necessary to balance each positive statement made about the Absolute with a corresponding negative one. If God is called the All, he is also to be called the Nothing. If God is called the Ground of being, he is also to be called the Abyss (*Ungrund*).

While the *via negativa* as an approach to God has a long tradition, preoccupation with nothingness or the void is very evident in this century and would seem to be the consequence of a mood of revulsion against Christian theism. Several of the most widely publicized religious viewpoints of the day, though conflicting in much, are united in the belief

---

1. C. J. Armbruster, *The Vision of Paul Tillich* (New York, 1967), p. 151.

Kenneth Hamilton is Professor of Theology at the University of Winnipeg, Manitoba, and is the author of many volumes on theology and the theological dimensions of contemporary literature. Hamilton, in his contribution, faces the question of God's presence in a world of catastrophe, asking whether there is a God to worship and, implicitly, a God to obey. Paul Tillich is his foil, as he examines the meaning of the divine abyss as a substitute for the God whose reality is a union of essence and existence. What is at stake is whether, in the absence of genuine transcendence, there can be a religion of worship and obedience.

that there is nothing to worship. This phenomenon can hardly be ignored by anyone concerned with contemporary witness to the Christian faith, and it may well indicate an area in which Christians should be doing some hard thinking if they are to bring clarity rather than confusion into the present "debate about God." In the present essay I shall look in some detail at Tillich's explication of God as ground and abyss, using Armbruster's comments as a string on which to run my argument. I shall then turn to Richard Rubenstein's understanding of God as holy nothingness, and glance briefly at his comments about the course of religious thinking in the "time of the death of God." From this analysis I hope to indicate the leading implications of the nontheistic stance that turns towards nothingness.

The description of the pantheistic God in terms of polar opposites is to be found even in the most popular expositions of religious monism. An instructive example is to be found in J. D. Salinger's short story "Teddy."[2] Teddy McArdle, the small boy, wonder-hero of this story, explains how, when he was six years old, he "saw that everything was God." His young sister Booper was drinking her milk at the time, and Teddy realized that "all she was doing was pouring God into God, if you know what I mean." But Teddy also explains how he followed this experience by the discovery that it is easy to "get out of the finite dimensions" once you understand that there are no individual objects—"Everybody just *thinks* things keep stopping off somewhere. They don't." Here the positive statement that all things, including milk and sisters, are God, is balanced over against the negative one that none of the things we think we see, including milk and sisters, exists in itself.

The necessity of thus opposing the divinity and the unreality of things arises out of the absurdity of supposing that God can be the All in the sense of being the sum of things. Obviously, God cannot simply be the result obtained by taking a complete inventory of the contents of the universe and adding them together. If God *is* both milk and small sister, he cannot be divided and parceled out among things, found partly in the milk and partly in the girl. Tillich points out that no pantheistic doctrine, in identifying God with nature, asserts him to be "the totality of natural objects," but rather claims that he is "the creative power and unity of nature, the absolute substance which is present in everything" (*ST,* I, 233).[3] Tillich himself distinguishes "being as a whole" from "the whole of being." His metaphors of ground and abyss are used, therefore, to

2. In *Nine Stories* (Boston, 1953).
3. References to *Systematic Theology* (Chicago, Vol. I, 1951; Vol. II, 1957; Vol. III, 1963) appear in the body of the text, using the abbreviation *ST*.

establish the divine in all things on the one hand and the relative unreality of all things on the other. As he says in his "Reply to Interpretation and Criticism," "ground of being" means "the creative source of everything that has being" and "abyss of being" means "the depth in which everything finite disappears."[4]

In regard to the nonultimacy of individual things, Tillich makes the same point as Teddy McArdle, namely, that everybody just *thinks* things keep stopping off somewhere—though he uses slightly more technical language: "Everything we encounter appears to us as real, as true being. But we soon notice that its reality is only transitory."[5] When we try to penetrate beneath the surface "toward the ultimate reality of a thing" we find that "no thing is isolated from all other things." He continues:

> In our search for the "really real" we are driven from one level to another to a point where we cannot speak of any level any more, where we must ask for that which is the ground of all levels, giving them their structure and their power of being. The search for ultimate reality *beyond everything that seems to be real* is the search for being-itself, for the power of being in everything that is.[6]

To the religious consciousness being-itself manifests itself as God. The double-sidedness of God appears in the experience of the holy, which Rudolph Otto described as *tremendum* and *fascinosum,* thus displaying, says Tillich, the experience of the ultimate "in the double sense of that which is the abyss and that which is the ground of man's being" (*ST*, I, 216).

Armbruster has a second argument against attributing pantheism to Tillich:

> But is it possible that, although God is not identified with finite beings, they are identified with him? Against this possibility Tillich erects the bulwark of freedom by which man has the power to contradict even the ground of being.[7]

The bulwark cannot be particularly effective, since Teddy McArdle's pantheistic views embrace the same notion. Teddy complains, "The trouble is most people don't want to see things the way they are. They don't even want to stop getting born and dying all the time they just want new bodies all the time, instead of stopping and staying with God, where it's really

---

4. In C. W. Kegley and R. W. Bretall (ed.), *The Theology of Paul Tillich* (New York, 1959), p. 341.
5. *Biblical Religion and the Search for Ultimate Reality* (Chicago, 1955), p. 12.
6. *Ibid.,* p. 13.
7. *Op. cit.,* p. 151.

nice." Tillich, indeed, does not place the freedom of man "outside" God, since human freedom is grounded in the freedom-destiny polarity of everything that is; and the exercise of freedom leads to the "split in reality between potentiality and actuality" (*ST*, II, 21), which is the "fall" (*ST*, II, 23). Once again, Tillich does not deviate from the traditional pantheistic understanding of human existence as a partial falling away from the divine ground "where it's nice." In the world man knows here and now, being is finite, existence is contradictory, and life is ambiguous (*ST*, I, 81); consequently, man's experience in the here and now is often far from "nice."

What differentiates Tillich and Teddy McArdle is not their pantheism, which they hold in common, but their estimate of the value of the "split in reality" which results in the historical world of space and time. Salinger's Teddy opts for a wholly Eastern form of religion in which the goal is the extinction of desire, making possible a return to the featureless divine all, which is also nothingness. Teddy explains how his reincarnation into his present life-destiny is the result of his failure in his former existence (as an Indian sage) to detach himself from the world of things. "I met a lady and I sort of stopped meditating." He would have had to return to existence anyway, since he was not sufficiently advanced spiritually to have "gone straight to Brahma." "But I wouldn't have had to get incarnated in an *Ame*rican body if I hadn't met that lady," he avers.

Tillich, however, did not find coming to live in America a hindrance to his development as a thinker about spiritual matters. As he mentions in *On the Boundary, An Autobiographical Sketch* (1966), he found it a help towards further insight. But then, he was already committed to a Western outlook. As he sees it (*ST*, II, 87), the crucial distinction between the Eastern and the Western approach to salvation is this: the East, turning away from history, seeks to negate all beings in order to affirm the Ground of Being alone; while the West considers salvation to be the goal of history, and finds religion to be a social rather than a purely individual enterprise.

Note that Tillich does not find the difference between East and West in the understanding of God as such. God is assumed to be truly known, both in Eastern and Western religious thought, as the ground and abyss of being. The parting of the ways lies in whether the split in reality resulting in the material universe and human existence is to be regarded as a wholly unfortunate episode or one with creative possibilities. At this point he believes that Hegel shows us the way to the truth, since the Hegelian dialectic relates the Absolute positively to existence. Thus, he writes of Hegel's dynamic view of "the idea":

The idea becomes concrete; it becomes individualized; it enters into history; it experiences a fate. Here, and nowhere as much as here, the greatness of Hegelian thinking is manifest.[8]

Yet even Hegel, Tillich thinks, stops short of giving full expression to the dynamic of the idea. Although he refuses to regard the Absolute as wholly contained in the concept of an unchanging essence, he allows essence to have the final word.

> In the last moment essence triumphs over existence, completion over infinity, and the static over the dynamic.... The possibility that the whole process gets a new meaning by a new realization of the infinite idea is denied.[9]

So Tillich looks to Jacob Boehme and to Schelling for a more dynamic understanding of the relation of the Absolute to the universe than Hegel's philosophy provides.

Armbruster brings forward a third argument in order to show that Tillich should not be labeled a pantheist:

> Finally, Tillich's God is beyond potentiality and actuality, beyond essence and existence, a doctrine which, although not entirely limpid to the understanding, is hardly pantheistic immanence.[10]

The limpidity to the understanding of Tillich's God, however, would seem to be fully assured by reference to Hegel. In Hegel's thinking philosophy comes to perfection in the Absolute as Idea, which is found in his own *Logic*. It begins with the imperfect understanding of the Absolute as pure being—or pure nothingness, the two being identical—as conceived by the Eleatics. The limitation of early Greek thought is in conceiving being as essence. Similarly, in the history of religions, Hinduism identifies being with essence, and therefore is forced to negate the whole of existence in its view of salvation. But Christianity, displaying the same teaching as that of absolute philosophy in content though not in form, shows itself to be the absolute religion. For Christianity arrives at the view of God as the Concrete Spirit, in which God and humanity are found to be at one. Thus the Hegelian understanding of God is one seeing God to be beyond both essence and existence, including both concepts in its overview of what Tillich calls "the whole process."

That Tillich's quarrel with Hegelianism is not a major one can be seen from the fact that the last lecture he delivered, on the day before his

---

8. *The Interpretation of History* (New York, 1936), p. 166.
9. *Ibid.*, pp. 166f.
10. *Op. cit.*, p. 151.

death, was devoted to showing that the theologian must see the whole history of religions "as a fight for the Religion of the Concrete Spirit."[11] For him the basic truth given insufficient prominence in Hegel is the element of real creativity which Boehme found to be latent in the divine abyss, a creativity to be explained by recognizing a dynamic element in God making the world process necessary. Hence he values the Christian "symbol" of the Logos. The Logos introduces "the element of otherness into the Divine Life without which it would not be life" (*ST*, III, 421). Because of the Logos "the universe of essence is given, the 'immanence of creative potentiality' in the divine ground of being.... In this view the world process means something for God" (p. 422).

II

Father Armbruster's three-point argument against pantheism in Tillich serves quite nicely to guide us to the main features of Tillich's pantheistic doctrine of God the Absolute, as this Absolute is conceived in relation to "the world process." The chief reason for looking in some detail at Tillich's Absolute, however, is to see how, religiously, Tillich deals with its negative aspect, namely, with God as the Abyss of Being.

David Kelsey has discussed how Tillich's theology appears in his sermons. Kelsey points out, "By far, the greatest number of Tillich's published sermons urge us to adopt certain attitudes toward the world as a whole."[12] Very little in the sermons deals directly with what is contained in the Christian Scriptures, and the greater part is taken up with "sermonic proposals of attitudes" based on "one's coming to a sudden insight."[13] Kelsey finds that the sermons exhibit a characteristic pattern. First, they draw attention to our existential state of estrangement and disruption, showing how the result is an experience of meaninglessness. Next, they draw attention "to the passion with which we protest that state of affairs in the name of an overriding concern for wholeness." From the tension generated between the existential predicament and the concern,

> Tillich tries to elicit a new insight, a new perspective or attitude on life as a whole: The world is not simply characterized by existential estrangement; in addition, there is present to me a grasp of eternally valid standards of the good, the true, and the beautiful or I should not have had any basis for my protest or the courage to be concerned in an ultimate way.[14]

---

11. "The Significance of the History of Religions for the Systematic Theologian," in *The Future of Religions* (New York, 1966).
12. *The Fabric of Paul Tillich's Theology* (New Haven, 1952), p. 177.
13. *Ibid.,* p. 188.
14. *Ibid.,* p. 190.

Kelsey's analysis is particularly interesting in showing how Tillich's basic concern is that of pantheistic faith, namely, to relate ourselves rightly to the All, as beings to Being. Tillich is not primarily concerned about the actual teachings of Christianity. It is enough for him that we adopt a religion of the Concrete Spirit enabling us to grasp, from where we stand (concretely) in history, a perspective on "life as a whole" or, in other words, on our relation as finite beings to being-itself. And the conclusion towards which Tillich directs us is that we ought to realize how the existential predicament is one which threatens our being yet does not exclude us from the Ground of our being. Although we are estranged from the Absolute, at all times we can be confident that we have not wholly left the divine Ground.

Tillich stresses, nevertheless, that our confidence is not to be lightly gained. He speaks of Boehme's belief in the unfolding of the divine Abyss. This unfolding of the "light" and "dark" principles in the depth of God contains within itself a threat. Therefore "there can be no comprehension of the essential nature of things except in decision, because the nature of things itself stands in fate and ambiguity."[15] Although this is an early statement, originally published in 1926, the conviction it enshrines continues to appear in subsequent writings. As Kelsey notes, Tillich is always urging us to keep ourselves open for the creative moment in the midst of what seems to be barrenness, when we may act with courage. Kelsey remarks that, on the basis of New Testament teaching, we might have expected Tillich to commend to us love rather than courage. Yet, Tillich's choice of courage rather than love can readily be understood if we consider it in connection with God as Abyss. The Abyss need never do more than threaten us so long as we are certain about our participation in the divine Ground. However, since "the nature of things" is known only in decision, we must meet the threat of "ultimate as Abyss" *decisively* (courageously) in order to know that, in spite of the threat to our being, nothing that has being in us can be annihilated and plunged into non-being.[16]

In *The Courage to Be* Tillich tells us that, in the last resort, nothing can save us except "absolute faith." It is fitting, of course, that faith in an absolute should be termed absolute faith. What is particularly interesting, though, is how Tillich describes this absolute faith. It is faith "in the God above the God of theism"—naturally, because the Absolute cannot be *a* being. In addition, since Tillich's Absolute is beyond essence as well as beyond existence, "the God above God" reached in absolute faith is more

---

15. *The Interpretation of History*, p. 162.
16. Kelsey, *op. cit.*, pp. 179f.

than the pure All which is identical with the pure Nothing. Tillich argues:

The God above the God of theism is not the devaluation of the meanings which doubt has thrown into the abyss of meaninglessness; he is their potential restitution. Nevertheless absolute faith agrees with the faith implied in mysticism in that both transcend the theistic objectivation of a God who is a being. For mysticism such a God is not more real than any finite being, for the courage to be such a God has disappeared in the abyss of meaninglessness with every other value and meaning.[17]

Commenting on the concern of Tillich's sermons to inculcate an attitude towards life as a whole on the basis of human experience in general, Kelsey concludes that Tillich makes no truth-claim that could possibly be confirmed or disconfirmed.[18] This is correct only to the extent that all ultimate commitments cannot be objectively confirmed. The truth-claim Tillich makes is that being lies beyond all possible doubt; even in our trying to doubt being we confirm it. So he refers us constantly to this supreme certainty: we all experience the Ground of our being in that we are compelled to ask the question, "Why is there something and not nothing."[19] This is, as he sees it, sufficient evidence to warrant our taking the step of faith and *deciding* courageously to trust ourselves to the Ground of our being.

Nevertheless, there is a religious estimate involved here which Tillich assumes rather than argues. If we grant that doubt establishes the Ground of our being, it does not follow that we are right in thinking that any of the "meanings" that doubt has thrown into the abyss of meaninglessness will be even potentially restituted. It may well be that maintaining this hope is exactly what must separate us effectively from the Ground of our being.

This viewpoint, indeed, is put forward in an article, from the perspective of Buddhism, by Yoshinori Takeuchi. He quotes from Heidegger the statement of the "ontological problem" of why there is any being and not rather nothing. Then, taking up this statement of the problem common to both Heidegger and Tillich, he criticizes it for being chiefly a philosophical rather than a religious approach to the question.

---

17. *The Courage to Be* (New Haven, 1952), pp. 186f.
18. Kelsey, *op. cit.*, p. 182.
19. See *ST*, I, 163. In his posthumously published lectures *My Search for Absolutes* (New York, 1967) Tillich writes of a conversation with Otto at Marburg in the 1920s, describing how Otto found the experience of the Holy to be "a mystery of man's own being in universal being" driving him to ask the question "Why is there something and not nothing?" (p. 129).

From a religious point of view, the formulation of the problem should rather be the converse: "Why is there any nothing and why not rather being." And with this question we come nearer to the meaning of Buddha's teaching: All created things are impermanent.[20]

Takeuchi argues that for the religious consciousness there can be no salvation in the decision of finite beings to avoid the abyss of meaninglessness. It would appear that "strictly speaking, this decision is meaningless, for all beings, including ourselves and therefore our decisions, are meaningless."[21] The only solution lies in the discovery that "God is at once Being-itself and Absolute Nothingness."[22] Through this discovery alone can come the realization that the Absolute shares in our experience of non-being as well as in our experience of being, leading to the religious "existential awakening" that achieves "emancipation from our conscious and subconscious attachment to the represented 'I' and the objective world."[23]

III

It is the problem of suffering that leads us to God the Absolute Nothingness, so Takeuchi declares. With Tillich the problem of meaninglessness occupies the central place, and this accounts for the relatively small place that the cross occupies in his theology. While he mentions the divine participation in suffering as a symbolic assertion to be made by theology because it is a type of biblical statement (*ST*, II, 175), he takes the primary meaning of the cross to be that the Christ is not separated by "the ultimate negativities of existence" from unity with God (*ST*, II, 158). In contrast with Tillich's confidence that we have a perpetual positive foundation for meaning in God as being-itself, Richard Rubenstein adopts the view that we can know God only as Holy Nothingness. He writes, "Religion is the way in which we share our predicament; it is never the way in which we overcome our condition."[24]

Rubenstein groups himself with those who believe that our era is a time of "the death of God." His point of departure is that of the magni-

---

20. Yoshinori Takeuchi, "Buddhism and Existentialism: The Dialogue between Oriental and Occidental Thought," in Walter Leibrecht (ed.), *Religion and Culture: Essays in Honor of Paul Tillich* (New York, 1959), p. 296.
21. *Ibid.*, p. 297.
22. *Ibid.*, p. 302. Takeuchi adds, "In the case of Absolute Negativity the significance of transcendence and participation is of course different from that in the case of being-itself."
23. *Ibid.*, p. 305.
24. *After Auschwitz: Radical Theology and Contemporary Judaism* (Indianapolis, 1966), p. 263.

tude of the suffering of the Jewish people under Hitler. After Auschwitz it is no longer possible to believe, as both Jews and Christians have believed, that God is the Lord of history, the one who has chosen Israel and whose will is declared in the special destiny of the Jewish people. "The real objections against a personal or theistic God come from the irreconcilability of the claim of God's perfection with the hideous human evil tolerated by such a God."[25] To acknowledge such a God means to assert that Hitler was God's chosen instrument. Also, corroborating this testimony from suffering is the understanding of modern man, in the tradition stretching from Nietzsche to Tillich and Erich Fromm, that a personal God is dead and deserves to die because he opposes human freedom and responsibility.

For his understanding of a God freed from the limitations of theism Rubenstein goes to the Kabalistic doctrine of R. Isaac Luria, a sixteenth-century Palestinian mystic. According to Luria,

The primal Godhead creates both the world and God out of its own nothingness.... It is also of consequence that the first act of creation is a *fall* or an original catastrophe. The ultimate goal of the created world is the reparation of the catastrophe and a return of all things to God as He was in the beginning.[26]

Rubenstein states that such a myth (which, we may note, is strikingly similar to the cosmic myth of the Gnostic Basilides) expresses all that we most need to know in order to express our deepest feelings about our existence. In Tillich's terminology, it opens to us "questions of ultimate concern."

The form of religion which Rubenstein recommends for a "time of the death of God" is a "mystical paganism." The final fact is that "God the Holy Nothingness offers us only dissolution and death as the way out of the dilemmas of earthly existence."[27] Yet, for our present existence, there is given to us a knowledge of our human responsibility for our existence. "God, as the ultimate measure of human truth and human potentiality, calls upon each man to face both the limitations and the opportunities of his finite predicament without disguise, illusion or hope."[28] In the face of the continuing evil in man, Rubenstein rejects all liberal optimism seeking to work for a society which shall one day outgrow its "immature" stage of internal and external strife and put behind it man's inhumanity to man. He sees in religion the need to choose between the "prophetic

---

25. *Ibid.*, p. 86.
26. *Ibid.*, p. 231.
27. *Ibid.*, p. 205.
28. *Ibid.*, p. 240.

moralist" and the "cultic participant." The former hopes to persuade men to be better, while the latter realizes that men are more likely to repeat in each generation their customary failings than they are to be weaned from them. In ritual and the religious practices hallowed by community history he sees the best means both for making life tolerable for the individual and for restraining the excesses of his communal behavior. The "cultic participant" draws on the inherited wisdom of a religious tradition in matters of "ultimate concern" and thence, consciously or unconsciously, derives support for the demands of his day-to-day existence. This attitude towards existence is mystical in that it believes the whole of existence to be oriented towards God the Holy Nothing; and it is pagan in that it sees no transcendent purpose in living—our lives must justify themselves, since each life is destined to be swallowed up in death.

It is evident that Rubenstein's positing of the true God as the Holy Nothing does not lead to any pure existence-fleeing, world-denying vision. Strongly influenced by Tillich, he refers in particular to Tillich's *The Courage to Be*,[29] and takes from both Tillich and Freud insights which he believes to be relevant to "human strivings." Because ritual is also relevant to "the most important human strivings"[30] he considers it to be so important an element in our existence. And, so far is he from embracing the mystical aspiration to experience oneness with the Absolute Nothingness that he can write, "We enter God's Kingdom only when we enter his Holy Nothingness.... I do not desire to enter God's Kingdom, because I prefer the problematics of finitude to their dissolution in the nothingness of eternity."[31]

Although his explicit world-view is monistic, understanding creation as a catastrophe, Rubenstein's religious attitude is to prefer catastrophe to the reparation of catastrophe. Perhaps, after all, he has not departed so far as he thinks from the Old Testament belief in a personal Creator, one who made the world good and in spite of human wickedness still guides it for his good purposes. At any rate, his religious horizons seem to encircle the world of existence as though this world continued to be of decisive importance. His faith lies at the furthest remove from the concept of mystical salvation through the stilling of the will to be, with its consequent discovery of a redemptive compassion that frees one from the ground of sin and death engulfing all earthly being. It is a strange sort of acknowledgement of the Godhead that he makes: knowing where God's Kingdom is to be found, and yet disliking the thought of entering that

29. *Ibid.*, pp. 87, 125, 232.
30. *Ibid.*, p. 233.
31. *Ibid.*, p. 198.

Kingdom. Can it be that he has called his new cosmic deity to occupy the throne of the universe in place of a personal God who has failed men's expectations, only to find that his God, too, is irrelevant to our ultimate concerns? Having decided that God is properly to be described as Holy Nothingness and that the goal of the world is "a return of all things to God as He was in the beginning," Rubenstein can hardly claim, as Tillich does, that the world process means something for God. He calls his attitude one of "tragic acceptance"[32] rather than one of eschatological hope, such as the Christian entertains. Yet, if the created world is a flaw in the ground of nothingness, it is hard to understand what there is to accept. Rubenstein seems bent on denying to historical existence any determinate being, while at the same time clinging to this existence as the sole locus of value and meaning.

IV

In the end Rubenstein, like Tillich, has no message of salvation to communicate, merely an attitude to commend. His "tragic resignation" parallels Tillich's "courage to be," though in a more somber vein. Instead of sharing Tillich's philosophic confidence in our essential participation in the Absolute as the Ground of our being, he is oppressed by our existential predicament. "We are alone in a silent, unfeeling cosmos."[33] Thus his sense of life as a lonely "exile" impels him to call God Nothingness rather than Being, and brings him near to the Buddha's teaching about the impermanence of all created things. Yet he does not follow through this concept with the logic of Eastern religious thought that sees in the revelation of God as Nothingness the compassionate response of the Absolute to our experience of non-being and the beginning of our liberation from suffering through the annihilation of the phenomenal self.

If we start from the presuppositions of a monistic philosophy where God in his dual aspect of being and nothingness (ground and abyss) is the sole reality and the world is the result of God's self-estrangement, then the Eastern view is the only one that faces directly the problem of suffering and promises a hope that is more than tragic resignation. Takeuchi touches on this aspect of the matter when he writes,

> If we were to transcend the personal God (trinity of God), it would not be toward Being-itself, but rather toward Absolute Nothingness. The concept of the Godhead or Being-itself as standing behind the

---

32. *Ibid.*, p. 264.
33. *Ibid.*, p. 225.

trinity of God arises, according to my view, from misunderstanding the personal God as the God of deism.[34]

Takeuchi emphasizes that encounter with suffering awakens us to an awareness of our responsibility for evil, and so compels us to take seriously our sin and guilt. Sin reveals itself as the presentness of death that brings us to despair and leads us to ask for conversion through repentance. Presumably, it is Buddhism's concern with the need of the individual to discover a radical transformation of his existence that causes Takeuchi to say that the personal God cannot be transcended by God as being-itself but only by God as Nothingness. Being-itself, because it stands ultimately secure from the threat of non-being, cannot enter into our predicament to help us. In this connection it is relevant that Tillich believes sin to be best described by the Hegelian term estrangement—the appropriateness of this term residing in its indication that we belong essentially to that from which we are estranged (*ST*, II, 45). Hence for Tillich sin is a negativity presenting a threat which is not finally serious. Takeuchi, on the other hand, states that the fact of sin produces a realization of guilt and condemnation "which does not simply stare at or peep into the threatening non-being."[35]

The price to be paid for transcending the personal God in the God of Absolute Nothingness, however, is the abandonment of created being, the dissolution of the personal self, and a religious discipline calculated to permit us to "get out of the finite dimensions." It is unlikely that those who have learned to view the world as God's creation will ever accept the Eastern world-renouncing vision. We have seen how Rubenstein shrinks back from the worship of Holy Nothingness, preferring a "pagan" understanding of man's place in the world and hoping that life may bring some brief joys to compensate for its unavoidable sorrows. (In keeping with his "paganism" he has nothing to say about sin.) Nevertheless, Rubenstein equally refuses to join in the easy optimism of a Thomas Altizer, a William Hamilton, or a Harvey Cox. The common conviction of these thinkers is, he says, "rooted in the American success story," and that is why they can imagine, contrary to all the evidence, that tragedy lies behind us and a creative future awaits only our strenuous efforts. "Will we have," he asks, "the tragic dignity, the stoicism, and the inner courage to meet the challenge of national disaster?"[36]

Yet a stoic resignation cannot be a lasting solution either, once the

34. *Loc. cit.*, p. 304.
35. *Ibid.*, p. 298.
36. Rubinstein, *op. cit.*, p. 253.

Stoic belief in a rational universe is denied. Where life is perpetually menaced by the omnipotence of death, and where the whole human enterprise lies under the shadow of final annihilation, men must either collapse into despair or reach out to find a faith offering hope beyond tragedy. Humanity confronted with the abyss cannot hold back from asking the religious question, "Why is there any nothing?" and asking it in the personal style of Shakespeare's Juliet, who cries out:

> *Is there no pity sitting in the clouds,*
> *That sees into the bottom of my grief?*
> (*Romeo and Juliet*, III.v.198f.)

Finally, the choice remains: absolute nothingness, or the personal God. The experience of the abyss is acknowledged in Christian faith also, but here the abyss is not seen as one side of God himself. Rather it is the Unholy Nothingness rooted in the dark mystery of evil and separating us from God. T. S. Eliot's *Murder in the Cathedral* expresses this encounter with the Abyss in the chorus of the priests before Becket's martyrdom:

> *...only is here*
> *The white flat face of Death, God's silent servant,*
> *And behind the face of Death the Judgement*
>
> *And behind the Judgement the Void, more horrid than active*
>   *shapes of hell;*
> *Emptiness, absence, separation from God;*
> *The horror of the effortless journey, to the empty land*
> *Which is no land, only emptiness, absence, the Void,*
> *Where those who were men can no longer turn the mind*
> *To distraction, delusion, escape into dream, pretence,*
> *Where the soul is no longer deceived, for there are no objects,*
>   *no tones,*
> *No colours, no forms to distract, to divert the soul*
> *From seeing itself, foully united forever, nothing with nothing,*
> *Not what we call death, but what beyond death is not death,*
> *We fear, we fear. Who shall then plead for me,*
> *Who intercede for me, in my most need?*

As Eliot is careful to insist, the experience of the abyss is one which isolates each person. The priests speak together of the Void; yet each speaks for himself, asking for the salvation that may come to "me, in my most need."

Where the personal God is considered to be *beyond* the abyss, there is a personal center of pity and of saving grace to which each may appeal. So Eliot's priests continue,

Dead upon the tree, my Saviour,
Let not be in vain Thy labour;
Help me, Lord, in my last fear.

That the last fear may be faced and overcome, even if the symbol of that fear be Auschwitz, is the claim of a faith turning towards a personal God. Such is the theme of a recent book which, like Rubenstein's, takes its title from the death camp: Ulrich E. Simon's *A Theology of Auschwitz.* Simon writes:

> Without the great transcendental "Nevertheless" non-existence over-takes being.... An existentialist decision raises no one from the dead. Only He Who Is, God, creates and sustains such an order of things as fulfils the aspiration of the believer's hopes. The God of Auschwitz is not made in the image of our despair, but rather meets our despair by his total Otherness and Reality. He is not the ground of our rotten and rotting being, but the Ground of what we are not and must yet become.... The transcendental "Nevertheless" is, therefore, always known in our repudiation of sin and unreality, which is the first step in faith.[37]

This is no easy escapism, but the only valid alternative to "the cynical thesis that all things remain as they have always been." And Simon's book, like Eliot's priests' chorus, ends on the appeal to the one who is beyond the abyss, and so able to reach us in our time of despair: *"Libera nos, Domine...!"*[38]

---

37. *A Theology of Auschwitz* (London, 1967), pp. 107f.
38. *Ibid.,* p. 160.

Can a Man Bless God?

JAMES DAANE

Although I never sat in a Henry Stob classroom, on many less formal occasions I have sat a learner at his feet. I suspect I have learned as much from him as did any tuition-paying student who sat in his classes. On these informal occasions my taking leave of him was often something like a descent from a mount of theological tranfiguration. He would give my theological thought a new shape and a greater depth. Thanks to the new insights into Christian truth he opened up, I would go my way with a brightened mind and more radiant spirit. Not that he always gained my total agreement. But even when I did not give his thought my total endorsement, his wide vision and Christian wisdom usually tempered and corrected my too narrow and unseeing theological commitments. Even today he is my teacher. When he writes, I read and learn. When he talks theology in my presence, windows open for me on aspects of Christian truth that I have seen only darkly, if indeed at all. I am therefore happy to make this small contribution in acknowledgment of the very considerable contribution that he has made not only to me but to many others. My concern in this essay, which involves both philosophical and theological considerations, is with the question whether Reformed theology is a conditional or unconditional theology. I will use the phrase 'unconditional theology' as shorthand for a theology of a God whose decisions and actions are unconditioned by human decisions and human actions.

* * *

The concept "unconditional" came into common use in connection with the Reformed view of election. Though the concept does not appear in that classic Reformed credal statement of election, the Canons of Dort,

James Daane is professor of theology and ministry at Fuller Theological Seminary. He is the author of The Freedom of God: A Study of Election and Pulpit. *In his essay he discusses the relationship of divine election and God's responsiveness to man. Around this problem cluster such questions as: Does the doctrine of unconditional election entail a doctrine of an unconditioned God? Does God really repent? Does God actually respond to conditions not of his making? Or, can man bless God so truly that God would not be blessed had man not blessed him?*

165

"unconditional election" became theological shorthand for the Reformed rejection of the Arminian contention that God's act of election is contingent on man's act of faith. Within this context, the term unconditional carries a religious meaning expressive of a central feature of Reformed theology.

Because unconditional election is so distinctive of Reformed thought, a tendency arose to regard Reformed theology as a theology of an unconditional God. This tendency was fed both by a general carelessness and by a self-conscious supralapsarianism. The uncomplicated, nontheological lay mind combined with sophisticated theological supralapsarianism to expand the doctrine of unconditional election into a theology of an unconditional God. If election is unconditional, the God who elects, it was thought, must also be unconditional. This mistaken expansion of the idea of unconditionality from its quite proper religious meaning into a theological-philosophical unconditionality has been the source of considerable confusion and error.

Classical, credal Reformed theology is not an unconditional theology. This is evident from the infralapsarian character of Reformed creeds. While supralapsarian theology explains, accounts for, and validates whatever comes to pass in terms of God himself, Reformed creeds, by virtue of their infralapsarian character, define neither election nor reprobation wholly in terms of God. On the contrary, they define both concepts with reference to a fallen, sinful world. Thus, reprobation in Reformed creeds is legitimately accounted for only within and with reference to a sinful context. Reprobation indeed is not conditional in the essentially Arminian sense; a man can no more reprobate himself than elect himself. Only God can elect and only God can reprobate. But in credal Reformed thought, the total meaning of election and reprobation does not lie exclusively in God. The total meaning of each can only be defined within the context of and with reference to the fallen, sinful world, that is, in terms of a context that contains what is other than God and is not God, namely, sin. Thus the Canons of Dort define election as that purpose of God to redeem in Christ some *sinful* men, and as that divine act which chooses such men out of the *fallen* race. It is impossible within the tradition of Reformed creeds to define election solely in terms of God himself, apart from the condition of fallen, sinful reality. In terms of what the Reformed creeds mean by election, God can elect only if that condition obtains which is called a fallen, sinful world. Election in Reformed thought is God's gracious *response* to a sinful world.

In the same sense reprobation, as taught in the Reformed creeds, is conditional. Reprobation is not wholly definable in terms of God. It is, indeed, an act of God; but even God, according to the Reformed creeds, can reprobate only within the context of and in response to a sinful world. The Reformed creeds, accordingly, define reprobation not as a divine act wholly definable in terms of God himself, but as an act of God which can only be properly defined in reference to a sinful condition—to that which is not God, and is indeed wholly foreign to his nature. Hence reprobation in the Reformed tradition is conditional; it is God's response to what is not God, to a fallen, sinful creation, and is thus regarded as an act of divine *justice.*

Since justice is not, strictly speaking, an attribute of God but rather that form of judgment in which the holiness of God responds to the reality of sin, reprobation as a *responsive* act of God is not an unconditional act. It is, like election, conditional precisely because, like election, it is divine *response* to a concrete condition, to something other than God.

The concept of the sovereignty of God has had a large place in the Reformed theological vocabulary. Divine sovereignty, too, is a relational concept, meaningless except in reference to that over which God is sovereign. Sovereignty is how God responds to that which is other than himself; hence, it has meaning only in reference to this "other." God is not sovereign in terms of himself, as though the meaning of the concept could be defined wholly in terms of what God is in himself. For all its insistence on the sovereignty of God and for all its usage of the economic trinity (in contrast to the ontological trinity), Reformed theology does not urge that the Father is sovereign over the Son, or the Son over the Spirit. God is rather said to be sovereign over that which, lying outside himself, is other than himself. Thus God is not unconditionally sovereign, but sovereign over conditions external to himself. Only within the sphere and with reference to these conditions is God sovereign, and only within that limitation does the term carry any meaning at all.

Absolute unconditionality is a philosophical concept, not a religious, biblical one. The Absolute of the philosophers is not the God of the Bible. The Absolute of the philosophers is, by definition, that which accounts for everything other than itself in terms of itself. Aristotle's Absolute is the Unmoved Mover. In itself the Absolute is unmoved and unmovable. As such it is unconditional. It hears no prayers; it has no pity for man; it neither creates nor re-creates. How, we ask Aristotle, can the Unmoved move? The best Aristotle can do is to regard the Absolute as the (fourfold) cause of all that is conditional and relative, of all that is not Absolute. Thus the Absolute is regarded as the cause which causes all things but is itself wholly unaffected by what it effects. The unconditional Absolute of the philosophers is not the God of the Bible, and Reformed theology is not the unconditional theology of such an unconditional God. The God of the Bible can be affected by what lies external to him. The wrath of God against sin is clear and fearful evidence of this.

Credal Reformed theology is infralapsarian. The *distinctive* mark of infralapsarian theology is its insistence that God's redemptive action is a response to the fallen, sinful condition. It is a theology of response and, therefore, a conditional theology. Everything that is meant by God's salvific action is a gracious divine response to the sinful, death-ridden world. For all its recognition of the sovereignty of the gracious God, classic Reformed theology was unwilling to *account for* mankind's fall. This basically distinguishes it from supralapsarianism, for which all things, including the fall, are accounted for in terms of God himself. Infralapsarian theology is, therefore, essentially incompatible with supralapsarianism which, when consistent, insists that God as he is in himself is the explanation, the cause of whatever comes to pass. Infralapsarian theology regards the contention that God is the cause of sin as blasphemous, and eschews as rationalism the view that regards God as the rationale for all that is and all that occurs.

Some Reformed theologians have defended their supralapsarianism by pointing out that there were many supralapsarian theologians at the Synod of Dort. The fact that they were not read out of the Reformed churches, as the Arminians were, appears to carry greater significance to supralapsarians than the fact that the Canons of Dort are an instrument of infralapsarian theology. The real significance of the presence of eminent supralapsarian delegates at the Synod of Dort lies in the fact that the Canons in one, perhaps two, places bear the marks of compromising concessions to their presence. No doubt this contributed to the (remarkably) unanimous adoption of the Canons by the Synod. It also made the Reformed churches somewhat vulnerable to the pressures of later supralapsarians. In 1903 the Synod of Utrecht granted tolerance to supralapsarians, permitting them residence within the Dutch Reformed Churches. This concession, however, was in fact an act of credal compromise, made to restore peace to churches deeply disturbed by a supra-infralapsarian controversy.

Some supralapsarians used their newly gained toleration in the manner of the proverbial camel permitted to put his nose in the tent. Supralapsarians in our day often boldly assert that God is the "source," the "ultimate cause," the "creator" of sin. They insist that God is an unconditional God, that authentic Reformed theology is supralapsarian, that infralapsarian theology grazes on the edge of Arminianism, that supralapsarianism is both true to Reformed infralapsarian creeds *and* a refined development of their deepest motifs. Those critical of the unconditional supralapsarian theology of an unconditional God are often regarded as persons who have lost all their defenses against Arminianism, or, indeed, capitulated to it. Any insistence on the biblical teachings of God's mutability as regards judgment, that is, his change of mind or repentance, or of the divine pathos shown in the tears of Jesus, or of prayer truly answered, so that it becomes an instrument that changes things; any insistence that Christian truth (the gospel) is not eternal truth but truth that became true and is only true by its occurrence; any insistence that it is not God as he is in himself that is the explanation and rationale for whatever is and happens; any insistence that our knowledge of God only obtains in and is qualified by God in relationship to what is not God, that is, in relationship to the world—all of these are regarded as surrendering the Reformed faith and accepting a conditional God who really is not sovereign, and thus endorsing a world run by chance, whose future is open-ended.

The question of conditional or unconditional theology is a question of how God is related to the world; and that in turn is a question of the nature of our knowledge of God. According to Calvin, all true knowledge of God is an ingredient of our true knowledge of man (and thus of his world), and all true knowledge of man is an ingredient of a true knowledge of God. In the thought of G. C. Berkouwer, this understanding of our knowledge of God is called the "principle of correlation"; one can know God and understand the gospel only within the terms of faith in the gospel. Any knowledge of God and of man sought outside the boundaries of faith is a form of theological speculation.

If this view of our knowledge of God is a proper view, then our knowledge of God is conditional and our theology is a conditional theology; that is, it only obtains, and thus is only valid, within the fact and the nature of God's relationship to the world of created and fallen reality. A conditional knowledge is that kind of knowledge that is contingent upon God's relationship to the world, and thus not a knowledge of God as he is in himself, and not a knowledge of a world whose clue lies in the nature of God himself.

One of the deepest sources of unconditional theology, a theology in which God is not conditioned or affected by any condition because he himself is regarded as the cause of every condition, lies in the period of seventeenth-century Reformed scholasticism. Reformed scholasticism identified God's decree, and thus all that happens in time and history, with God's essence. Francis Turretin urged that God's decree exists in him *essentially* and not, as he says, *accidentally*. The decree is not something added to God, that is, the decree is not something that is not God, for, if it were, Turretin says, it would bespeak change, something new. The decree, he contended, is "nothing other than the divine essence itself, as it is known by God." Thus the divine decree is not the product of the divine freedom, but the form and content of the divine essence, as it is also the form and content, he says, of the divine self-knowledge. In this doctrine of God lies the deepest source of the contention that Reformed theology is an unconditional theology.

This identification of the divine decree with the divine essence has played a long and persistent role in much Reformed theology. Because of this deification of the decree, the decree took on the attributes of God himself. Thus it was urged that the divine decree is a single decree, not with reference to other decrees, but with reference to the nature of God's essence. Since the divine essence has no parts, and since God does not think discursively, the decree has no parts or moments. Since God is eternal, the decree is eternal in the same essential and necessary sense in which God is eternal. Thus the idea of an unconditioned God gave rise to a Reformed theology of the unconditional.

This identification of the divine decree with the divine essence, with all its serious consequences, has played a long and persistent role in much Reformed thought; and its influence lingers on into the present, where it is seen especially in supralapsarian theology. For if God's decree is identical with his essence, if its content is identical with God's self-knowledge of his essence, if God's will is merely the volitional form of his essence, then it surely follows that authentic theology is a theology of the unconditional, and that all that is and all that happens necessarily is and necessarily happens, having its cause and its rationale in terms of God's necessary nature and being. Such a God could rightly be regarded as an unconditional God. But God is only that kind of unconditional God if his decree is a mode of his essence.

*   *   *

Should we think of God's relationship to the world in terms of his decree or plan? Not if we conceive of the decree as issuing solely from the divine *thought*. Indeed, God did not decree thoughtlessly; but the decree is more than thought, being an act of the divine freedom. Hence God's relationship to the world cannot be described in terms of a decree whose content is exhaustively and comprehensively definable in terms of rationality, even if this be God's rationality. For the same reason God's relationship to the world cannot be defined in terms of a plan that rationally determines whatsoever comes to pass, so that whatsoever happens is, if not wholly moral, at least wholly rational. What is totally lacking in such conceptions of God's relationship to the world is the element of divine freedom.

That God should have a decree that relates to both creation and re-creation is a cause for wonder, surprise, and praise. Such a decree bespeaks something new, something Turretin called an "addition" to God, an addition not to be rejected precisely because God's decree is not God but the product of his freedom. Such a decree is indeed rational, not irrational, but as an act of God's freedom it is more than rational and thereby creates that dimension of wonder and surprise which belongs to the fabric of Christian worship and praise.

What has been said about God's decree must also be said about God's creation of the world, and about his re-creation of the world in its sinful condition. Both are rational, not irrational, divine acts, but both are acts of his freedom. In creating the world God *became* a creator. As respects God's necessary essence and being, this is something new. In becoming the Creator or, if you will, the Father or maker of the world, God, being by nature a Father, did not violate his nature. Nonetheless, that God can become something that he was not, something that is not a mere mode of his divine essence, but something new, the Father of creation, is a tremendous wonder; moreover, that God became the Creator in order to bestow divine beneficences on man is the wonder of grace.

And what is here said about God's free act of becoming our creator could be raised to its highest exponent in an attempt to describe God's becoming the Father of our Lord Jesus Christ and our Father through him. The God who became the God of Abraham, Isaac, and Jacob, the God who was in Christ reconciling the world to himself, is the God who created conditions and in Christ entered into and identified with the man-wrought sinful condition of the fallen world. Such a God is himself involved in conditionality; he is provoked to wrath by man's sin; he responds in pity to a death-ridden world; he hears and responds to the cries of the needy; he becomes the Father of the fatherless; he strives with men, restraining their sinful resistance; he hears and responds to the prayers of men; he is the God of those "who receive not because they ask not."

This God of the Bible is not unresponsive to finite human conditions. His freedom does not consist in being free from the touch of what is not God, nor is his immutability a change of relationship to the world that involves no change in God, as Protestant scholasticism maintained.

The God of the Bible creates conditions and responds to them both in a sinless and in a fallen creation. Judgment and grace both attest to this. Both judgment and grace, however, slip away in the measure in which a theologian attempts to define God as absolute without reference to such conditionality as constitutes a created, and no less, a sinful, redeemed world.

Reformed theology is a conditional theology. It sees election and reprobation, judgment and grace, indeed the incarnation itself, as God's free response to the condition of the fallen world. Indeed, it even understands God's free creation of the world as an act of divine self-giving to man through which God can share himself with man. In the classical Reformation tradition God is said to have created man so that man may "enjoy" God, "know" God, "love" God, and "live with Him in eternal blessedness," and that God may be "glorified" by man forever. Classical Reformed theology knows nothing of a God who is the Absolute who accounts for the conditional but is not himself involved in the work of his hands, a notion that gives supralapsarianism its most distinctive feature but is more Aristotelian than biblical. Those who define the God of the Bible as the Unconditional Absolute have lingered too long at the waterholes of Western rationalism.

God is, indeed, related to the world in terms of his decree. But this decree is the product of his freedom, not a form of his essence. It is, in biblical thought, a dynamic, responsive, redemptive decree, not to be confused with a general plan that accounts for everything. The character of this decree is drawn in the description of the enthronement of Israel's messianic king in Psalm 2 and indicated by Paul when he speaks of God's "eternal purpose which he purposed in Christ Jesus our Lord."

Reformed theology must continue its battle against Arminian theology with its God who can save only on the condition that the sinner is willing. But in a zeal to protect its own best heritage against Arminianism it must not naively use concepts that more aptly describe the absolute of the philosophers than the God of the Bible. Let the Reformed churches continue to speak of unconditional election but not without recalling that what they here mean by unconditional derives from their historic controversy with Arminianism, not from Aristotle. Reformed men must not unwittingly turn God into a static Absolute, the divine freedom into the divine essence, nor divine sovereignty into a principle of necessity. To do so would be to destroy the biblical dynamics of their own rich Reformed theological tradition, and thereby make Arminianism an increasingly attractive option and give modern process theologians a greater excuse for being.

*   *   *

The terms 'conditional' and 'unconditional' can both be properly used in describing the God of Reformed theology. When so used they do not diminish the force of the biblical teaching that in freedom God *became* Creator and re-Creator, a God who both creates conditions and overcomes sinful conditions, a God who responds to conditional, contingent reality in judgment and in grace. In the biblical view God hears and responds to the cries of the needy, and is indeed so involved in conditional, contingent reality that he can be both sinned against and, no less, blessed by man in such a way that it makes a difference to God himself. But a God who is unconditional because he himself accounts for all conditions by virtue of his essence or decree is a God who cannot hear, let alone answer prayer.

On God and Evil

DAVID H. FREEMAN

I remember Henry Stob, my friend and teacher, saying in the classroom that a philosopher who cuts himself off from reality by doubt will never be able to return. I would like to suggest that language that is ripped away from its moorings, from where it was originally anchored, may founder on the shoals of confusion.

In this essay I wish to examine an oft-repeated thesis: that the existence of inexplicable evil virtually precludes that God exists.[1] I shall first try to show that the expression 'the existence of inexplicable evil,' far from implying anything about God, has no clear meaning in this and similar contexts. And I shall seek to examine a context where the expression is at home—within the framework of the biblical text. Here the expression does not imply that God does not exist but the use of such a term as 'evil' derives its intelligibility from a context where God is presupposed.

The assumption that the presence of inexplicable evil in the universe virtually precludes the existence of God makes sense if a sense can be given to the term 'evil' that would render God's existence impossible, or at least so improbable that it would require a superstitious credibility to believe in him. For those who deny God and do not use the term 'evil' there is no problem. There is no need to reconcile God and evil if the reality of both is simply denied. It is our contention, however, that the denial of God at least presents difficulties to those who would still use the word 'evil.' The nonexistence of God may imply the nonexistence of evil. At the very least anyone who would use the term 'evil' while denying God must give this term an intelligible sense. To hold that the presence

---

1. Cf. Michael Scriven, *Primary Philosophy* (New York: McGraw Hill, 1966), p. 158.

David H. Freeman is Professor of Philosophy at the University of Rhode Island, and has written several books on the philosophy of religion. Freeman, in this essay, argues that, far from rendering the existence of God doubtful, evil can be understood only on the assumption of God's existence. The word 'evil,' he contends, can have a moral meaning only if a God with moral will and judgment exists; to deny God is virtually to deny the existence of evil as a moral category.

of evil is incompatible with the existence of God requires that the word 'evil' have a comprehension and an extension, that it both connote and denote. To understand what any term means, we need first discover how people use it; we must look to see whether the term functions in a way that adequately conveys sense, that it describes what it purports to describe, that it is applicable, is at home, in the context in which it is used. Does the term 'evil' clarify, does it convey meaning, does it have an intelligible sense, or is it a mere sound that delights or offends the ear? Is it, perhaps, a furious sound, signifying nothing, but nevertheless capable of sending terrifying doubts up our spines?

Consider again the sentence: *The presence of inexplicable evil virtually precludes the existence of God.*

I shall restrict my analysis to instances in which 'God' refers to the biblical God, and I shall not consider cases where 'God' may be used to refer to an all-encompassing, impersonal absolute which makes evil to be an illusory consequence of regarding things and events as independent of that one reality. I shall not consider that sense of 'evil' which refers to the perception by an individual self-consciousness that there exist different things, this perception allegedly arising out of desire and cravings. My concern is with a notion of evil that is supposedly incompatible with God who in the beginning created the heavens and the earth.

The term 'evil' is sometimes used to refer to what is detrimental to or destructive of certain living organisms. Evil may refer to the suffering experienced by both human and nonhuman organisms, and it may also refer to the decay or disintegration of what appears to be order within the inorganic realm. Happenings such as floods and earthquakes may be regarded as evil, since such events may produce physical pain in animals and both physical pain and mental anguish in man. Bacteria, viruses, cells that grow in such a way as to produce cancer are regarded as somehow unnatural, as producing pain and ultimately death, and therefore as being evil.

Now whatever gave rise to the notion that earthquakes, floods, tidal waves, volcanic eruptions, and plague-spreading bacteria are evil? To live and to die, to suffer pain and to be free of pain, are simply what is there, are what happens. A person may not like this world as it is, but it is not his. He does not own it, nor can he control it. He did not make it. Man can shake his fist at the stars; shout in defiance at the waves; whimper and cry when he feels pain; mourn at the thought of his own impending death; weep at the death of other lumps of clay to which he has become attached. But why does he call such happenings evil? Why does he call them unnatural, and act as if they were abnormal? Where does he get the notion of what is normal, of what is not evil?

There is a context where 'evil' is often applied to such happenings. The notion of disorder in our world, of physical suffering and death, of the unharmonious and the unnatural, of physical evil, has a use within the Scriptures. In the beginning God created the heavens and the earth. What he made was good. We have, at least to a large extent, learned to use the term 'evil' in the context of biblical faith. Physical suffering, death, and disorder are not at home, do not belong in God's creation. Within the Scriptures physical evil is connected with man's sin. It is God who ultimately uses pain, suffering, and disaster to punish our wickedness.

> I am the Lord, and there is none else, there is no God beside me....
> I form the light, and create darkness: I make peace and create evil:
> I the Lord do all these things (Isa. 45:5,7).

We get what we deserve:

> Wherefore doth a living man complain, a man for the punishment of his sins? (Lam. 3:39).
> . . . shall there be evil in the city and the Lord hath not done it? (Amos 3:6).

Evil—*ra* in Hebrew; *kakos, poneros, phaulos* in Greek—refers to what is the disagreeable, the offensive, to what is hurtful. Suffering and pain are not necessarily connected in individual cases, but the presence of evil in the world is ultimately due to God's using pain and death as a punishment of wrongdoing.

Ezekiel told Israel that because of their abominations God would "send upon them the evil arrows of famine . . . for their destruction" (Ezek. 5:6). Paul said that the whole of creation groans and waits for the redemption of God. Certain moderns who learned to use the term 'evil' in a context where evil is God's punishment for sin, now use this very punishment as an objection to God. "God punishes, therefore, there is no God" is indeed a strange argument. What we know about God from Scripture is that man's sin is punished by physical evil. To disbelieve the Scriptures, to be an unbeliever is, for the Psalmist, to be a fool; to speak of certain physical events as evil without giving the word 'evil' a sense is to speak nonsense.

Evil is not inexplicable within the biblical context; it is the consequence of sin. To what does the term refer in a context that denies God as revealed in Scripture? The term 'evil 'may still be used to denote such events as earthquakes, floods, pain, and death, but there is no reason to regard such events as being unnatural, as being abnormal. To die is the 'norm'; to live is the exception.

The world is a meaningless, purposeless sea of absurdities, a chance combination of unplanned happenings devoid of any significance except what we for a brief time project, ascribe to it; a tale told by idiots, signifying nothing. "Evil" is what Adam and his kinfolk do not like. No one except a sadist enjoys pain. But neither likes nor wishes, neither beliefs nor desires, neither longings nor strivings can change a single hair on our head, let alone preclude the existence of the Almighty. If 'evil' refers to what we find unpleasant and nasty, to what causes us pain, the term is simply a way of expressing our feelings, and feelings are simply auto-biographical "facts" that have no bearing on anything beyond our own subjective emotional states.

One may not believe in the God revealed in Scripture, but in the biblical context evil in the physical sense is not inexplicable. Instead of virtually precluding God, the notion of physical evil presupposes a world that God has made and controls.

The term 'evil' may be used in a second sense when it is said that a particular person is evil or that a certain act is evil. Here the term is used in a moral sense to describe an act which ought not to have been performed or to describe someone whose character we find reprehensible.

Now there have been other cultures, other times, other places where the word 'evil' was used in a moral sense without referring to man in his relation to God and to God's moral law. However, where the biblical tradition has exerted a strong influence, our very notion of moral evil has, at least to a large extent, grown out of a situation in which God as revealed in the Scriptures is presupposed. For centuries it was believed that the moral law is written in the hearts of men, that man's awareness of right and wrong is due to what man is, to his being a creature, an image-bearer of God. Some people still believe this and others do not; but those who reject God and his moral laws still have—at least to a large extent—based their moral principles on the belief that God said "Thou shalt not."

Nietzsche saw that business would not be conducted as usual after "God's funeral"; Sartre has seen as much. Our century has marched beyond good and evil; it has sought cleansing in the showers of Dachau, while dancing to the pitter-patter of falling bombs; it has waltzed with the new order, where pride, hate, and war replace humility, love, and peace.

Moral evil is clearly defined within the context of the biblical text. Here moral evil arises from man's sinful inclinations. God is in no way responsible for it; God is holy, removed from all depravity.

Let no one say when he is tempted, "I am tempted by God"; for God cannot be tempted with evil, and he himself tempts no one; but each person is tempted when he is lured and enticed by his own desire. Then desire when it has conceived gives birth to sin; and sin when it is full-grown brings forth death (James 1:13-15).

The entire saving activity, the redemption accomplished on the cross, is God's way of dealing with the internal malignity of sin. Moral evil is ultimately direct enmity against God, despising his goodness, expressing contempt of his omniscience, rejecting his love, repudiating his justice and power. To transgress against God's law, to fail to love and obey God, leads to transgressions against our neighbors, to a lack of neighbor love.

Moral evil within the biblical context has a clearly defined sense. It refers to man's failure to keep God's laws; moral "evil" here presupposes God; it does not in any way preclude his existence.

What sense can the term 'moral evil' have outside of a context where God is presupposed? There are three possible sources of moral standards: God, man, and physical nature. If God is eliminated, man and nature alone remain. Moral standards can then be derived from man or nature. But it is difficult to see how nature can help. Neither rocks, rivers, rattlesnakes, planets, plants, nor even little fish can tell man what he ought to do. What is "nature"? The word is sometimes hypostatized and used as though it referred to something other than sticks and stones. "Mother Nature," indeed! To formulate a standard as to what ought to be done requires nothing less than a person.

Unless nature is personified when God is rejected, man alone is the standard of what is right and wrong. Since men differ in what they want, there are then as many possible standards as there are human differences. The terms 'right' and 'wrong' may then be used to refer to the feelings that a particular person has, to what pleases an individual or a group of individuals.

If there is no God, everything is possible in a moral sense. There are then no objective nonhuman standards. Of course, it is still possible to act to some degree as if there was a holy and righteous God. In business, honesty may still be the best policy. Stealing, lying, murder, rape, and pillage are options; but if stability is preferred to chaos, such options will be rejected by most people most of the time. When a particular individual or group of individuals persists in acting contrary to the norms accepted by the majority, or by those in power, sanctions may be imposed against the nonconformists. To say that Eichmann and Hitler were wrong, then, simply means that they violated the usually professed standards of Western society. To say that what they did was morally evil is simply to express strong disapproval. *We* do not like what they did. Killing innocent people evokes a feeling of revulsion in us. Moral evil is what certain people do not like. 'Moral evil' like 'physical evil' refers in the final analysis to emotive states; moral terms are emotive vehicles enabling us to express our feelings, enabling us to move freely up and down the scale of our own human values. The world we live in, on this view, has no plan or purpose; there are only men, "idiots" strutting like players engaged in a meaningful game of Scrabble, forming words like 'good,' 'bad,' 'right,' 'wrong,' 'evil'; deceiving themselves into thinking that such words refer to some objective order, to something other than their own sentiments. Thus, sometimes it would appear that to say there is no God is to become foolish, to talk nonsense, by disguising our feelings in terms which purport to be about something other than feelings.

On the assumption that there is no God the conclusion that should be reached is that the intelligibility of the term 'evil' is virtually precluded, except as a synonym for expressions of intense feelings of disapproval. Instead of *evil* precluding God's existence the denial of God reduces physical evil—pain and death—to a normal happening and moral evil to the study of psychology and sociology, to the study of emotive states and group behavior.

What, then, lies behind such cavils? Why would anyone want to say that pain, death, and men like Hitler virtually preclude the existence of God?

There is an answer that is intelligible within the context of Scripture. To raise such an objection is an act of rebellion. It is to call the Almighty into judgment. Now, I suppose that a Platonist might censure the behavior of the gods in terms of some external standard that even the gods ought to obey. And for a while Job and his friends engaged in such speculations. But Job kept silent after God set him straight.

> Then the Lord answered Job out of the whirlwind: "Who is this that darkens counsel by words without knowledge? Gird up your loins like a man, I will question you, and you shall declare to me. Where were you when I laid the foundation of the earth? Tell me, if you have understanding . . . " (Job 38:1-4).

> "Shall a faultfinder contend with the Almighty? He who argues with God, let him answer it.... Will you even put me in the wrong? Will you condemn me that you may be justified? (Job 40:2, 8).

Job was not a philosopher, or rather he was a good philosopher in that he at least knew when to keep silent.

"Behold, I am of small account; what shall I answer thee? I lay my hand on my mouth" (Job 40:4).

The righteous do not suffer; there are no righteous. All have sinned and come short of God's glory.

To call the Almighty to account, to bring the ways of God to judgment, is to introduce contradictory premises by first disguising them as questions that need to be answered, as objections that need to be met. Job believed in the God who made heaven and earth, in a God whose very nature was just: to question God is to deny God. It is to accept and to reject him at the same time; to believe, to trust, to love, and to serve the Almighty, and not to believe, not to trust, not to love and not to serve the Almighty— to believe and not to believe at the same time.

To question the ways of God, as if there were some standard by which God can be judged, is to fall into the trap laid by the serpent; it is to try to be like God; to presume to judge God. "If we had made the world, it would be a lot different." A modest admission, indeed. If evil is what simply happens and what some men don't like, it is difficult to see how man's likes or dislikes can preclude the existence of anything.

The sentence 'The existence of inexplicable evil virtually precludes the existence of God' can be rewritten in two ways: (1) 'The existence of what some men don't like virtually precludes the existence of God,' and (2) 'The existence of God's punishment for sin virtually precludes the existence of God.' The first of these is hardly plausible, while the second is scarcely intelligible.

To deny God is virtually to deny evil; to believe in the God revealed in Scripture renders evil intelligible, and offers that hope which culminates in knowing that all things work together for good to them that love God, to them who are called according to his purpose.

When you hear the term 'evil' thrown around, remind yourself where you first learned to use it. Was it in the Scriptures? If so, go back there. This is where the term is at home. Here you will find other words, too, words like forgiveness, redemption, goodness, mercy, and love. Within this context, such words do have a sense: they point to what God has done for those who love and serve him.

God Everlasting

NICHOLAS WOLTERSTORFF

All Christian theologians agree that God is without beginning and without end. The vast majority have held, in addition, that God is *eternal,* existing outside of time. Only a small minority have contended that God is *everlasting,* existing within time.[1] In what follows I shall take up the cudgels for that minority, arguing that God as conceived and presented by the biblical writers is a being whose own life and existence is temporal.

The biblical writers do not present God as some passive factor within reality but as an agent in it. Further, they present him as acting within *human* history. The god they present is neither the impassive god of the Oriental nor the nonhistorical god of the Deist. Indeed, so basic to the biblical writings is their speaking of God as agent within history that if one viewed God as only an impassive factor in reality, or as one whose agency does not occur within human history, one would have to regard the biblical speech about God as at best one long sequence of metaphors pointing to a reality for which they are singularly inept, and as at worst one long sequence of falsehoods.

More specifically, the biblical writers present God as a redeeming God. From times most ancient, man has departed from the pattern of responsibilities awarded him at his creation by God. A multitude of evils has followed. But God was not content to leave man in the mire of his misery. Aware of what is going on, he has resolved, in response to man's sin and its resultant evils, to bring about renewal. He has, indeed, already been acting in accord with that resolve, centrally and decisively in the life, death, and resurrection of Jesus Christ.

What I shall argue is that if we are to accept this picture of God as

---

1. The most noteworthy contemporary example is Oscar Cullmann, *Christ and Time* (Eng. tr., Philadelphia, 1950).

Nicholas Wolterstorff is Professor of Philosophy at Calvin College. He is the author of several articles in professional journals and a recent book, On Universals. *He has also written and lectured extensively on the Christian approach to cultural issues. In "God Everlasting" he carries forward the project of "de-Hellenizing" Christian theology by arguing, on philosophical and biblical grounds, that God is not eternal but temporal.*

acting for the renewal of human life, we must conceive of him as ever-lasting rather than eternal. God the Redeemer cannot be a God eternal. This is so because God the Redeemer is a God who *changes*. And any being which changes is a being among whose states there is temporal succession. Of course, there is an important sense in which God as presented in the Scriptures is changeless: he is steadfast in his redeeming intent and ever faithful to his children. Yet, *ontologically*, God cannot be a redeeming God without there being changeful variation among his states.

If this argument proves correct the importance of the issue here confronting us for Christian theology can scarcely be exaggerated. A theology which opts for God as eternal cannot avoid being in conflict with the confession of God as redeemer. And given the obvious fact that God is presented in the Bible as a God who redeems, a theology which opts for God as eternal cannot be a theology faithful to the biblical witness.

Our line of argument will prove to be neither subtle nor complicated. So the question will insistently arise, why have Christian theologians so massively contended that God is eternal? Why has not the dominant tradition of Christian theology been that of God everlasting?

Our argument will depend heavily on taking with seriousness a certain feature of temporality which has been neglected in Western philosophy. But the massiveness of the God eternal tradition cannot, I am persuaded, be attributed merely to philosophical oversight. There are, I think, two factors more fundamental. One is the feeling, deep-seated in much of human culture, that the flowing of events into an irrecoverable and unchangeable past is a matter for deep regret. Our bright actions and shining moments do not long endure. The gnawing tooth of time bites all. And our evil deeds can never be undone. They are forever to be regretted. Of course, the philosopher is inclined to distinguish the mere fact of temporality from the actual pattern of the events in history and to argue that regrets about the latter should not slosh over into regrets about the former. The philosopher is right. The regrettableness of what transpires in time is not good ground for regretting that there is time. Yet where the philosopher sees the possibility and the need for a distinction, most people have seen none. Regrets over the pervasive pattern of what transpires within time have led whole societies to place the divine outside of time—freed from the "bondage" of temporality.

But I am persuaded that William Kneale is correct when he contends that the most important factor accounting for the tradition of God eternal within Christian theology was the influence of the classical Greek philosophers on the early theologians.[2] The distinction between eternal being and everlasting being was drawn for the first time in the history of thought by Plato (*Timaeus* 37-38), though the language he uses is reminiscent of words used still earlier by Parmenides. Plato does not connect eternity and divinity, but he does make clear his conviction that eternal being is the highest form of reality. This was enough to influence the early Christian theologians, who did their thinking within the milieu of Hellenic and Hellenistic thought, to assign eternity to God. Thus was the fateful choice made.

A good many twentieth-century theologians have been engaged in what one might call the dehellenization of Christian theology. If Kneale's contention is correct, then in this essay I am participating in that activity. Of course, not every bit of dehellenization is laudatory from the Christian standpoint, for not everything that the Greeks said is false. What is the case, though, is that the patterns of classical Greek thought are incompatible with the pattern of biblical thought. And in facing the issue of God everlasting versus God eternal we are dealing with the fundamental pattern of biblical thought. Indeed, I am persuaded that unless the tradition of God eternal is renounced, fundamental dehellenizing will perpetually occupy itself in the suburbs, never advancing to the city center. Every attempt to purge Christian theology of the traces of incompatible Hellenic patterns of thought must fail unless it removes the roadblock of the God eternal tradition. Around this barricade there are no detours.

I

Before we can discuss whether God is outside of time we must ask what it would be for something to be outside of time. That is, before we can ask whether God is eternal we must ask what it would be for something to be eternal. But this in turn demands that we are clear on what it would be for something to be a temporal entity. We need not be clear on all the features which something has by virtue of being temporal—on all facets of temporality—but we must at least be able to say what is necessary and sufficient for something's being in time.

For our purposes we can take as the decisive feature of temporality the exemplification of the temporal ordering-relations of precedence, succession, and simultaneity. Unless some entities did stand to each other in one or the other of these relations, there would be no temporal reality. Conversely, if there is temporal reality then there are pairs of entities whose

2. William Kneale, "Time and Eternity in Theology," *Proceedings of the Aristotelian Society* (1961).

members stand to each other in the relation of one occurring before (precedence) or one occurring after (succession) or one occurring simultaneously with (simultaneity) the other.

We must ask in turn what sort of entity is such that its examples can stand to each other in the relations of precedence, succession, and simultaneity. For not every sort of entity is such. The members of a pair of trees cannot stand in these relations. The golden chain tree outside my back door neither occurs before nor after nor simultaneously with the shingle oak outside my front door. Of course, *the sprouting of the former* stands in one of these relations to *the sprouting of the latter;* and so too does *the demise of the latter* to *the demise of the former.* But the trees themselves do not. They do not occur at all.

We have in this example a good clue, though, as to the sort of entity whose examples can stand in the relations of precedence, succession, and simultaneity. It is just such entities as *the demise of my golden chain tree* and *the sprouting of my shingle oak.* It is, in short, what I shall call events that stand in these relations.

As I conceive of an event, it consists in something's actually having some property, or something's actually performing some action, or something's actually standing in some relation to something. Events as I conceive them are all actual occurrences. They are not what *can have* occurrences. They are, rather, themselves occurrences. Furthermore, as I conceive of events, there may be two or more events consisting in a given entity's having a given property (or performing a given action). For example, my golden chain tree flowered last spring and is flowering again this spring. So there are two events each consisting in the flowering of my golden chain tree. One began and ended last year. The other began and will end this year.

Such events as I have thus far offered by way of example are all temporally limited, in the sense that there are times at which the event is not occurring. There are times at which it has not yet begun or has already ended. Last year's flowering of my golden chain tree is such. It began at some time last spring and has now for about a year or so ceased. But there are other events which are not in this way temporally limited; *3's being prime,* for example. If time itself begins and ends, then this event, too, occurs wholly within a finite interval. Yet even then there is no time at which it does not occur.

I said that every event consists in something's actually having some property, actually performing some action, or actually standing in some relation to something. So consider some event *e* which consists in some entity *a* having some property or performing some action or standing in some relation. Let us call *a*, a *subject* of *e*. And let us call *e* an *aspect* of *a*. A given event may well have more than one subject. For example, an event consisting of my sitting under my shingle oak has both me and the shingle oak as subjects. Indeed, I think it can also be viewed as having the relation of *sitting under* as subject. I see nothing against regarding an event consisting of my sitting under my shingle oak as identical with an event consisting of the relation of *sitting under* being exemplified by me with respect to my shingle oak.

Now consider that set of a given entity's aspects such that each member bears a temporal order-relation to every member of the set and none bears a temporal order-relation to any aspect not a member of the set. Let us call that set, provided that it is not empty, the *time-strand* of that entity. I assume it to be true that every entity has at most one time-strand. That is, I assume that no entity has two or more sets of temporally interrelated aspects such that no member of the one set bears any temporal order-relation to any member of the other. I do not, however, assume that each of the aspects of every entity which has a time-strand belongs to the strand. And as to whether every entity has at least one time-strand—that of course is involved in the question as to whether anything is eternal.

Consider, next, a set of events such that each member stands to every member in one of the temporal order-relations, and such that no member stands to any event which is not a member in any of these relations. I shall call such a set a *temporal array*. A temporal array is of course just the union of a set of time-strands such that every member of each member strand bears some temporal order-relation to every member of every other member strand, and such that no member of any member strand bears any temporal order-relation to any member of any strand which is not a member of the set. In what follows I assume that there is but one temporal array. I assume, that is, that every member of every time-strand bears a temporal order-relation to every member of every time-strand.

Now suppose that there is some entity all of whose aspects are such that they are to be found in no temporal array whatsoever. Such an entity would be, in the most radical way possible, outside of time. Accordingly, I shall define "eternal" thus:

Def. 1: *x* is eternal if and only if *x* has no aspect which is a member of the temporal array.

An alternative definition would have been this: "*x* is eternal if and only if *x* has no time-strand." The difference between the two definitions is that, on the latter, an entity is eternal if none of its aspects bears any temporal order-relation to any of those events which are *its* aspects;

whereas on the former, what is required of an entity for it to be eternal is that none of its aspects be related by any temporal order-relation to *any event whatsoever*. Of course, if every event which bears any temporal order-relation to any event whatsoever is also simultaneous with itself, then everything which fails to satisfy the "temporal array" definition of "eternal" will also fail to satisfy the "time-strand" definition.

At this point, certain ambiguities in the concepts of precedence, succession, and simultaneity should be resolved. By saying that event e_1 occurs *simultaneously with* event e_2, I mean that there is some time at which both e_1 and e_2 are occurring. I do *not* mean—though indeed this might reasonably also have been meant by the words—that there is *no* time at which one of e_1 and e_2 is occurring and the other is not. When two events stand in that latter relation I shall say that they are *wholly simultaneous*. By saying that e_1 *precedes* e_2, I mean that there is some time at which e_1 but not e_2 is occurring, which precedes all times at which e_2 is occurring. I do not mean that every time at which e_1 occurs precedes every time at which e_2 occurs. When e_1 stands to e_2 in this latter relationship, I shall say that it *wholly precedes* e_2. Lastly, by saying that e_1 *succeeds* e_2, I mean that there is some time at which e_1 but not e_2 is occurring which succeeds all times at which e_2 is occurring. This, as in the case of precedence, allows for overlap. And, as in the case of precedence, an overlapping case of succession may be distinguished from a case in which one event *wholly succeeds* another.

When 'simultaneity,' 'precedence,' and 'succession' are understood thus, they do not stand for exclusive relations. An event e_1 may precede, occur simultaneously with, and succeed, another event e_2. But of course e_1 cannot *wholly* precede e_2 while also being *wholly* simultaneous with it, and so forth for the other combinations.

Reflecting on the consequences of the above definitions and explanations, someone might protest that the definition of eternal is altogether too stringent. For consider, say, the number 3. This, no doubt, was referred to by Euclid and also by Cantor. So, by our explanation of "aspect," *3's being referred to by Euclid* was an aspect of the number 3, and *3's being referred to by Cantor* was another aspect thereof. And of course the former preceded the latter. So, by our definition, 3 is not eternal. But— it may be protested—the fact that something is successively referred to should not be regarded as ground for concluding that it is not eternal. For after all, successive references to something do not produce any change in it. Although they produce variation among its aspects, they do not produce a changeful variation among them.

In response to this protest it must be emphasized that the concept of an eternal being is not identical with the concept of an unchanging being. The root idea behind the concept of an eternal being is not that of one which does not change but rather that of one which is outside of time. And a question of substance is whether an unchanging being may fail to be eternal. The most thoroughgoing and radical way possible for an entity to be outside of time is that which something enjoys if it satisfies our definition of "eternal." And it must simply be acknowledged that if an entity is successively referred to, then it is not in the most thoroughgoing way outside of time. There is temporal succession among its aspects.

However, the idea of change could be used by the protester in another way. It is indeed true that not every variation among the aspects of an entity constitutes change therein. Only variation among some of them— call them its *change-relevant* aspects—does so. So on the ground that the change-relevant aspects of an entity are more basic to it, we might distinguish between something being *fundamentally* noneternal and something being *trivially* noneternal. Something is *fundamentally* noneternal if it fails to satisfy the concept of being eternal by virtue of some of its change-relevant aspects. Something is *trivially* noneternal if its failure to satisfy the concept of being eternal is not by virtue of any of its change-relevant aspects.

Now in fact it will be change-relevant aspects of God to which I will appeal in arguing that he is not eternal. Thus my argument will be that God is *fundamentally* noneternal.

II

In order to present our argument that God is fundamentally noneternal we must now take note of a second basic feature of temporality; namely, that all temporal reality comes in the three modes of past, present, and future.[3]

An important fact about the temporal array is that some events within it are *present*: they *are occurring*; some are *past*: they *were occurring*; some are *future*: they *will be occurring*. Indeed, every event is either past or present or future. And not only *is* this the case now. It always was the case in the past that every event was either past or present or future. And it always will be the case in the future that every event is either past or present or future. Further, every event in the array is such that it either

---

3. There are two other basic features of temporality: one is the phenomenon of temporal location—the fact that events occur at or within intervals. The other is the phenomenon of temporal duration—the fact that intervals have lengths. In our preceding discussion we repeatedly made appeal to the phenomenon of temporal location without calling attention to our doing so.

was present or is present or will be present. No event can be past unless it was present. No event can be future unless it will be present. Thus the present is the most basic of the three modes of temporality. To be past is just to have been present. To be future is just to be going to be present. Further, if an event is past, it *presently* is past. If an event is future, it *presently* is future. In this way, too, the present is fundamental.

The reason every event in the temporal array is either past, present, or future is as follows: in order to be in the array at all, an event must occur either before or after or at the same time as some other event. But then, of course, it must occur sometime. And when an event is occurring it is present. So consider any event *e* which is to be found in the temporal array. If *e* is occurring, *e* is present. If, on the other hand, *e* is not occurring, then *e* either precedes or succeeds what is occurring. For *some* event is presently occurring. And every event in the array either precedes or succeeds or is wholly simultaneous with every other. But if *e* were wholly simultaneous with what is occurring, *e* itself would be occurring. So *e* either succeeds or precedes what is occurring if it is not itself occurring. Now for any event *x* to precede any event *y* is just for *x* sometime to be past when *y* is not past. So if *e* precedes what is occurring and is not itself occurring, then *e* is past. On the other hand, for any event *x* to succeed any event *y* is just for *x* sometime to be future when *y* is not future. So if *e* succeeds what is occurring and is not itself occurring, then *e* is future. Hence everything to be found in the temporal array is either past, present, or future.

In contemporary Western philosophy the phenomenon of temporal modality has been pervasively neglected or ignored in favor of the phenomena of temporal order-relationships, temporal location, and temporal duration. Thus time has been "spatialized." For though space provides us with close analogues to all three of these latter phenomena, it provides us with no analogue whatever to the past/present/future distinction.[4]

Perhaps the most fundamental and consequential manifestation of this neglect is to be found in the pervasive assumption that all propositions expressed with tensed sentences are mode-indifferent and dated. Consider for example the tensed sentence 'My golden chain tree is flowering.' The assumption is that what I would assert if I now (June 5, 1974) assertively uttered this sentence with normal sense is *that my golden chain tree is or*

4. A recent example of the neglect of temporal modality in favor of temporal location is to be found in David Lewis, "Anselm and Actuality," *Noûs*, 4 (May 1970). Concluding several paragraphs of discussion he says, "If we take a timeless view and ignore our own location in time, the big difference between the present time and other times vanishes."

was or will be flowering on June 5, 1974. And that the proposition I would be asserting if I assertively uttered the same sentence on June 4, 1975, is *that my golden chain tree is or was or will be flowering on June 4, 1975*. And so forth.

In order to see clearly what the assumption in question comes to, it will be helpful to introduce a way of expressing tenses alternative to that found in our natural language.[5] We begin by introducing the three tense operators, *P, T,* and *F*. These are to be read, respectively, as "it was the case that," "it is the case that," and "it will be the case that." They are to be attached as prefixes either to sentences in the present tense which lack any such prefix,[6] or to compound sentences which consist of sentences in the present tense with one or more such prefixes attached. And the result of attaching one such operator to a sentence is to yield a new sentence. For example: P (my golden chain tree is flowering), to be read as, *"it was the case that my golden chain tree is flowering."* And: F[P (my golden chain tree is flowering)], to be read as: *"it will be the case that it was the case that my golden chain tree is flowering."*

So consider any sentence *s* which is either a present tense sentence with no operators prefixed or a compound sentence consisting of a present tense sentence with one or more operators prefixed. The proposition expressed by P(*s*) is true if and only if the proposition expressed by *s* was true (in the past). The proposition expressed by T(*s*) is true if and only if the proposition expressed by *s* is true (now, in the present).[7] And the proposition expressed by F(*s*) is true if and only if the proposition expressed by *s* will be true (in the future).

Any proposition expressed by a tensed sentence from ordinary speech can be expressed by a sentence in this alternative language. Thus "My golden chain tree was flowering" has as its translational equivalent "P (my golden chain tree is flowering)." And "My golden chain tree will have been flowering" has as its translational equivalent "F[P (my golden chain tree is flowering)]."

Let us now introduce a fourth tense operator, *D,* defining this one in terms of the preceding three thus:

5. See the writings of Arthur Prior, especially *Time and Modality* (Oxford, 1957); *Past, Present and Future* (Oxford, 1967); and *Time and Tense* (Oxford, 1968).
6. This reflects the fact that the past is what was *present;* the future what will be *present.*
7. Thus, strictly speaking, the *T* operator is unnecessary. Attaching *T* to any sentence *s* always yields a sentence which expresses the same proposition as does *s* by itself. This reflects the fact that what is past is *presently* past, what is future is *presently* future, and, of course, what is present is *presently* present.

Def. 2: D(...), if and only if P (...) or T(...) or F(...).

And let us read it as: "It was or is or will be the case that...." Let us call this the *tense-indifferent* tense operator. And, correspondingly, let us call a sentence which has at least one tense operator and all of whose tense operators are tense-indifferent, a *wholly tense-indifferent* sentence. Furthermore, as the ordinary language counterpart to the tense-indifferent operator let us use the verb in its present tense with a bar over it, thus: "My golden chain tree is flowering." Or "My golden chain tree flowers."

Finally, let us add to our linguistic stock a certain set of modifiers of these tense operators—modifiers of the form "at *t*," "before *t*," and "after *t*," where *t* stands in for some expression designating a time which is such that that expression can be used to designate that time no matter whether that time is in the past, present, or future. These modifiers are to be attached to our tense operators, thus: *P at 1974* (...). The result of attaching one to an operator is to yield an operator of a new form—what one might call a *dated* tense operator. The proposition expressed by a sentence of the form *P at t(s)* is true if and only if the proposition expressed by *s* was true at or within time *t*. The proposition expressed by *T at t(s)* is true if and only if the proposition expressed by *s* is true at or within time *t*. And the proposition expressed by *F at t(s)* is true if and only if the proposition expressed by *s* will be true at or within time *t*. Thus the proposition expressed by "P at 1973 (my golden chain tree is flowering)" is true if and only if my golden chain tree was flowering at or within 1973. Similarly, the proposition expressed by a sentence of the form *P before t(s)* is true if and only if the proposition expressed by *s* was true before *t*; likewise for *T before t(s)* and *F before t(s)*. And the proposition expressed by a sentence of the form *P after t(s)* is true if and only if the proposition expressed by *s* was true after *t*; likewise for *T after t(s)* and *F after t(s)*. Let us call a sentence which has tense operators and all of whose tense operators are dated ones, a *fully dated* sentence.

The assumption underlying a great deal of contemporary philosophy can now be stated thus: every proposition expressed by a sentence which is not wholly tense-indifferent and not fully dated is a proposition which can be expressed by some sentence which is wholly tense-indifferent and fully dated. Consider, for example, the sentence 'T (my golden chain tree is flowering)'—the translational equivalent of the ordinary sentence, 'My golden chain tree is flowering.' Suppose that I assertively utter this sentence on June 5, 1974. The assumption is that the proposition I assert by uttering this sentence is that which is expressed by 'D at June 5, 1974 (my golden chain tree is flowering).' And in general, where *s* is some present tense sentence, the assumption is that the proposition asserted by assertively uttering s at time t is just that which would be asserted by assertively uttering D at $t(s)$. Similarly, it is assumed that the proposition asserted by assertively uttering $P(s)$ at time t is that which would be asserted by assertively uttering D before $t(s)$. And it is assumed that the proposition asserted by assertively uttering $F(s)$ at time t is that which would be asserted by assertively uttering D after $t(s)$.

On this view, tense-committed sentences are characteristically used to assert different propositions on different occasions of use. For example, if the sentence 'My golden chain tree is flowering' is assertively uttered on June 5, it is being used to assert that it is or was or will be the case on June 5 that my golden chain tree is flowering; whereas, if uttered on June 4, it is being used to assert that it is or was or will be the case on June 4 that my golden chain tree is flowering. Whether this view is correct will be considered shortly. If it is, then tense-committed sentences are in that way different from wholly tense-indifferent sentences. For these latter are used to assert the same proposition on all occasions of utterance.

I think we now have the assumption in question clearly enough before us to weigh its acceptability. It is in fact clearly false. To see this, suppose that I now (June 5, 1974) assertively utter the sentence 'My golden chain tree is flowering' and 'D at June 5, 1974 (my golden chain tree is flowering).' The proposition asserted with the former entails that the flowering of my golden chain tree is something that *is* occurring, *now, presently*. But the latter does not entail this at all. In general, if someone assertively utters a present tense sentence s at t, what he asserts is true if and only if the proposition 'D at $t(s)$' is true. Yet 's' and 'D at $t(s)$' are distinct propositions. So also, if I now assertively utter 'My golden chain tree was flowering,' what I assert entails that the flowering of my golden chain tree is something that *did* take place, in the past. Whereas the proposition asserted with 'D before June 5, 1974 (my golden chain tree is flowering)' does not entail this. And this nonidentity of the propositions holds even though it is the case that if someone assertively utters $P(s)$ at t, what he asserts is true if and only if the proposition D before $t(s)$ is true.

Just as a wholly tense-indifferent sentence is used to assert the same proposition no matter what the time of utterance, so, too, the proposition asserted with such a sentence does not vary in truth value. If it is ever true, it is always true, that D at June 5, 1974 (my golden chain tree is flowering). And if it is ever false, it is always false. Such a proposition is constant in its truth value. But an implication of the failure of the contemporary assumption is that the same cannot be said for the propositions expressed by tense-committed sentences. At least some of these are such that they are sometimes true, sometimes false. They are variable in their truth value. For example, 'My golden chain tree is flowering' is now true; but two weeks ago it was false.

So the situation is not that in successively uttering a tense-committed sentence we are asserting distinct propositions, each of which is constant in truth value and each of which could also be expressed with wholly tense indifferent, fully dated, sentences. The situation is rather that we are repeatedly asserting a proposition which is variable in its truth value. Contemporary philosophers, along with assuming the dispensability of the temporal modes, have assumed that all propositions are constant in truth value. Plato's lust for eternity lingers on.

Though philosophers have ignored the modes of time in their theories, we as human beings are all aware of the past/present/future distinction. For without such knowledge we would be lost in the temporal array. Suppose one knew, for each event x, which events $\overline{occur}$ simultaneously with x, which $\overline{occur}$ before x, and which $\overline{occur}$ after x. (Recall the significance of the bar over a present-tense verb.) Then with respect to, say, Luther's posting of his theses, one would know which events $\overline{occur}$ simultaneously therewith, which $\overline{occur}$ before it, and which $\overline{occur}$ after it. And so forth, for all other temporal interrelations of events. There would then still be something of enormous importance which one would not on that account know. One would not know where we are in the array of temporally ordered events. For one would not know which events are occurring, which were occurring, and which will be occurring. To know this it is not sufficient to know, with respect to every event, which events $\overline{occur}$ simultaneously therewith, which $\overline{occur}$ before, and which $\overline{occur}$ after.

Nor, as we have seen above, is such knowledge gained by knowing what $\overline{occurs}$ at what time. If all I know with respect to events $e_1 \ldots e_n$ is that they all $\overline{occur}$ at the time, say, of the inauguration of the first post-Nixon President, then I do not yet know whether those events are in the past, in the present, or in the future. And if all my knowledge with respect to every event and every interval is of that deficient sort, I do not know where we are in the temporal array. For I do not know which events are present, which are past, and which are future.

III

It might seem obvious that God, as described by the biblical writers, is a being who changes, and who accordingly is fundamentally noneternal. For God is described as a being who *acts*—in creation, in providence, and for the renewal of mankind. He is an agent, not an impassive factor in reality. And from the manner in which his acts are described, it seems obvious that many of them have beginnings and endings, that accordingly they stand in succession relations to each other, and that these successive acts are of such a sort that their presence and absence on God's time-strand constitutes changes thereon. Thus it seems obvious that God is fundamentally noneternal.

God is spoken of as calling Abraham to leave Chaldea and later instructing Moses to return to Egypt. So does not the event of *God's instructing Moses* succeed that of *God's calling Abraham?* And does not this sort of succession constitute a change on God's time-strand—not a change in his "essence," but nonetheless a change on his time-strand? Again, God is spoken of as leading Israel through the Red Sea and later sending his Son into the world. So does not his doing the latter succeed his doing the former? And does not the fact of this sort of succession constitute a change along God's time-strand?

In short, it seems evident that the biblical writers regard God as having a time-strand of his own on which actions on his part are to be found, and that some at least of these actions vary in such a way that there are changes along the strand. It seems evident that they do not regard changes on time-strands as confined to entities in God's creation. The God who acts, in the way in which the biblical writers speak of God as acting, seems clearly to change.

Furthermore, is it not clear from how they speak that the biblical writers regarded many of God's acts as bearing temporal order-relations to events which are not aspects of him but rather aspects of the earth, of ancient human beings, and so forth? The four cited above, for example, seem all to be described thus. It seems obvious that God's actions as described by the biblical writers stand in temporal order-relations to all the other events in our own time-array.

However, I think it is not at all so obvious as on first glance it might appear that the biblical writers do in fact describe God as changing. Granted that the language they use suggests this. It is not at once clear that this is what they wished to say with this language. It is not clear that this is how they were describing God. Let us begin to see why this is so by reflecting on the following passage from St. Thomas Aquinas:

> Nor, if the action of the first agent is eternal, does it follow that His effect is eternal, . . . God acts voluntarily in the production of things, . . . God's act of understanding and willing is, necessarily, His act of making. Now, an effect follows from the intellect and the will according to the determination of the intellect and the command of the will.

Moreover, just as the intellect determines every other condition of the thing made, so does it prescribe the time of its making; for art determines not only that this thing is to be such and such, but that it is to be at this particular time, even as a physician determines that a dose of medicine is to be drunk at such and such a particular time, so that, if his act of will were of itself sufficient to produce the effect, the effect would follow anew from his previous decision, without any new action on his part. Nothing, therefore, prevents our saying that God's action existed from all eternity, whereas its effect was not present from eternity, but existed at that time when, from all eternity, He ordained it (*SCG* II.35; cf. II.36, 4).

Let us henceforth call an event which neither begins nor ends an *everlasting* event. And let us call an event which either begins or ends, a *temporal* event. In the passage above, St. Thomas is considering God's acts of bringing about temporal events. So consider some such act; say, that of God's bringing about Israel's deliverance from Egypt. The temporal event in question, Israel's deliverance from Egypt, occurred (let us say) in 1225 B.C. But from the fact that what God brought about occurred in 1225 it does not follow, says Aquinas, that God's act of bringing it about occurred in 1225. In fact, it does not follow that this act had any beginning or ending whatsoever. And in general, suppose that God brings about some temporal event *e*. From the fact that *e* is temporal it does not follow, says Aquinas, that God's act of bringing about *e*'s occurrence is temporal. The temporality of the event which God brings about does not infect God's act of bringing it about. God's act of bringing it about may well be everlasting. This can perhaps more easily be seen, he says, if we remember that God, unlike us, does not have to "take steps" so as to bring about the occurrence of some event. He need only will that it occur. If God just wants it to be the case that *e* occur at *t*, *e* occurs at *t*.

Thus God can bring about changes in our history without himself changing. The occurrence of the event of Israel's deliverance from Egypt constitutes a change in our history. But there is no counterpart change among God's aspects by virtue of his bringing this event about.

Now let us suppose that the four acts of God cited above—instructing Moses, calling Abraham, leading Israel through the Red Sea, and sending his Son into the world—regardless of the impression we might gain from the biblical language used to describe them, also have the structure of God's bringing about the occurrence of some temporal event. Suppose, for example, that God's leading Israel through the Red Sea has the structure of God's bringing it about that Israel's passage through the Red Sea occurs. And suppose Aquinas is right that the temporality of Israel's passage does not infect with temporality God's act of bringing about this passage. Then what is strictly speaking the case is not that God's leading Israel through the Red Sea occurs during 1225. What is rather the case is that Israel's passage through the Red Sea occurs during 1225, and that God brings this passage about. And the temporality of the passage does not entail the temporality of God's bringing it about. This latter may be everlasting. So, likewise, the fact that the occurrence of this passage marks a change in our history does not entail that God's bringing it about marks a change among God's aspects. God may unchangingly bring about historical changes.

It is natural, at this point, to wonder whether we do not have in hand here a general strategy for interpreting the biblical language about God acting. Is it not perhaps the case that all those acts of God which the biblical writers speak of as beginning or as ending really consist in God performing the everlasting event of bringing about the occurrence of some temporal event?

Well, God does other things with respect to temporal events than bringing about their occurrence. For example, he also *knows* them. Why then should it be thought that the best way to interpret all the temporal-event language used to describe God's actions is by reference to God's action of bringing about the occurrence of some event? May it not be that the best way to interpret what is said with some of such language is by reference to one of those other acts which God performs with respect to temporal events? But then if God is not to change, it is not only necessary that the temporality of *e* not infect God's act of *bringing about* the occurrence of *e*, but also that *every* act of God such that he performs it with respect to *e* not be infected by the temporality of *e*. For example, if God *knows* some temporal event *e*, his knowledge of *e* must not be infected by the temporality of *e*.

So the best way of extrapolating from Aquinas' hint would probably be along the lines of the following theory concerning God's actions and the biblical speech about them. All God's actions are everlasting. None has either beginning or ending. Of these everlasting acts, the structure of some consists in God's performing some action with respect to some event. And at least some of the events that God acts with respect to are temporal events. However, in no case does the temporality of the event that God acts with respect to infect the event of his acting. On the contrary, his acting with respect to some temporal event is itself invariably an everlasting event. So whenever the biblical writers use temporal-event language to describe God's actions, they are to be interpreted as thereby claiming that God acts with respect to some temporal event. They are not to be interpreted as claiming that God's acting is itself a temporal event. God as described by the biblical writers is to be interpreted as acting, and as acting with respect to temporal events. But he is not to be interpreted as changing. All his acts are everlasting.

This, I think, is a fascinating theory. If true, it provides a way of harmonizing the fundamental biblical teaching that God is a being who acts in our history, with the conviction that God does not change. How far the proposed line of biblical interpretation can be carried out, I do not know. I am not aware of any theologian who has ever tried to carry it out, though there are a great many theologians who might have relieved the tension in their thought by developing and espousing it. But what concerns us here is not so much what the theory can adequately deal with as what it cannot adequately deal with. Does the theory in fact provide us with a wholly satisfactory way of harmonizing the biblical presentation of God as acting in history with the conviction that God is fundamentally eternal?

Before we set about looking for a refutation of the theory it should be observed, though, that even if the theory were true God would still not be eternal. For consider God's acts of bringing about Abraham's leaving of Chaldea and of bringing about Israel's passage through the Red Sea. These would both be, on the theory, *everlasting* acts. Both are always occurring. Hence they occur simultaneously. They stand to each other in the temporal order-relation of simultaneity. And since both are aspects of God, God accordingly has a time-strand on which these acts are to be found. Hence God is not eternal. Further, these are surely change-relevant aspects of God. Hence God is fundamentally noneternal.[8]

Though I myself think that this argument is sound, it would not be decisive if presented to Aquinas. For Aquinas held that God is simple. And an implication of this contention on his part is that all aspects of God are identical. Hence in God's case there are no two aspects which are simultaneous with each other; for there are no two aspects at all.

A reply is possible. For consider that which is, on Aquinas' theory, God's single aspect; and refer to it as you will—say, as *God's being omnipotent.* This aspect presumably occurs at the same time as itself. Whenever it occurs, it is itself occurring. It is simultaneous with itself. Furthermore, it occurs simultaneously with every temporal event whatsoever. Since God's

---

8. By a similar argument the number 3 can be seen to be fundamentally noneternal. Surely *3's being odd* and *3's being prime* are both change-relevant aspects of 3. If either of these were for a while an aspect of 3 and then for a while not, we would conclude that 3 had changed. But these two aspects occur simultaneously with each other. They stand to each other in the temporal order-relation of simultaneity. Hence 3 is fundamentally noneternal.

being omnipotent is always occurring, it "overlaps" all temporal events whatsoever. So once again we have the conclusion: God is noneternal, indeed, he is fundamentally noneternal.

It is true, though, that even if Aquinas were to accept this last argument he would not *say*, in conclusion, that God was noneternal. For Aquinas defined an eternal being as one which is without beginning and without end, and which has no *succession* among its aspects (*ST*, I.I q 10 a 1). Thus as Aquinas defined eternal, an eternal being may very well have aspects which stand to each other in the temporal order-relation of simultaneity. What Aquinas ruled out was just aspects standing in the temporal order-relation of succession. Our own definition of "eternal," which disallows simultaneity as well as succession, is in this way more thoroughgoing than is Aquinas'. For a being at least one of whose aspects occurs simultaneously with some event is not yet, in the most radical way possible, outside of time. However, in refutation of the extrapolated Thomistic theory sketched out above I shall now offer an argument against God's being eternal which establishes that there is not only simultaneity but succession among God's aspects, and not just succession but *changeful* succession. This argument will be as relevant to the issue of God's being eternal on Aquinas' definition of eternal as it is on my own definition.

To refute the extrapolated Thomistic theory we would have to do one or the other of two things. We would have to show that some of the temporal-event language the biblical writers use in speaking of God's actions cannot properly be construed in the suggested way—that is, cannot be construed as used to put forth the claim that God acts in some way with respect to some temporal events. Or, alternatively, we would have to show that some of the actions that God performs with respect to temporal events are themselves temporal, either because they are infected by the temporality of the events or for some other reason.

One way of developing this latter alternative would be to show that some of God's actions must be understood as a response to the free actions of human beings—that what God does he sometimes does in response to what some human being does. I think this is in fact the case. And I think it follows, given that all human actions are temporal, that those actions of God which are "response" actions are temporal as well. But to develop this line of thought would be to plunge us deep into questions of divine omniscience and human freedom. So I shall make a simpler, though I think equally effective objection to the theory, arguing that in the case of certain of God's actions the temporality of the event that God acts on infects his own action with temporality.

Three such acts are the diverse though similar acts of knowing about some temporal event that it is occurring (that it is *present*), of knowing about some temporal event that it was occurring (that it is *past*), and of knowing about some temporal event that it will be occurring (that it is *future*). Consider the first of these. No one can know about some temporal event *e* that it is occurring except when it is occurring. Before *e* has begun to occur one cannot know that it is occurring, for it is not. Not after *e* has ceased to occur can one know that it is occurring, for it is not. So suppose that *e* has a beginning. Then P's knowing about *e* that it is occurring cannot occur until *e* begins. And suppose that *e* has an ending. Then P's knowing about *e* that it is occurring cannot occur beyond *e*'s cessation. But every temporal event has (by definition) either a beginning or an ending. So every case of knowing about some temporal event that it is occurring itself either begins or ends (or both). Hence the act of knowing about *e* that it is occurring is infected by the temporality of *e*. So also, the act of knowing about *e* that it *was* occurring, and the act of knowing about *e* that it *will be* occurring, are infected by the temporality of *e*.

But God, as the biblical writers describe him, performs all three of these acts, and performs them on temporal events. He knows what is happening in our history, what has happened, and what will happen. Hence, some of God's actions are themselves temporal events. But surely the nonoccurrence followed by the occurrence followed by the nonoccurrence of such knowings constitutes a change on God's time-strand. Accordingly, God is fundamentally noneternal.[9]

It is important, if the force of this argument is to be discerned, that one distinguish between, on the one hand, the act of knowing about some event *e* that it $\overline{occurs}$ at some time *t* (recall the significance of the bar) and, on the other hand, the act of knowing about *e* that it is occurring or of knowing that it was occurring or of knowing that it will be occurring. Knowing about *e* that it $\overline{occurs}$ at *t* is an act not infected by the temporality of the event known. *That Calvin's flight from Geneva $\overline{occurs}$ in 1537* is something that can be known at any and every time whatsoever. For it is both true, and constant in its truth value. But *that Calvin's flight from Geneva is occurring* is variable in its truth value. It once was true, it

---

9. This line of argument is adumbrated by Arthur Prior here and there in his essay "Formalities of Omniscience," in *Time and Tense*. It is also adumbrated by Norman Kretzmann, "Omniscience and Immutability," *Journal of Philosophy*, 63 (1966). The essence of the argument is missed in discussions of Kretzmann's paper by Hector Castaneda, "Omniscience and Indexical Reference," *Journal of Philosophy*, 64 (1967); and Nelson Pike, *God and Timelessness* (New York, 1970), ch. 5. Castaneda and Pike fail to take the *modes* of time with full seriousness; as a partial defense of them it should perhaps be admitted as not wholly clear that Kretzmann himself does so.

now is false. And since one can know only what is true, this proposition cannot be known at every time. It cannot be known now. God can know, concerning every temporal event whatsoever, what time that event occurs at, without such knowledge of his being temporal. But he cannot know concerning any temporal event whatsoever that it is occurring, or know that it was occurring, or know that it will be occurring, without that knowledge being itself temporal.

Similarly, we must distinguish between, on the one hand, the act of knowing about some temporal event e that it occurs simultaneously with events $e_1 \ldots e_n$, after events $f_1 \ldots f_n$, and before events $g_1 \ldots g_n$; and, on the other hand, the act of knowing about e that it is occurring or of knowing that it was occurring or of knowing that it will be occurring. Knowledge of the former sort is not infected by the temporality of the event whose temporal order-relationships are known. Knowledge of the latter sort is. I know now that Calvin's flight from Geneva occurs after Luther's posting of his theses occurs. But once again, I do not and cannot now know that Calvin's flight is occurring. Because it is not. So too, God once knew that Calvin's flight from Geneva was occurring. But he no longer knows this. For he, too, does not know that which is not so. Thus, in this respect his knowledge has changed. But God always knows that Calvin's flight from Geneva occurs after Luther's posting of his theses occurs. Only if time lacked modes and only if propositions were all constant in truth value could God's knowledge be unchanging—assuming that God's knowledge comprises temporal as well as everlasting events.

The act of *remembering* that e has occurred is also an act infected by the temporality of e (remembering is, of course, a species of knowing). For one can only remember that e has occurred after e has occurred. 'P remembers that e occurs' entails that e has occurred. So if e is an event that has a beginning, then the act of remembering that e has occurred has a beginning. But some events with beginnings are such that God remembers their occurrence. Consequently this act on God's part is also a temporal event. It too cannot be everlasting.

God is also described by the biblical writers as planning that he would bring about certain events which he does. This, too, is impossible if God does not change. For consider some event which someone brings about, and suppose that he planned to bring it about. His planning to bring it about must occur before the planned event occurs. For otherwise it is not a case of planning.

So in conclusion, if God were eternal he could not be aware, concerning any temporal event, that it is occurring nor aware that it was occurring nor aware that it will be occurring; nor could he remember that it has occurred; nor could he plan to bring it about and do so. But all of such actions are presupposed by, and essential to, the biblical presentation of God as a redeeming God. Hence God as presented by the biblical writers is fundamentally noneternal. He is fundamentally in time.

IV

As with any argument, one can here choose to deny the premises rather than to accept the conclusion. Instead of agreeing that God is fundamentally noneternal because he changes with respect to his knowledge, his memory, and his planning, one could try to save one's conviction that God is eternal by denying that he knows what is or was or will be occurring, that he remembers what has occurred, and that he brings about what he has planned. It seems to me, however, that this is clearly to give up the notion of God as a redeeming God; and in turn it seems to me that to give this up is to give up what is central to the biblical vision of God. To sustain this latter claim would of course require an extensive hermeneutical inquiry. But lest someone be tempted to go this route of trying to save God's eternity by treating all the biblical language about God the redeemer as either false or misleadingly metaphorical, let me observe that if God were eternal he could not be the object of any human action whatsoever.

Consider, for example, my act of referring to something, X. The event consisting of *my referring to* X is a temporal event. It both begins and ends, as do all my acts. Now the event of *my referring to* X is identical with the event of *X's being referred to by me.* And this event is an aspect both of X and of me. So if X is a being which lasts longer than my act of referring to X does, then for a while X has this aspect and for a while not. And thus X would have *succession* on its time-strand. And so X would not be eternal. Thus if God were eternal, no human being could ever refer to him—or perform any other temporal act with respect to him. If he were eternal, one could not know him. In particular, one could not know that he was eternal, or even believe that he was. Indeed, if God were eternal one could not predicate of him that he is eternal. For predicating is also a temporal act. So this is the calamitous consequence of claiming of God that he is eternal: if one predicates of him that he is eternal, then he is not.

V

I have been arguing that God as described by the biblical writers is a being who changes. That, we have seen, is not self-evidently and obviously so, though the mode of expression of the biblical writers might lead one to think it was. Yet it is so nonetheless.

But are there not explicit statements in the Bible to the effect that God does not change? If we are honest to the evidence, must we not acknowledge that on this matter the biblical writers contradict each other? Let us see.

Surprisingly, given the massive Christian theological tradition in favor of God's ontological immutability, there are only two passages (to the best of my knowledge) in which it is directly said of God that he does not change. One of these is Malachi 3:6. The prophet has just been saying to the people that God is wearied by their hypocrisy; however (he goes on), God will send his messenger to clear a path before him; and "he will take his seat, refining and purifying." As a result of this cleansing, the "offerings of Judah and Jerusalem shall be pleasing to the Lord as they were in days of old." And then comes this assurance: "I am the Lord, unchanging; and you, too, have not ceased to be sons of Jacob. From the days of your forefathers you have been wayward and have not kept my laws. If you will return to me, I will return to you, says the Lord of Hosts" (NEB).

Surely it would be a gross misinterpretation to treat the prophet here as claiming that God is ontologically immutable. What he says, on the contrary, is that God is faithful to his people Israel—that he is unchanging in his fidelity to the covenant he has made with them. All too often theologians have ontologized the biblical message. Malachi 3:6 is a classic example of a passage which, cited out of context, would seem to support the doctrine of God's ontological immutability. Read in context, however, it supports not that but rather the doctrine of God's unswerving fidelity. No ontological claim whatever is being made.

The other passage in which it is said of God that he is unchanging is to be found in Psalm 102:27. Again we must set the passage in its context:

My strength is broken in mid course;
the time allotted me is short.
    Snatch me not away before half my days are done,
    for thy years last through all generations.
Long ago thou didst lay the foundations of the earth,
    and the heavens were thy handiwork.

They shall pass away, but thou endurest;
    like clothes they shall all grow old;
    thou shalt cast them off like a cloak,
    and they shall vanish;
but thou art the same and thy years shall have no end;
    thy servants' children shall continue,
and their posterity shall be established in thy presence (NEB).

Here, too, it would be a gross misinterpretation to regard the writer as teaching that God is ontologically immutable. The Psalmist is making an ontological point of sorts, though even so the ontological point is set within a larger context of religious reflection. He is drawing a contrast between God on the one hand and his transitory creation on the other. And what he says about God is clearly that God is without end—"Thy years shall have no end." He does not say that God is ontologically immutable.

In short, God's ontological immutability is not a part of the explicit teaching of the biblical writers. What the biblical writers teach is that God is faithful and without beginning or end, not that none of his aspects is temporal. The theological tradition of God's ontological immutability has no explicit biblical foundation.[10]

VI

The upshot of our discussion is this: the biblical presentation of God presupposes that God is everlasting rather than eternal. God is indeed without beginning and without end. But at least some of his aspects stand in temporal order-relations to each other. Thus God, too, has a time-strand. His life and existence is itself temporal. (Whether his life and existence always was and always will be temporal, or whether he has taken on temporality, is a question we have not had time to consider.) Further, the events to be found on God's time-strand belong within the same temporal array as that which contains our time-strands. God's aspects do not only bear temporal order-relations to each other but to the aspects of created entities as well. And the aspects and succession of aspects to be found on God's time-strand are such that they constitute *changes* thereon. God's life and existence incorporates changeful succession.

Haunting Christian theology and Western philosophy throughout the centuries has been the picture of time as bounded, with the created order on this side of the boundary and God on the other. Or sometimes the metaphor has been that of time as extending up to a horizon, with all creaturely reality on this side of the horizon and God on the other. All such metaphors, and the ways of thinking that they represent, must be discarded. Temporality embraces us along with God.

This conclusion from our discussion turns out to be wholly in accord with that to be found in Oscar Cullmann's *Christ and Time.* From his

---

10. "I am that I am" (Exod. 3:13) has also sometimes been used to support the doctrine of God's immutability. However, this is one of the most cryptic passages in all of Scripture; and—to understate the point—it is not in the least clear that what is being proclaimed is God's ontological immutability. There is a wealth of exegetical material on the passage, but see especially the comments by J. C. Murray, *The Problem of God* (New Haven, 1967), ch. 1.

study of the biblical words for time Cullmann concluded that, in the biblical picture, God's "eternity" is not qualitatively different from our temporality. Cullmann's line of argument (though not his conclusion) has been vigorously attacked by James Barr on the ground that from the lexicographical patterns of biblical language we cannot legitimately make inferences as to what was being said by way of that language.[11] Verbal similarities may conceal differences in thought, and similarities in thought may be clothed with verbal differences. Barr's objection is *apropos*. But though we have traveled a very different route from Cullmann's we have come out at the same place. We have not engaged in any word studies. Yet, by seeing that God's temporality is presupposed by the biblical presentation of God as redeemer, we too have reached the conclusion that we share time with God. The lexicographical and philosophical cases coincide in their results.

Though God is within time, yet he is Lord of time. The whole array of contingent temporal events is within his power. He is Lord of what occurs. And that, along with the specific pattern of what he does, grounds all authentically biblical worship of, and obedience to, God. It is not because he is outside of time—eternal, immutable, impassive—that we are to worship and obey God. It is because of what he can and does bring about within time that we mortals are to render him praise and obedience.

---

11. *Biblical Words for Time* (London, 1962).

The Behavior of Robots

CLIFTON J. ORLEBEKE

I

Robots, like Hamlet, are fictitious beings. Unlike Hamlet, robots have no hearts, not even fictitious ones. Hamlet, though he had a heart, slew his stepfather. What will robots do to *their* parents?

Speculations along the lines of this question are still principally in the custody of creative story-tellers. It is they who postulate societies with extended memberships—extended, that is, by the addition of mechanical intelligent artifacts, or robots—in order to explore the new "interpersonal" relationships that arise. Many of their stories are artful, some are amusing, and a fair number are downright scary. Mary Shelley's invention of the monster in *Frankenstein* (1818) set going a typical scenario: man assembles a humanoid creature, the creature is dissatisfied with its lot, the creature turns pitilessly upon its originator to destroy him. Karel Capek, whose 1921 play *R.U.R.* introduced the term 'robot' into the language, likewise ends his story apocalyptically with a revolution, where the robots prevail against the humans.[1] It was not until the 1940s that fictional robots were tamed by the ever-ingenious Isaac Asimov, whose Three Laws of Robotics, incorporated into the design of every "positronic" robot brain, provided the necessary technological safeguard.[2]

1. For brief historical surveys of robot literature, see the Introductions of Sam Moskowitz (ed.), *The Coming of the Robots* (New York, 1963) and Isaac Asimov, *The Rest of the Robots* (New York, 1966).
2. The Three Laws of Robotics are: (1) A robot may not injure a human being, or, through inaction, allow a human being to come to harm. (2) A robot must obey the orders given it by human beings except where such orders would conflict with the First Law. (3) A robot must protect its own existence as long as such protection does not conflict with the First or Second Law.

Clifton J. Orlebeke is Professor of Philosophy at Calvin College and the author of several articles on the relation between science and the Christian religion. His essay explores some of the technical, philosophical, and theological implications of "artificial intelligence" research, which attempts to simulate features of intelligent human behavior by means of computing machines. He concludes that sanguine predictions about the future existence of humanoid robots are not at present adequately justified.

We cannot be assured that the Three Laws of Robotics will really suffice for the job, given the rather poor behavioral record of us humans, who have been favored with over three times as many Commandments. But of course there is a prior question: before we concern ourselves overmuch with preventing a takeover of man by robots, we might ask whether there are going to be any robots capable of such monstrous deeds. The robots of science fiction may be ever so clever or winsome or ferocious, but being fictional, their powers are severely limited. Among the things that they cannot do we must surely include the feat of conquering the human race.[3]

When philosophers discuss the possibility of robotic beings, it is not because they are deluded or confused by the authors of science fiction but because they are impressed with the factual underpinnings of this fiction and the claims made by respectable scientists in the field of artificial intelligence. (Marvin Minsky, in one of the racier examples of the latter, reportedly called the human brain "just a computer that happens to be made out of meat," eventually to be superseded by electronic intelligences which make all of society's major decisions. "Once computers get control we might never get it back. . . . If we're lucky, they might decide to keep us as pets.")[4] Intrigued by such claims, an increasing number of philosophers have inquired into the perceptual, volitional, cognitive, affective, linguistic, and other humanoid capabilities of machines; have speculated about the likelihood that machines can be conscious, can have minds or souls, or can sin; and have seriously entertained the possibility that machines can be persons ("persots"—Gunderson) and have civil rights. The opinions now being registered in the philosophic literature concerning these matters warrant at least this cautious generalization: some philosophers find no reason in principle why robots should not become members of an extended human community at some future time. So far, at least, has philosophy come in the direction of science fiction.[5]

II

In the remainder of this essay I will pursue some of the ramifications of this futuristic question: can humanoid robots be built? As already noted, there are some researchers and philosophers in the field of artificial in-

---

3. I do not intend to deny that (a) thinking about fictional beings can have psychological impact upon human actions, or (b) that human beings can become "enslaved" to artifacts as an alcoholic is enslaved to alcohol.
4. Quoted by Brad Darrach in "Meet Shaky, The First Electronic Person," *Life*, Nov. 20, 1970.
5. Cf. the thesis defended by Arthur W. Burks in his presidential address at the meeting of the Western Division of the American Philosophical Association: "A finite determinist automaton can perform all natural human functions." *Proceedings and Addresses of the American Philosophical Association*, 46 (1972-73).

telligence (i.e., *artifactual* intelligence) who are persuaded that they *can* be built. Almost everyone else, including most college students I have met, disagree. They regard the hypothesis of conscious, moral, rational machines as simply preposterous.

Who is right? My own view leans toward the negative, as the sequel will show. But the question is complicated. Many answers already given have been too hasty. Some depend on unsound general principles of philosophy or theology; some depend on sound principles misapplied (as I believe) to this case; some depend on premature estimates of future technology; and some depend on altogether too simplistic a conception of the task itself.

The last-mentioned point should concern us immediately. What is the nature of the task called robot-building? What are the specifications of a humanoid machine? What does it take to be *like* a human being—enough like a human being, that is, to become a member of a community of persons? These are good questions not merely for futurists, but for anyone who desires a theoretically adequate account of human nature. Through biology we have learned something about humans, based on recognized similarities between humans, animals, and plants; so, I suggest, should research in cybernetics provide opportunity to learn about humans, based on our similarities with information processing machines ("computers").

To begin, let us consider references to robots in three recent articles on the philosophy of artificial intelligence. Hilary Putnam has offered this brief definition of robots: "machines that simulate human behavior, often with an at least roughly human appearance...."[6] In developing his definition Putnam ascribes to these hypothetical robots the ability to speak a language, develop a religion, and publish papers on philosophy; he equips them with sense organs, and postulates that their behavior obeys psychological laws. About such robots Putnam raises the questions: are they alive? conscious? eligible for civil rights?

Similarly, Keith Gunderson raises the "repredication problem" for a robot that was manufactured with a "teeny mechanical brain which from the outset was endowed with a highly self-corrective micro-program . . . and 'clothed and masked' in such a way that it was 'virtually indistinguishable from men in all respects: in appearance, movement, in the utterances it uttered, and so forth.'"[7] The repredication problem arises from the un-

6. Hilary Putnam, "Robots: Machines or Artificially Created Life?", in F. J. Crosson (ed.), *Human and Artificial Intelligence* (New York, 1970), p. 178.
7. Keith Gunderson, *Mentality and Machines* (New York, 1971), p. 64. The interior quotation is from Paul Ziff, "The Feelings of Robots," in Alan Anderson (ed.), *Minds and Machines* (Englewood Cliffs, N. J., 1964), p. 99.

masking of such a robot: whereas formerly we had ascribed to it thoughts, feelings, etc., we now are inclined to wonder whether any or all of these predicates still apply.

Finally, Michael Scriven's influential article "The Compleat Robot: A Prolegomena to Androidology"[8] formulates the problem of robots in terms of two levels of possible achievement. Assuming that the robot's body size and shape are no great challenge, Scriven proceeds to discuss whether various human capacities such as choosing, creating, learning, understanding, etc. can be simulated in a machine with respect to performance and personality. By the "performatory" element Scriven means the behavioral; to succeed at this level the robot must effect the same input-output transformation as does a human being. The "personality" element is that elusive characteristic by virtue of which we may use human-achievement vocabulary in characterizing the robot's performance. When the robot acts *as if* (for example) it is making a choice, then it meets the performatory criterion. When and if it actually *does* make a choice, it meets the personality criterion as well.

These three statements are representative both of the concept of robot and the type of questions raised about robots in recent artificial intelligence (AI) philosophy. Putnam's concern about civil rights, Gunderson's about repredication, and Scriven's about personality are all direct descendants of A. M. Turing's question, "Can machines think?" Turing had proposed *replacing* that question with another, behavioral question: "Can a machine successfully play the imitation game?"[9] But none of the aforementioned philosophers is willing to accept this replacement *simpliciter*. Their stance is this: no matter how well a robot simulates human behavior, there is still another issue to be reckoned with, and that is moreover the crucial one, the one that determines whether the robot is merely a fancy piece of hardware or a member of the community. Scriven, for example, says that it is the question of being a person, which he understands to depend on whether the robot has *feelings* as well as a full repertoire of humanoid performatory skills.

In their understandable occupation with the "extra ingredient" that robots must possess beyond behavioral competence in order to qualify as more than mere simulators, mere "as if" behavers, AI philosophers have paid relatively less attention to the achievability of the simulation level that is *presupposed* by the "extra ingredient." AI philosophy has focused primarily on Turing's "replacement thesis" with regard to the question

---

8. Much anthologized, e.g. in Crosson, *op. cit.*
9. A. M. Turing, "Computing Machinery and Intelligence," in Anderson, *op. cit.*, pp. 4ff.

whether machines can think (namely, the thesis that another question, about behavior, can stand in its stead), and only secondarily on the question whether machines can even be built which can, for example, play the imitation game.

In taking this tack, AI philosophers have probably been influenced in part by a feeling about where their competence lies. Knowing what computers can do requires technical expertise that not all philosophers possess. Moreover, when they look to the experts, they hear repeated reassurances that computer-controlled artifacts can be built to perform marvelously well. Ziff, for instance, cites D. M. MacKay as authority for the claim that "any test for mental or any other attributes to be satisfied by the observable activity of a human being can be passed by automata." [10] In another article MacKay asserts:

> I think it is fair to say that no barrier of principle prevents an artificial opponent [in chess] from showing as many characteristic human features as we care to specify, including the crucial ability to develop and employ an internal running representation of "what is going on", so as to be able to converse intelligently and purposefully *about* his own activity and experience.[11]

MacKay claims that the construction of a robot that simulates human behavior is contingent solely on one's ability to state precisely, in terms of a stochastic process, the behavior pattern in question.[12] The only limitation on what can be simulated, says K. M. Sayre, "is imposed by our understanding of the function."[13] And John Von Neuman, generalizing McCulloch and Pitts' work with model neural networks, asserted: "Any functioning in this sense [that is, a specific input-output function] which can be defined at all logically, strictly, and unambiguously in a finite number of words can also be realized by such a formal neural network."[14]

In view of such assurances it is hardly surprising that philosophic attention has been diverted toward the "personality" issue as distinguished from the "behavioral" issue—notwithstanding the failure of actual AI artifacts to yet fulfill many of the promises made on theoretical grounds. As Keith Gunderson has remarked, toward the end of the nineteenth cen-

10. Ziff, *loc. cit.*, p. 101.
11. D. M. MacKay, "The Use of Behavioral Language to Refer to Mechanical Processes," in Crosson, *op. cit.*, p. 152.
12. "Mentality in Machines, III," *Proceedings of the Aristotelian Society*, Suppl. XXVI (1952), p. 85.
13. K. M. Sayre and F. C. Crosson (eds.), *The Modeling of Mind* (New York, 1968), p. 12.
14. J. H. Von Neuman, "The General and Logical Theory of Automata," in J. R. Newman (ed.), *The World of Mathematics* (New York, 1956), IV, 2090.

tury it was vehemently maintained that a subject could not be both wholly mechanistic and exhibit self-adaptive behavior. "This . . . had the flavor of an analytic truth before various negative feedback machines were developed. . . ."[15] So, too, it would seem foolhardy to deny *a priori* that certain behavioral goals for robots can be met, especially when we are given detailed stories about how an automaton can be built to do such-and-such.

Before returning to a further discussion of those behavioral skills usually associated with mentality or personhood, I propose to advert briefly to some of the more homely virtues a robot ought to possess.

Let us say that a robot is a machine directed by a computer-brain—a physical object, then, possessing a body (or, possibly, being identical with a body, though it is not my intention here to beg the question whether robots can have souls). It may be pointed out in passing that because robots are material artifacts they must be *built*. As every development engineer knows, there is always a gap between finely wrought designs and working hardware; thus, a proof that a Turing machine can do such-and-such does not suffice to show that an actual robot can do it.

The robot's body should be a plausible replica in size, form, and general appearance of the human body. (These requirements probably will not exceed the limits of a future technology of robotics, and they will surely minimize the problems of social acceptability that nonstandard representatives of personhood invariably suffer from.) Ms. Julie Newmar, who played the robot heroine of a long-defunct television series, was acceptable in spite of the control panel on her back (no one is perfect); but even one such as the Tin Woodman of Oz might be thought to satisfy a somewhat more relaxed version of this requirement.

More importantly, I propose that for social reasons a robot's body ought to *function* similarly to the functioning of the human body. Thus, though it would hardly be fair to require that robots eat and drink and breathe and reproduce sexually (would they be robots if they did?), it is not unfair to ask that robots be able to run and walk with appendages that resemble legs; push, pull, and otherwise manipulate objects with mechanical arms and hands; respond to the same ranges of auditory and visual stimuli as humans by use of head-mounted receptors; and coordinate their effector capacities such as grasping and running under the direction of information received through sensory stimuli.

As is known to readers of the popular press, there are robots such as Stanford Research Institute's "Shakey" which exhibit a fair amount of ingenuity within a severely limited range of sensori-motor tasks. Shakey,

---

15. *Op. cit.*, p. 79.

a wheeled vehicle equipped with feelers, TV camera, and a radio link to
its computer brain, is able to carry out instructions such as "push a box off
a platform," where this requires scanning the room to locate the box, scanning the room to find a ramp, shoving the ramp up to the platform, climbing the ramp, and then pushing the box off. A machine as sophisticated
as this, incorporating advanced applications of pattern-recognition, problem-solving, and feedback techniques, certainly ought not to be scorned.
Yet, compared with a fairly average human physical achievement such as
playing table tennis, Shakey's accomplishment is very primitive.

It has been observed by several hands, particularly in recent years by
Hubert Dreyfus, that the bodiliness of human beings poses a larger challenge to simulation engineers than some aspects, at least, of mentality. And
if (as Dreyfus further contends) some aspects of mentality depend essentially on body functions that cannot be duplicated in a robot, we would
indeed have encountered limitations on the behavioral repertoire of future
robots.[16] The issue is, however, an unresolved one which I note only to pass
on.

Finally, a robot ought to behave *as if* it were a person. This is Scriven's
"performatory" test, not his "personality" test. The behavior in question is
publicly observable behavior; a robot can pass this "as if" condition regardless of what is under its epidermis. So, for example, if a robot successfully occupies the first-desk oboe position in an orchestra it would not
be fair to quibble about its using (say) a small internal blower instead of
lungs to generate its wind.

A fair analogy, though not an exact one, is provided by (imaginary)
beasts that are mysteriously qualified to function as persons in human
society—such as Puss-in-Boots, who makes a splash in the royal court, or
the sleek and seal-like *hrossa* in C. S. Lewis' *Out of the Silent Planet*. The
physiological givens of such beasts resemble our own much more than a
robot's is likely to; yet for them, too, there is an acceptability-problem
because we have learned to account for distinctively human behavioral
skills in terms of physiological traits that such beasts lack. Nevertheless, this
explanatory gap does not seem to be insurmountable. When we learn about
the *hrossa* that they use a developed language and exhibit religious awareness, we agree with Ransom that they are rational after all. So, I presume,
if some bench-made artifact should launch into a discerning conversation

---

16. Hubert Dreyfus, *What Computers Can't Do* (New York, 1972), pp. 163ff. See
also the exchange between Dreyfus and K. M. Sayre in *Review of Metaphysics:*
"Why Computers Must Have Bodies in Order to be Intelligent" (Sept. 1967) and
"Intelligence, Bodies, and Digital Computers" (June 1968).

with me about the problem of personal identity in robots, I would be inclined to overlook the strange metallic quality of its voice.

There is no question whether a robot's behavior should simulate human behavior in every detail and for an indefinite span of time. Obviously it need not and cannot. Human beings spend a fair portion of their time in eating and drinking and sleeping, which makes us from one point of view (advanced by Socrates in *Phaedo*) inefficient; why duplicate such weakness in an artificial person? On the other hand, a robot ought to be permitted a few weaknesses and ineptitudes of its own. Robots would very likely prove much superior in computation to their human counterparts, as digital computers already are; but it may be impossible to build a robot that can discriminate between Coke and Dr. Pepper. None of these behavioral variants bears profoundly on the credentials of robots.

What forms of behavior, what skills and capabilities, are then crucial for a robot to possess if it is to be regarded as a candidate for being a *thou,* not merely an *it?*

Surely a robot must be able to use a natural language. Turing—and Mortimer Adler after him[17]—have made this the one behavioral test of reason, and if we look at a choice sample conversation between a human and an artifact like Turing's, it is not hard to understand why.[18] Yet there are existing computer programs already which respond in grammatical English to English-language inputs[19]—not randomly, but in a way that would be counted responsive and relevant by a human monitor—which does not at all incline us to call these computers humanoid robots.

Why not? A commonplace but nevertheless pertinent observation about such conversational programs is that they produce only those responses which they are programmed to produce. One feature of this programming involves building in rules for grammatically correct output sentences; another involves equipping the computer store with a vocabulary; another involves scanning procedures for detecting specific words and word sequences in the input; and another involves rules for selecting which response to give in the light of the input's content. Once these program-

---

17. Adler, *The Difference of Man and the Difference It Makes* (New York, 1967).
18. *Interrogator:* In the first line of your sonnet which reads "Shall I compare thee to a summer's day," would not "a spring day" do as well or better?
Witness: It wouldn't scan.
Int.: How about "a winter's day." That would scan all right.
Wit.: Yes, but nobody wants to be compared to a winter's day.
etc.
19. E.g., Joseph Weizenbaum, "ELIZA—A Computer Program for the Study of Natural Language Communication Between Man and Machine," *Communications of the ACM,* 9 (Jan. 1966), 36ff.

ming features are understood, we can see just why any given linguistic response of the machine is what it is, even though it is quite possible that some of these responses may not in fact have been anticipated by the programmer.

Yet it is not my purpose to focus on such considerations about *how* the computer "says" what it says, but rather on *what* it says. If a robot is competent enough behaviorally at conversation, it will not count as a put-down to declare that "you were programmed to say what you say, and moreover I know what the program is." Today's conversational programs fail not because they are programs, but because they enable the computer to produce only a *specific range* of linguistic responses. The programmer's aim is to simulate the responses of a nondirective therapist, or of a manic-depressive psychotic, or of a translator from Russian to English—the responses, that is, of persons standing in just such roles, performing just such functions, and nothing else. It is utterly impossible for a machine so programmed to drop out of that role without vitiating the very basis on which its vocabulary and input-output rules of transformation were selected.

What the robot talks about, and when, are thus much more important than its being able to talk *per se*. Range counts a lot: even the philosophizing robot of a couple of pages back fails to simulate the behavior of a human if it talks about nothing but philosophy. But there is more. For suppose that a given robot can simulate human conversation about a number of topics such as physics, the World Series, international trade, or any other in a finite series of subject matters—*depending on which button I push*. If I push Button B, I get World Series conversation until I stop it, and so on. This will not do either, for all I have now is a composite machine housing a set of one-dimensional talkers. A plausible humanoid robot must somehow *integrate* its linguistic behavior; it must be able to enter and leave conversational topics on its own, or in natural response to shifts made by other parties to the conversation.

There is yet more. So far I have pretended that language is used by humans only literally and indicatively, to convey information or to conduct inquiry. But of course this is not so. Language is also used to express the speaker's attitudes and emotions, to evoke responses in others, to display wit or craftsmanship with words themselves. It thus bears witness to the speaker's own sense of himself and others, to his aspirations and memories and imperatives, to the whole range of his private and social experience. In speech a person bares himself to another; in genuine dialogue, two persons are in a relation of mutual self-revelation.

I want to insist, now, that a humanoid robot must use language in that way. For if it does not speak *as though* it comprehends what I am revealing about my own self; and if it does not speak *as though* it, too, possessed an integral identity that was being communicated to me; then I shall perforce regard it as only a clever simulation of a person and not a person itself.

This point may immediately be generalized beyond the robot's *linguistic* behavior to its *overall* pattern of behavior. Taking a walk, flying an airplane, arranging furniture in a room—all of these conceivably simulable manifestations of human behavior cannot merely be concatenated in a robot's career if it is to simulate human behavior. That is: while all of these may be pieces of humanoid behavior, they are not yet segments in the behavior of a humanoid. For "the behavior of a humanoid" must have the benefit of an integrating principle that constitutes selfhood.

In "The Feelings of Robots" Paul Ziff argues persuasively that a certain kind of robot cannot sensibly be said to feel anything. The kind of robot Ziff had in mind can be programmed to act in any way we want it to act: to act tired when it lifted a feather but not when it lifted a ton; to act tired when it lifted blue things but not green things; to require more work, not less, when it acted tired; any or all of these, in any sequence, just as the programmer pleases. The behavior of such robots is the behavior of passive instruments, submissive to their programmers as the hammer is to the carpenter who wields it. Such robots, says Ziff, unlike organisms, are "merged with their environment," having no uniqueness, no individuality.[20]

Ziff's case, I believe, is plausible, but it does not matter to my argument whether *such* robots can feel or not. And oddly enough, it ought not to matter to Ziff's argument either. For Ziff begins by hypothesizing quite another sort of robot. These genuinely humanoid robots "when clothed and masked . . . may be virtually indistinguishable from men in practically all respects: in appearance, in movement, in the utterances they utter, and so forth."[21] And of such robots it could not be said that they had no individuality, for their behavior simply cannot be manipulated arbitrarily. A humanoid robot cannot today love strawberries and tomorrow hate them, where the change is brought about merely by a programmer's whim, and still be "virtually indistinguishable" from a human being in behavior.

The point is important. Ziff fails to realize fully the implications of the convenient recipe: "virtually indistinguishable" in behavior. For a robot it is a strong recipe indeed. It includes—or so I infer—indistinguishability of behavior over more than a few moments, or days, or months. It takes

---

20. Ziff, *loc. cit.*, pp. 98ff.
21. *Ibid.*, p. 99.

human beings longer than that to collect some experience, to develop a conception of the world, to formulate some short- and long-range objectives for themselves. The behavior of a humanoid robot must then simulate all these complexities of learning, deciding, goal-setting, execution of plans; and it must simulate the behavior associated in humans with joy, disappointment, frustration, satisfaction. The robot should exhibit joy after success and frustration after defeat, not vice versa. There should be some robot objectives that take what looks like effort, ingenuity, persistence, and time. I cannot take seriously a robot·for which every task is easy, or every task is nearly impossible, or for which task A is easy today and nearly impossible tomorrow, or which would submit without challenge to manipulations of its powers and perquisites by someone whose credentials consist solely of being a programmer.

There must indeed *be* a programmer somewhere in the humanoid robot's past. It could not be a robot unless there were. The programmer has great power over his artifact, though this power has limits. He cannot, for example, make his robot organically alive. But he can and must equip his robot to behave *as if* it were living its own life, which means among other things that the robot will resist arbitrary reprogramming. (What the programmer does for his robot, humans try to do for their children by nurture and education.) There is no special problem with anomalous components in such an overall program, such as Ziff's robot that acts tired when lifting blue things but not green things, as long as the robot can cope with its abnormality as does a human being with a physical handicap or a psychological anomaly.

A humanoid robot, then, is behaviorally a marvelous contrivance. If I take it home, it will play with my children not as their toy but as their playmate. (They can teach it a new game; it can beat them after a few tries but will not, to spare their feelings.) It will not eat dinner with the family, but might spend the dinner hour sampling my record collection or, as a favor, figuring out my income tax. It will express political opinions, help me to interpret a passage in Kant, perhaps read aloud a poem it has composed. It may express wonder at my praying, as an aborigine wonders about the reverence of Americans for their cars, but through hearing my explanations can be brought to register comprehension. All the while I will know that it is an artifact and has been programmed; but there will come a juncture in our relationship where I will stop wondering *whether* it is doing what its behavior indicates it is doing (Gunderson's repredication problem) and begin wondering *how* a programmed artifact such as he does do these things. Then will come the further realization that I don't know how people do their "things" either, if "knowing how" entails pos-

sessing a predictively adequate biological, behavioral, or cybernetic theory of human behavior. If it is permissible to suppose that in some sense human beings are themselves programmed without thereby being prevented from behaving as humans, *mutatis mutandis* the same could well be true of a well-formed humanoid robot.

III

Can robots of this sort be built? I do not know. There are enough considerations on both sides of the question to make it interesting. In what follows I shall merely sketch and appraise three arguments for the affirmative case.

1. *The extrapolation argument.* This argument begins by exhibiting the accomplishments of actual hardware, whether robots like Shakey or goal-seeking artifacts like radar-directed missiles or (most frequently) programmed computers, and inferring from these demonstrated accomplishments that the problems of simulating human behavior are in principle solved. There is, according to this view, no reason why existing chess-playing programs (some fairly competent) cannot be improved to the grand master level, or why simulation models of a neurotic personality cannot be indefinitely refined, or why the two cannot be merged into a model of a neurotic chess grand master, or why some super-program could not be devised to make a complete neurotic grand master chess-playing robot.

If this is an argument at all, it is most likely *ad ignorantiam.* An uninformed enthusiast of AI may propose it, and thereby reveal little more than his credulity. It is not sufficient simply to extrapolate; one can't support the claim that he can climb a fifty-foot tree by climbing a ten-foot tree. One needs to show that the skills exhibited in the short climb are sufficient to enable the long climb.

The extrapolation argument makes an assumption about the burden of proof. It says, "Here is what can be done already; show me why we cannot do the rest." To which the obvious response is, "Show me why you can." In an actual research project one seldom knows what can be done until it is done, or even, *in particular,* what *needs* to be done to complete the project. In 1957 Herbert Simon predicted that within ten years a digital computer would be the world's chess champion, unless the rules barred it from competition.[22] In 1972, Professor Monty Newborn of Columbia University predicted that in possibly fifteen years computers will be able

---

22. Dreyfus, *op. cit.,* p. xxix.

to beat the likes of Bobby Fischer.[23] Evidently the lot of the AI extrapo-
laters is hazardous.[24]

One of the objectives of Section II was to show that the extrapolation
argument must cross not one but several gaps. One gap lies between the
minimal simulation and the full-scale simulation of some specific human
skill, such as pattern-recognition or problem-solving. Dreyfus has argued
at length that these gaps are much harder to span than some AI researchers
admit. But there is a second gap, between a simulation (however impres-
sive) of some specific human skill or disposition and the *integration* of
many such skills or dispositions into a single humanoid personality-
simulator.

Consider the assignment indicated above, of simulating the behavior of
a neurotic chess grand master. A chess-playing program transforms inputs
consisting of board descriptions at a given state of the game into chess
moves; one existing "neurotic process" computer model transforms input
sentences employing terms such as 'mother,' 'hates,' and 'old' into so-called
distortion sentences that exhibit Freudian mechanisms.[25] It is now necessary to combine features of both.

As these programs stand, the task is impossible, for board descriptions
in chess do not employ the vocabulary of the neurotic simulator. Neither
program knows what to do with "mother moves her king one square to
the left." The chess program, if that is the one we try to modify, needs
to be made responsive to a wider range of input messages (such as the
above) and equipped with a wider assortment of responses (such as making a stupid move or just refusing to move). And still such a program is
painfully handicapped, for a human neurotic chess player responds not to
verbal inputs only but to an indefinite variety of features at the site of
the match, and responds in far more possible ways than can be expressed
in a repertoire of chess moves or refusals to move.

These observations go some way toward stating a design problem, the
problem of *integrating* skill-simulating programs with attitude-simulating
programs. They do not show that the design problems will never be solved,

---

23. Reported in the *Grand Rapids Press*, Aug. 18, 1972.
24. Cf. Richard Purtill: ". . . that any computer might be able to play [Turing's
imitation game] in the foreseeable future is so immensely improbable as to make
the whole question academic." "Beating the Imitation Game," *Mind*, 80 (Apr.
1971), 294.
25. Kenneth Colby's program. See John Loehlin, *Computer Models of Personality*
(New York, 1968), pp. 91ff. Sample input: "I hate my father but I must like him";
output: "I hate Joe" (deflection), "My mother hates my father" (projection), "My
father hates me" (projection).

but neither does the extrapolation argument show that they will.

2. *The argument from materialism.* There are some persons who believe that no entities exist other than material ones, and that all explanations of what these entities do can be subsumed wholly under the laws of physics. On this view the human body is all there is to a human being, and physics is the only science necessary to explain human behavior.[26] But if the foregoing are true, one might infer that humanoid robots differ only accidentally from human beings and therefore eventually can be built to do all that human beings do.

In response to this argument it is only necessary to remark (a) that a physical theory capable of generating explanations of all behavior is so remote from existing physical theories as to make its existence and character wholly conjectural; (b) that the explanatory laws necessary to account for the functioning of digital computers are not physical but logical, and there is in principle no way to derive the logical features of an information processing system from the physical laws that govern a physical embodiment of that system;[27] and (c) that the truth of metaphysical materialism is no less disputed than the conclusion which it is supposed to support.

3. *The all-purpose argument.* This is the argument cited in Section II on the authority of D. M. MacKay, John Van Neuman, Kenneth Sayre, and others. One premiss, which I will call the *machine premiss,* is this: a general purpose information processing (IP) artifact, such as a Turing machine, can simulate any input-output transformation function provided that this function be described unambiguously. A second premiss, which I will call the *behavior premiss,* is this: all the things that humans do can be described without loss of essential content in terms of IP. Examples of "what humans do" would include riding a bicycle, playing checkers, remembering what happened yesterday, composing a poem, making an investment decision, or praying—insofar as the evidence relevant to whether or not someone *is* doing these things is in principle public. The behavior premiss does not include the claim that feeling a toothache in a Cartesian mind is describable in terms of IP, but that the observable behavior by which we tell whether another person is feeling a toothache is so describable. In this way I shall once again try to avoid the question whether a humanoid robot can be built to be conscious, and concentrate instead on the question whether the robot can simulate the behavior of persons that are conscious.

---

26. This seems to be the view held by Dean Wooldridge, *Mechanical Man* (New York, 1968).
27. A point also made by Burks, *loc. cit.*

It will be useful to distinguish two versions of this argument, a stronger and weaker version. The stronger version affirms both premisses categorically, while the weaker version affirms the machine premiss categorically and the behavior premiss dialectically. With regard to the behavior premiss, the dialectical position is this: no successful counter-example can be provided, for any such alleged counter-example will either be clear and unambiguous or not. If it is clear and unambiguous, a machine can be designed to simulate the behavior. If it is not, then "no clear meaning can be attached to the claim that no machine can accomplish it."[28]

I call this the all-purpose argument for a double reason: it depends on a property of all-purpose IP networks, and it purportedly refutes *any* given challenge of the sort: "no machine can do such and such." I regard the behavior premiss as the more disputable, and will confine my comments to it in the weaker version of the argument.

To achieve any sort of purchase on a counter-example to the behavioral premiss one must raise this question: are there patterns of behavior such that we can at the same time determine with reasonable assurance how to characterize them, and yet not know how to describe them as functional transformations of input data? It would appear that there are.

For example: no machine can match the letter-recognition abilities of an average literate human being. The "inputs" here are occurrences of (for instance) the letter *a* in a large variety of cursive handwriting samples, and the "outputs" are indications (however expressed) that all the *a*'s and only the *a*'s are picked out. Now a humanoid robot must surely be able to perform with facility equal to human beings the task of *recognizing cursive a's*. However, at this time no machine can match this human ability. This proves one of two things: either that no description of this behavioral skill *suitable for an IP system* exists, or that such a description does exist but has not yet been discovered. With regard to the second possibility my earlier comments about extrapolation are applicable.

A second example, of a much more important kind, is this: no machine can dispense justice in a court of law. I do not mean to deny that a machine can make legal decisions as to guilt or innocence, or make further decisions pertaining to the sentencing of those convicted. This is no harder for a machine than is playing a competent game of chess. Neither do I deny that a machine can act for the sake of a goal. Finally, I do not deny that people of good will may differ about how justice is best served in a given case. Rather, the problem of a designer of mechanical judges comes from the fact (as I allege) that it is impossible to anticipate all the pos-

---

28. K. M. Sayre, in *Philosophy and Cybernetics,* p. 25.

sible "inputs" and all the possible *weightings* of these inputs that will (ought to) influence the decision that justice demands.

In human affairs the situation is like this: we are inclined, in a given litigation, on the basis of all the facts and laws that we can possibly think of as relevant, to suppose that justice demands decision A; yet, after the judge gives some other decision B and we find out why, we acknowledge *ex post facto* that B was indeed the just decision. Such a power of judgment as we find in good judges is, as it seems to me, precisely the power that an automaton must lack. "Rendering a just decision" is a task that humans can comprehend but not describe in terms computable by an IP system.

The general point in both of these examples is as follows. The simulation of human behavior, if it is to proceed at all, must presuppose an agreed-upon conception of what behavior is to be simulated. Both failures and successes of simulation will be measured by this conception. Now it may be the case that a back-and-forth simulation research project will help to clarify that original conception *in a sense*. But that sense is a limited one, namely, the sense that is computable by a IP system and thereby simulable by a machine. It is entirely possible that the IP version of a human behavioral skill will consistently fail to reproduce the behavior that was indicated by the original conception (e.g., "recognizing cursive *a*'s," "rendering a just decision"). It would be a *non sequitur* then to infer that the human behavior in question was not understood, except in this special sense. And accordingly, the behavior premiss under discussion must be regarded as dialectically vulnerable.

IV

It may be of interest to append some remarks on the relevance of Christian theology to the question of robots.

I do agree with MacKay and Turing on this point: if a truly humanoid robot *were* to be built, it would be presumptuous to deny that the Creator of us all could confer a soul on it and treat it with the same I-thou respect as he does human persons. To claim otherwise, in an age when we are prepared to entertain the thought of nonhuman persons inhabiting other worlds, is merely parochial.

But the argument is not as straightforward with regard to the prospects for building humanoid robots in the first place. The question here, as it seems to me, is whether the degree of complexity manifested in human behavior can be penetrated by a level of analysis that is confined to computational categories. To put it in another, admittedly tendentious way: does God see human beings as information processors made of meat? For if he did, robots could be on the way, provided that we humans come to see ourselves in the same way that God does.

I see no reason to suppose that he does so regard human beings, except in the inconsequential sense that he also regards us as metabolizers of foodstuffs and members of communities. The IP analysis of human behavior lays down a preferred set of categories for understanding man that may well be useful for many purposes, including the design and manufacture of "intelligent" artifacts that profoundly alter the economic and political patterns of the future. But my theological instincts, like Socrates' *daimon,* restrain me from expecting more of robotics than that.

A Bibliography of Henry Stob

compiled by Peter De Klerk

abbreviations

Awsi	As we see it (in the *Reformed Journal*)
Ban	*The Banner*
CF	*The Calvin Forum*
CT	*Christianity Today*
CTJ	*Calvin Theological Journal*
Et	*Eternity*
FM	*The Federation Messenger*
RefRev	*The Reformed Review*
RevRéf	*La Revue Réformée*
RJ	*The Reformed Journal*
Strom	*Stromata*
TT	*Torch and Trumpet*
Wach	*De Wachter*
WTJ	*The Westminster Theological Journal*

1936

The Christian idea of revelation. ThM. thesis. Hartford, Conn.: Hartford Theological Seminary, 1936. (unpublished)

"Graeco-Roman and Christian ethics: a contrast" CF 2 (1936/37) 269-271.

1937

"The doctrine of God" in *Christian truth today.* A presentation and defense of historical supernatural Christianity for College Students. Ed. by Calvin Knox Cummings. Philadelphia: The League of Evangelical Students of America, 1937. Vol. 1, pp. 95-109.

"The Galilean conquers" CF 3 (1937/38) 5-8.

1938

Eine Untersuchung zu Max Webers Religionssoziologie. Dissertation zur Erlangung des Doktorgrades der Philosophischen Fakultät an der Georg-August-Universität zu Göttingen. Göttingen: Dieterichsche Universitäts-Buchdruckerei (W. Fr. Kaestner), 1938.

"A letter from Amsterdam" CF 4 (1938/39) 119-120.

"The Free Reformed University—Amsterdam" CF 4 (1938/39) 168.

1939

"Some antitheses in life" in *Educational theories and practices.* Annual conven-

221

tion papers. Chicago: The National Union of Christian Schools, 1939. Pp. 70-81.

"The antitheses in education" in *Educational theories and practices.* Annual convention papers. Chicago: The National Union of Christian Schools, 1939. Pp. 82-88.

"God's antithesis: the ultimate disjunction" *CF* 5 (1939/40) 170-171.

1940

"On peace" *CF* 6 (1940/41) 164.

1941

Review of *A sacramental universe,* by Archibald Allan Bowman. Ed. by J. W. Scott. Princeton, N.J.: Princeton University Press, 1941. *CF* 7 (1941/42) 30-31.

1943

"Philosophy" in *Calvin College faculty syllabi.* Ed. by J. Broene. Grand Rapids: Calvin College, 1943. Pp. 125-128.

"The Word of God and philosophy" in *The Word of God and the Reformed faith.* Addresses delivered at the second American Calvinistic Conference held at Calvin College and Seminary, Grand Rapids, Michigan, June 3, 4 and 5, 1942. Grand Rapids: Baker's Book Store, 1943. Pp. 102-111.

1947

Review of *Common grace,* by Cornelius Van Til. Philadelphia: The Presbyterian and Reformed Publishing Co., 1947. *CF* 13 (1947/48) 53-55.

Review of *Does God exist?* by Alfred E. Taylor. New York: The Macmillan Co., 1947. *WTJ* 10 (1947/48) 62-67.

1948

Review of *Transcendental problems of philosophic thought.* An inquiry into the transcendental conditions of philosophy, by Herman Dooyeweerd. Grand Rapids: Wm. B. Eerdmans Publishing Co., 1948. *CF* 14 (1948/49) 53-54.

1949

"Was Calvin a philosopher? a symposium" *CF* 14 (1948/49) 214.

1950

"A living theology" *CF* 15 (1949/50) 111-113.

"The kingdom world-wide" in *Kingdom frontiers.* Vital issues. Addresses given at the 27th Convention of the Young Calvinist Federation in Lynden, Washington, on August 20, 21, and 22, 1950. Grand Rapids: The Young Calvinist Federation, 1950. Pp. 15-21.

1951

"On the call for leadership" *RJ* 1 (March 1951) 6-7.

"Our people and their school" *RJ* 1 (April 1951) 3-5.

"'In all these things'" *RJ* 1 (May 1951) 1-2.

"What did 1928 say?" *RJ* 1 (May 1951) 11-13.

"The majority report examined . . . 'worldly amusements'" *RJ* 1 (June 1951) 5-9.

"Synod on worldly amusements" *RJ* 1 (July 1951) 5-7.
"Principle and practice" *RJ* 1 (October 1951) 10-12.
"Tradition and the church" *RJ* 1 (December 1951) 13-14.

1952

"On using and revising the compendium" *RJ* 2 (January 1952) 7-9.
"Movies, television and the Christian" *RJ* 2 (February 1952) 10-12.
"Truth, language, compendium revision" *RJ* 2 (May 1952) 4-6.
"Shall we expand catechesis?" *RJ* 2 (June 1952) 11-12.
"What think ye of the Christ?" *RJ* 2 (July 1952) 1-3.
"Academic freedom at Calvin" *RJ* 2 (August 1952) 4-6.
"Notes to a college freshman" *RJ* 2 (September 1952) 12-13. Also in *TT* 2 (February-March 1953) 6-7.

1953

"Too much philosophy?" *RJ* 3 (January 1953) 3-4.
"Reading the pagan writers" *RJ* 3 (February 1953) 6-7.
"Towards better understanding" *RJ* 3 (April 1953) 12-15.
"Lo, I am with you alway" *RJ* 3 (June 1953) 15-16.

1954

"The liberty of man" *RevRéf* 5 no. 17 (1954) 35-47. Also in *The Christian concept of freedom*. Grand Rapids: Grand Rapids International Publications, 1957. Pp. 13-33. French version in *RevRéf* 5 no. 17 (1954) 48-59.
"Waterink was here" *RJ* 4 (September 1954) 1-2.
"Christmas fear" *RJ* 4 (December 1954) 1-2.

1955

"Jesus and the Old Testament" *RJ* 5 (January 1955) 6-7; (February 1955) 6-7.
"Faith and science" *RJ* 5 (April 1955) 1-2.*
"Can physics be Christian?" *RJ* 5 (May 1955) 13-15.*
"Science and pure reason" *RJ* 5 (July-August 1955) 12-13.*
"Religion in science" *RJ* 5 (September 1955) 12-14.*
    *These articles reprinted under title "Calvinism and the philosophy of science" in *Calvinism 301X*. Grand Rapids: Calvin College, 1956.

1956

"Cecil DeBoer: the philosopher" *RJ* 6 (January 1956) 7-8.
"Admission into the church" *RJ* 6 (May 1956) 5-6.
"St. Paul, the pastor" *Ban* 91 (1956) 1361, 1364-1365.

1957

The Christian concept of freedom. Grand Rapids: Grand Rapids International Publications, 1957. First lecture "The liberty of man" also in *RevRéf* 5 no. 17 (1954) 35-47. French version of first lecture in *RevRéf* 5 no. 17 (1954) 48-49.
"Henry Zylstra: in memoriam" *RJ* 7 (January 1957) 3-4.
"The mind of the church" *RJ* 7 (March 1957) 3-6.
"The mind of safety" *RJ* 7 (April 1957) 4-9.
"Why did Jesus want to be baptized?" *Ban* 92 (April 12, 1957) 6-7.

"The militant mind" *RJ* 7 (June 1957) 3-7; (July-August) 3-6; (October 1957) 13-17.
"Mary and Jesus" *RJ* 7 (December 1957) 3-4.

1959
"Synod and Biblical infallibility" *RJ* 9 (May 1959) 3-8; (July-August 1959) 7-9.
"The absoluteness of Christianity" *RefRev* 13 (December 1959) 33-41.

1960
"Apologetics" *Ban* 95 (January 29, 1960) 9, 25; (February 12, 1960) 9, 16; (March 11, 1960) 9.
"It is finished" *RJ* 10 (April 1960) 3.
"A significant protest" *RJ* 10 (May 1960) 3-4. (Awsi)
"Gifts for TCNN?" *RJ* 10 (May 1960) 4. (Awsi)
"Prescription for heart disease" *RJ* 10 (July-August 1960) 4. (Awsi)

1961
"The positive mind" *RJ* 11 (March 1961) 5-9; (May 1961) 23-24; (September 1961) 3, 22-24.
"The way of love" *RJ* 11 (June 1961) 5-8.
"Miracles" *CT* 5 (1960/61) 850-851.
"Berlin" *RJ* 11 (September 1961) 4. (Awsi)
"Natural love" *RJ* 11 (September 1961) 5-9.

1962
"Miracles" in *Basic Christian doctrines*. Ed. by Carl F. H. Henry. Contemporary Evangelical Thought. New York: Holt, Rinehart and Winston, 1962. Pp. 82-88.
Principle and practice. Inaugural address delivered in Calvin Seminary Chapel, Friday 8 December 1961. Grand Rapids: Calvin Theological Seminary, 1962.
"Themes in Barth's ethics" *RJ* 12 (April 1962) 19-23.
"Moral education" *RJ* 12 (September 1962) 7-11.
"Clarence Bouma, 1891-1962" *Ban* 97 (November 2, 1962) 27.

1963
"Modernity and motherhood" *RJ* 13 (February 1963) 3-4. (Awsi)
"Does God hate some men?" *RJ* 13 (February 1963) 9-13.
"Madison Avenue" *RJ* 13 (March 1963) 3. (Awsi)
"Of self defense" *RJ* 13 (April 1963) 3. (Awsi)
"This month—a literary menu" *RJ* 13 (April 1963) 6. (Awsi)
"The old and the new" *RJ* 13 (May-June 1963) 4. (Awsi)
"Is nuclear war justifiable? An ethics professor's view" *CT* 7 (1962/63) 913-915, 1115-1116.
"Christian education: a sermon (Proverbs 22, 6)" *RJ* 13 (September 1963) 7-9; 14 (January 1964) 20-21.
"Christian organizations" *RJ* 13 (October 1963) 4. (Awsi)
"The Heidelberg Catechism in moral perspective" *RJ* 13 (October 1963) 6-9.
"Morality and public life" *RJ* 13 (November 1963) 4. (Awsi)
"The God-Man" *RJ* 13 (December 1963) 3. (Awsi)

"In memory & in prospect: prayer for the Nation" *RJ* 13 (December 1963) 6-7.

1964

"Foreword" in *Faith and philosophy*. Philosophical studies in religion and ethics. A collection of essays in honor of W. Harry Jellema. Ed. by Alvin Plantinga. Grand Rapids: Wm. B. Eerdmans Publishing Co., 1964. Pp. v-viii.

"The ethics of Jonathan Edwards" in *Faith and philosophy*. Philosophical studies in religion and ethics. A collection of essays in honor of W. Harry Jellema. Ed. by Alvin Plantinga. Grand Rapids: Wm. B. Eerdmans Publishing Co., 1964. Pp. 111-137.

"The nature of forgiving biblically described" in *Proceedings* of the eleventh annual convention of Christian Association for Psychological Studies. Grand Rapids: Christian Association for Psychological Studies, 1964. Pp. 6-12.

"Religion and the chapel" *RJ* 14 (January 1964) 5; (May-June 1964) 2, 24-25. (Awsi)

"Whither shall I flee?" *RJ* 14 (February 1964) 4. (Awsi)

"The synod and movies" *RJ* 14 (March 1964) 5-6. (Awsi)

"Christian organizations: power and strategy" *RJ* 14 (March 1964) 7-10.

"Robinson and Christ's sermon" *RJ* 14 (April 1964) 4. (Awsi)

"Are movies contraband?" *RJ* 14 (May-June 1964) 4-5. (Awsi)

"The Christian and neutral organizations" *RJ* 14 (May-June 1964) 14-17; (July-August 1964) 21-23.

"Senator Barry Goldwater" *RJ* 14 (July-August 1964) 3-4; (September 1964) 20-21; (October 1964) 3-4. (Awsi)

"Calvin College and Seminary" *RJ* 14 (September 1964) 4-5. (Awsi)

"What is theology?" *Ban* 99 (September 25, 1964) 16-17.

"Religion and the unions" *RJ* 14 (November 1964) 5. (Awsi)

"Calvin Theological Seminary—a convocation address" *RJ* 14 (November 1964) 6-10.

"Christ and the will to peace" *RJ* 14 (December 1964) 3. (Awsi)

"Our knowledge of God" *Ban* 99 (December 4, 1964) 16-17.

1965

"Justification and sanctification; liturgy and ethics" in *A reexamination of Lutheran and Reformed traditions*. Ed. by Paul C. Empie and James I. McCord. New York: Published jointly by representatives of the North American Area of the World Alliance of Reformed Churches holding the Presbyterian Order and the U.S.A. National Committee of the Lutheran World Federation, 1965. Vol. 3, pp. 5-17. Also in *Marburg revisited*. A reexamination of Lutheran and Reformed traditions. Ed. by Paul C. Empie & James I. McCord. Minneapolis, Minn.: Augsburg Publishing House, 1966. Pp. 105-127.

"Dooyeweerd and Vollenhoven" *RJ* 15 (January 1965) 4-5. (Awsi)

"The far right: fundamentalism & political rightism" *RJ* 15 (January 1965) 12-14.

"The church and society" *RJ* 15 (February 1965) 3-4. (Awsi)

"Rain makers" *RJ* 15 (March 1965) 4. (Awsi)

"The Christian in society: human freedom and political order" *RJ* 15 (April 1965) 22-24.
"Some issues in philosophy" *RJ* 15 (September 1965) 17-20.
"Fruits of the Reformation in the natural sciences... 'a firm foundation for modern science'" *CT* 10 (1965/66) 76-79.
"Christian freedom" *Ban* 100 (November 19, 1965) 14-15.

1966

"As we see it after 15 years" *RJ* 16 (March 1966) 3-6.
"The death-of-God theology" *RJ* 16 (March 1966) 23-28; (September 1966) 19-21; (November 1966) 7-11.
"The doctrine of revelation in St. Paul" *CTJ* 1 (1966) 182-204.
"William B. Eerdmans, Sr., 1882-1966" *Ban* 101 (May 20, 1966) 21.
"Synod, the committee, and Professor Dekker" *RJ* 16 (May-June 1966) 5; 17 (May-June 1967) 5-6; (October 1967) 3. (Awsi)

1967

"Polonius" *RJ* 17 (January 1967) 6. (Awsi)

1968

"Statement on fair housing" *RJ* 18 (January 1968) 3-4. (Awsi)
"War and the new morality" *RJ* 18 (February 1968) 31-33.
"Riots and guns" *RJ* 18 (March 1968) 3. (Awsi)
"The Christian and birth control" *FM* 40 (November 1968) 7-8.

1969

"Karl Barth en de ethiek" *Wach* 102 (7 januari 1969) 11-12.
"L. D. K." *RJ* 19 (September 1969) 2. (Awsi)
"Birth control" *Strom* 15 (December 1969) 12-13.

1970

"An event that shames us all: let us repent" *RJ* 20 (March 1970) 2-3.
"One of America's churches is in crisis: the church before decision" *RJ* 20 (May-June 1970) 5-6.

1971

"Is Chicago North in contempt?" *RJ* 21 (May-June 1971) 5-7. (Awsi)
"Abortion, yes or no?" *Ban* 106 (June 4, 1971) 10-13.
"The kingdom of God" *RJ* 21 (December 1971) 6-8; 22 (February 1972) 15-17.

1972

"Calley affair" *Et* 23 (January 1972) 13, 54.
"Calvin P. Bulthuis, 1924-1971" *RJ* 22 (February 1972) 3-4.
"Albertus C. Van Raalte (1811-1876)" *RJ* 22 (March 1972) 19-22.
"Biblical authority: a special section" *RJ* 22 (April 1972) 7.
"Civil disobedience" *RJ* 22 (April 1972) 22-23.
"He that cometh..." *RJ* 22 (December 1972) 2-3, 5.

1973

"Christian ethics and scientific control" in *The scientist and ethical decision*. Ed. by Charles Hatfield. Downers Grove, Ill.: Inter Varsity Press, 1973. Pp. 3-24.

"Social ethics" in *Baker's dictionary of Christian ethics*. Ed. by Carl F. H. Henry. Washington, D.C.: Canon Press, 1973. Pp. 635-637.

"Watergate: judgment, healing, and renewal" *RJ* 23 (July-August 1973) 6.

"Notes on the philosophy of St. Augustine" *CTJ* 8 (1973) 117-130.

1974

"Avenger of blood" in *The Zondervan pictorial encyclopedia of the Bible*. Ed. by Merrill C. Tenney. Grand Rapids: Zondervan Publishing House, 1974. Vol. 1, p. 422.

"Concupiscence" in *The Zondervan pictorial encyclopedia of the Bible*. Ed. by Merrill C. Tenney. Grand Rapids: Zondervan Publishing House, 1974. Vol. 1, p. 935.

"Content, Contentment" in *The Zondervan pictorial encyclopedia of the Bible*. Ed. by Merrill C. Tenney. Grand Rapids: Zondervan Publishing House, 1974. Vol. 1, p. 953.

"Courage" in *The Zondervan pictorial encyclopedia of the Bible*. Ed. by Merrill C. Tenney. Grand Rapids: Zondervan Publishing House, 1974. Vol. 1, pp. 992-993.

"Forbear, Forbearance" in *The Zondervan pictorial encyclopedia of the Bible*. Ed. by Merrill C. Tenney. Grand Rapids: Zondervan Publishing House, 1974. Vol. 2, p. 589.

"Judging, Judgment" in *The Zondervan pictorial encyclopedia of the Bible*. Ed. by Merrill C. Tenney. Grand Rapids: Zondervan Publishing House, 1974. Vol. 3, pp. 758-760.

"Calvin and Aquinas" *RJ* 24 (May-June 1974) 17-20.

"Observations on the concept of justice" *CTJ* 9 (1974) 133-148.